Profiting from Monetary Policy

Profiting from Monetary Policy

Investing through the Business Cycle

Thomas Aubrey

palgrave
macmillan

First published 2013 by
PALGRAVE MACMILLAN

Palgrave Macmillan in the UK is an imprint of Macmillan Publishers Limited, registered in England, company number 785998, of Houndmills, Basingstoke, Hampshire RG21 6XS.

Palgrave Macmillan in the US is a division of St Martin's Press LLC, 175 Fifth Avenue, New York, NY 10010.

Palgrave Macmillan is the global academic imprint of the above companies and has companies and representatives throughout the world.

Palgrave® and Macmillan® are registered trademarks in the United States, the United Kingdom, Europe and other countries.

ISBN 978–1–137–28969–8

This book is printed on paper suitable for recycling and made from fully managed and sustained forest sources. Logging, pulping and manufacturing processes are expected to conform to the environmental regulations of the country of origin.

A catalogue record for this book is available from the British Library.

A catalog record for this book is available from the Library of Congress.

10 9 8 7 6 5 4 3 2 1
22 21 20 19 18 17 16 15 14 13

Printed and bound in Great Britain by
CPI Antony Rowe, Chippenham and Eastbourne

For Yanina, Thea and Ethan

The futility of price level stabilization as a goal of credit policy is evidenced by the fact that the end-result of what was probably the greatest price-stabilization experiment in history proved to be, simply, the greatest and worst depression.

Banking and the Business Cycle – Phillips, McManus, Nelson 1937

Stock market bubbles don't grow out of thin air. They have a solid basis in reality, but reality as distorted by a misconception.

George Soros 2004 – Buzzflash Interview

Contents

Figures

Tables

Preface

When the Nobel Laureate Robert Solow gave evidence to the House Committee on Science and Technology in 2010, as part of an investigation into the limits of economic theory, he asserted that elements of modern macroeconomic theory did not pass the smell test. Either those supporters of modern macroeconomic theory, he argued, had stopped sniffing or they had lost their sense of smell altogether. I went back to university after a career in management consulting to study mathematical economics in an attempt to explain why the UK economy had been plagued by housing market bubbles. Much of what I was taught did not pass the smell test either, particularly the pervasiveness of the role of price stability in maintaining a general equilibrium. Worse still, this principle seemed to be guiding the investment community in the way it thought about asset returns through time.

As house prices boomed in the period leading up to the financial crisis, I returned to the problem using the framework of the Swedish economist Knut Wicksell, who had developed a dynamic, credit-based view of an economy. Using Wicksell's ideas of excess credit growth, with additional guidance from the writings of the 1974 Nobel Prize winners Gunnar Myrdal and Friedrich Hayek, I attempted to empirically measure the extent of disequilibrium in the US and UK economies. Initial estimates from analyses of both economies suggested that they had been operating significantly above equilibrium for a period of 20 years, despite the fact that inflation had remained subdued. This implied that the robust returns generated by financial assets during the Great Moderation were therefore an anomaly rather than the expected market rate of return. Hence, future returns would be much lower than the past given that the excess growth in credit was not sustainable with significant implications for pension schemes

The dramatic fall in asset prices that came about in 2008 has largely been responsible for a decade of poor returns. However, such a level of capital destruction could have been anticipated given that the economy had been operating at a level substantially above equilibrium since the early 1980s. As the investment community has attempted to avoid further capital destruction by moving into liquid and high-quality government bonds, it seemed logical that Wicksell's analytical approach could be applied by the investment community to avoid the peaks and troughs of the business cycle by monitoring the rise and fall of credit growth as an investment signal.

This book is thus an attempt to explain how investors can reduce the volatility of returns and invest through the business cycle to ensure that the capital tied up in pension schemes doesn't get periodically destroyed. During the 1930s, Hayek and Myrdal both argued that signals based on price stability and general equilibrium were misleading for market participants. They have been proven right, again. The challenge of funding future pension liabilities is a daunting prospect for policy makers, which has been exacerbated by a decade of poor returns. Until investors reject the prevailing monetary policy consensus as an investment framework and switch to credit-based investment strategies that track the business cycle, pension schemes will continue to suffer poor returns due to the periodic destruction of capital.

Acknowledgements

This book could not have been written without the support of some incredibly generous people who have given their time and knowledge and who have encouraged me in my endeavours in attempting to explain the nature of business cycles. In particular, I'd like to thank Meghnad Desai for introducing me to the work of Wicksell and Hayek, and Max Steuer for his encouragement to pursue my ideas. I'd also like to thank Charles Goodhart, Steve Nickell and George Selgin for their helpful comments and pointers on my empirical work. I'd also like to thank the numerous reviewers as well as Glenn Bedwin, Norman Bernard, Vit Bubak, Simon Commander, Joao Garcia, Tiziana di Matteo and William White for their comments on various sections and drafts of the manuscript. I would also like to thank Thomson Reuters and Fitch Solutions for allowing me to use their data to support my argument. I am also grateful to the Hayek estate, the Karl Popper library, Taylor & Francis Books and Buzzflash for permitting me to reproduce material.

Finally, this book could not have been written without Datastream. Empirical work is an almost never ending quest of trial and error, and the advice of the Datastream product and content experts, in conjunction with the vast array of available data, has been invaluable.

Introduction

In 2011, as the number of people on our planet surpassed 7 billion, the United Nations forecast that the world's population will keep on rising until around 2050, when it is expected to plateau at the 9 billion mark. Rising population statistics can often generate fear about the future of our civilisation. Are there really sufficient resources on our planet to support that many people without causing mass malnutrition? Will the increased CO_2 emissions from an extra 2 billion people cause the polar ice caps to melt, resulting in extensive flooding and forced migrations of entire populations?

Such anxiety about our future has led to the telling of gripping tales depicting life under a new climate or continents at war, battling for diminishing natural resources. These stories have begun to inform the debate about resource management and environmental issues and have, importantly, become part of our culture. There is however one major issue related to rising population that is largely absent from popular websites, newspapers, television and cinemas. And that is how pensions will be funded given there will be fewer workers to support an ever-increasing number of retirees. Perhaps not the stuff of a gripping thriller, although a recent attempt by Christopher Buckley, a speechwriter for Vice President George H.W. Bush, suggests even that might be beginning to change. In his novel *Boomsday*, a young blogger, angry at having to pay for the burgeoning social security budget, incites intergenerational warfare which amongst other things leads to the destruction of golf courses.

Pensions crisis

Although we might not think of this issue as a crisis given we haven't yet seen students and pensioners being kept apart by riot police in New York, Paris or Shanghai, the debate is reasonably well understood. Most of the world's pension systems are funded through the taxation of the working population, which is a good system when life expectancy beyond retirement is short and the rate of young people entering the workforce is increasing. This was the case when Bismarck set up the world's first universal pension system in Germany in the 1880s. Fortunately and unfortunately for society, the conditions of the 1880s and 2012 are rather different. Average life expectancy has almost doubled during this period and the rate of population growth in most developed economies has declined below its replacement rate, which means that fewer and fewer workers are supporting an ever-increasing number of pensioners. Politicians have largely avoided tackling this issue because it means alienating the pensioner vote which has proven to have been crucial in gaining re-election. However, the problem is becoming more obviously acute in many countries.

In the United States, unfunded public sector pension liabilities at the state level have been estimated to be as high as $3 trillion.[1] This is of particular concern from a future growth perspective, as public expenditure on pensions is already higher than that of education accounting for 16 per cent of total expenditure versus 15 per cent.[2] Recent experience in Europe suggests that these issues are unlikely to be tackled until there is a fiscal crisis. Dramatic increases in the retirement age for women and men across Southern Europe have only come about in an attempt to help avert a future default. Indeed, policies forced on the Greek government in 2010 meant that by 2060 the annualised pension bill will be an affordable 15.5 per cent of GDP instead of an unsustainable 24 per cent of GDP if the old system had continued. In China also, there is a growing concern about how to fund future pension liabilities given that a quarter of the population will be retired by 2050. China is already faced with the issue that fewer people are entering the workforce than retiring.

Besides the appropriate age of retirement being increased in order to help stave off a potential fiscal crisis, the concern around the kind of pensions on offer to the public sector is also being raised. Traditionally both private and public sector pensions offered what is known as defined benefit pensions, where retirees would be awarded an annualised pension generally based on their final salary. The private sector has found these challenging to fund, and has largely moved towards a defined contribution approach where the value of each pension is determined by the amount of money paid in, plus the investment return. Some public sector pensions are also moving towards defined contribution schemes although these remain the exception. Whatever the outcome of this debate, one issue that remains crucial to both systems is how best to invest the assets to ensure that sufficient returns are generated. Shortfalls in investment returns for defined benefit schemes generate an unfunded liability for the government or company, whereas low investment returns for a defined contribution scheme provides a much lower standing of living during retirement. The risk of low returns is bad for both systems; they are just borne by different people. Furthermore, low returns act as a disincentive for people to contribute more to their pension pots which would clearly help solve this challenge. It is not easy to convince someone to forego consumption today when the money that has been invested falls rather than rises in value.

The economic and financial crisis that started in the summer of 2007 has brought this issue to the fore due to a substantial and unexpected crash in the value of pension schemes. Indeed, some US pension funds saw losses of around 20 per cent in 2008 and in 2011 barely broke even. According to the OECD between 2007 and 2011, OECD countries' pension returns averaged –1.6 per cent per year.[3] Given the damage a prolonged period of poor investment returns can do in terms of increasing unfunded liabilities as well as lowering retirement income, tax payers and pensioners are clearly being let down by fund managers who are paid to manage pension assets. Fund managers of course still get paid despite the fact that their clients' money has fallen in value since the onset of the crisis.

An industry duped by a Great Myth

The investment management industry has largely escaped direct criticism from the analysis of the causes of the financial crisis that started in the summer of 2007. Indeed, a handful of investors have achieved an almost heroic status by betting on falling housing and equity markets, generating substantial returns for their clients.[4] However, most investors did not see it coming. The result of this failure is that investment returns for the vast majority of savers since the beginning of the new millennium have been awful. The OECD calculated that pension fund returns between 2001 and 2010 averaged a paltry 0.1 per cent per annum,[5] a far cry from the magical 8 per cent figure that savers have been led to expect. Given that ten years is roughly a quarter of someone's investment plan, something has clearly gone wrong with the way in which pension money is invested.

So why did the investment management sector, which is paid to manage the world's pension assets, not see the crisis coming? Most pension fund assets are invested in equities and bonds, where the assets are expected to increase in value over time despite economic fluctuations. Standard financial theory in the form of the capital asset pricing model (CAPM) argues that the expected rate of return for the market can be explained by how the market has performed historically. Today, most pension plans use an expected real return on assets of 8 per cent, as up until 1999 this was roughly the historical average of returns since 1945. Crucially, the ideas of CAPM are grounded in the notion of general equilibrium which has been one of the most important building blocks of modern macroeconomic theory. The theory argues that short-term price changes of goods and services, including money and interest, can be understood as deviations from long-term equilibrium prices which the economy will naturally tend towards. The fall in returns since 1999 are therefore seen as mere deviations from the long-run trend.

The assumption that the historical average of the return on assets should equate to an expected rate of return appears reasonable as long as sufficient deviations from equilibrium are taken into account. It also assumes that the economy over time has been operating around an equilibrium level. This is further justified by Rational Expectations theory, another core component of current macroeconomics, which argues that economic agents cannot be systematically wrong about the future. If information from the market is signalling economic imbalances of say output and inflation, expectations would shift to take account of the expected changes. This idea has become central to monetary policy with central banks communicating out to the market their views on the future trajectory of output and inflation in order to minimise future fluctuations around equilibrium.

This body of economic theory has thus been instrumental in the way that pension assets are managed by the investment management sector. As the theory assumed that future returns would be similar to historical returns, a significant amount of assets have been invested in passive funds, whose investments purely mimic an index such as the S&P 500. Thus pension funds can benefit from average market returns without the costs of investment advice. Actively managed funds where investors allocate assets in order to beat market benchmarks, which account for the majority of pension money, are also dependent on this economic theory. This is because key signals that are used to allocate equity and bond investments include stable and strong real GDP forecasts,[6] the idea being that robust real GDP growth ought to filter through to higher corporate earnings growth and therefore better returns, with the lower risk ensuring lower defaults for bond funds. Signals emanating from the world's central banks have therefore become central to the asset allocation decisions of the active investment management sector as well as an indicator of passive returns.

Hence in the summer of 2007, all seemed well to most investors. They were being informed by central bankers and economists that they had never had it so good. The 25 years prior to 2007 had been distinguished by a period of low inflation, low unemployment, robust growth and low interest rates. As a result the returns on pension fund assets had grown just above the 8 per cent that was expected by the market. It was the goldilocks economy, or in economists' jargon the 'Great Moderation'. Investors were led to believe that as long as inflation remained low, so would interest rates, and thus growth could be sustained. This in turn would maintain asset price growth and everyone would profit.

In the summer of 2007 the Fed was projecting real GDP growth of 2.50–2.75 per cent for 2008, slightly up from the 2007 full-year projection of 2.25–2.50 per cent.[7] The ECB's forecasts were also positive at 1.8–2.8 per cent for 2008, slightly down on the 2007 forecast of 2.3–2.9 per cent due to rising oil prices.[8] Other indicators were also supporting a continued positive growth rate. Equity markets in many countries were at all-time highs, including the United States, Germany, Canada, Brazil, Australia, India and China. Other major equity markets, including France and the United Kingdom, were almost back at the dizzy heights they reached during the tech bubble of 2000. Of the major markets only Japan remained significantly below previous highs.[9] Housing markets too were booming with a decade-long expansion in many countries, including the United States, Ireland, Spain and the United Kingdom.[10] Most other countries also saw a significant increase in housing market values. In tandem with this housing boom, credit markets continued their downward trend, with the market believing that credit risk had been largely conquered. Credit default swap indices which provide a good proxy for perceived credit risk reached all-time lows in early 2007.[11]

The onset of the financial crisis has highlighted that the investment community was duped by a Great Myth of modern economic and financial theory – a theory where large deviations from equilibrium are not possible due to the signalling framework of rational expectations, general equilibrium and stable inflation. The data since 2007 demonstrates that stable inflation has not maintained economic stability, and given the large fall in output, large deviations from equilibrium are indeed possible. As a result, investment returns over the last decade have had little in common with the returns from the latter half of the 20th century. This poor performance has clearly contributed to value destruction within the investment management sector which according to a draft report from IBM could be as high as $1.3 trillion.[12]

Thus for the investment management sector to provide investment products to help solve the pensions crisis, the current framework of modern economic and financial theory needs to be firmly rejected. Clearly for such a rejection to take place, an alternative and more robust approach needs to be developed and tested. Such an alternative has however been on offer for many years by a handful of global macro hedge funds.

The dissenters

Over the last 40 or so years, a handful of investors have been able to successfully invest through the business cycle by ignoring modern financial and economic theory. This not only suggests that current economic and financial theory is fundamentally flawed, but that there must be an alternative underlying theory that would permit investors to monitor the business cycle and reduce the volatility of returns. In a speech delivered at Trento in Italy in 2012, George Soros reiterated his stance that some of the key planks of modern financial theory, including General Equilibrium and Rational Expectations, were so unrealistic that he never bothered to study them. Given that he is one of the most successful investors ever, having generated returns of 20 per cent per annum over a 40-year period, it is somewhat surprising that his ideas have been largely ignored by mainstream economists. Soros' speech highlighted that an economy did not have a natural tendency to move towards equilibrium but developed a boom and bust scenario whose general trend and eventual reversal can be predicted, but not the magnitude and duration. Other global macro-hedge funds with expertise in credit, such as Bridgewater and Brevan Howard, have also shown that it is possible to invest through the business cycle, providing double digit returns to their clients over an extended period of time.

Besides these absolute return funds, a few high-profile economists, notably with deep knowledge of credit markets, have also been highly critical of the theory underlying the Great Myth. Both Hyman Minsky and Joseph Stiglitz attacked modern macroeconomic theory for largely ignoring credit and banking from its models. Given the central role of credit in the modern economy, this highlights a rather large crack in the foundations of the Great Myth.[13] Another idea central to the Great Myth was attacked in 2006 when William White, the former chief economist at the Bank of International Settlements (BIS), warned that the stability of prices might not be sufficient to ensure macroeconomic stability.[14] Since the crisis started, the level of criticism of the foundations of the Great Myth has unsurprisingly stepped up a few notches. In 2009 Willem Buiter in a Financial Times (FT) blog argued that the typical graduate macro and monetary economics training received at Anglo-American universities during the last 30 years was a waste of time, with its research programmes amounting to nothing more than self-referential, inward-looking distractions at best.[15] John Kay also attacked the foundations of modern economic and financial theory in an FT article particularly focussing on the futility of abstract and unrealistic models.[16]

No doubt the level of criticism will continue given that current monetary and macroeconomic theory has not helped with solving practical problems. Indeed it is ironic that the fund that manages the money which generates income for the Nobel Prizes, including that for economics, has generated such poor returns that for the first time since the 1940s it will be reducing the cash value awarded to its recipients. The challenge for the investment management industry is that the Great Myth has made the problem with regard to the funding of future pension liabilities worse. But what signals should the industry use when it comes to asset allocation decisions in order to rectify this? Those investors who made profitable asset allocation decisions ten years ago by ploughing into BRIC equity markets because of higher forecast real GDP growth have done substantially better compared to those who invested in developed market economies. But if output can slump in the developed world unexpectedly causing capital destruction, couldn't the same happen in emerging markets too? Given that the investment paradigm will be tougher over the next decade as interest rates rise, impacting the returns on bonds due to falling prices, challenges for the industry remain significant.

Fund managers have always had a multitude of ideas about where to invest, but without a systematic approach of being able to predict general trends and generate the returns after costs that the pension sector requires, it is not clear how the sector can provide the pensions industry with what it needs. One possible approach is to return to credit-based theories of the economy that were very much in vogue in the earlier part of the 20th century. These were unfortunately discarded by the post-war economics profession, largely because credit was too complex to model. However, increases in the availability of data and new modelling techniques have made this approach a strong candidate for providing an improved signalling framework.

A new hope?

For around 40 years, between 1898 and 1939, a substantial body of economic thought based on credit rather than on money and price stability was developed by economists in Austria and Sweden. These theorists also had the added benefit of having lived through the non-inflationary credit bubble of the 1920s and seeing at first hand its impact on the Great Depression. The movement was founded on the ideas of Knut Wicksell, the great Swedish economist who developed the first credit-based economic model in his book *Interest and Prices* published in 1898. His major contribution was the idea that equilibrium existed when the return on capital in an economy was equal to the cost of capital. Hence, when the return on capital was higher than the cost of capital, the increase in profits meant that demand for credit would grow generating an economic boom, but if the return on capital fell below the cost of capital it caused an economic slump as firms went out of business.

These ideas were carried forward by Hayek in the late 1920s and early 1930s before being refined by Myrdal, whose book on monetary equilibrium was published in English in 1939. Myrdal argued that Wicksell's framework could be used to assess where an economy was in relation to its equilibrium, thus defining the business cycle. Like Hayek, he argued that price stability was a cause of economic instability as it sent false signals to the wider economy. What mattered was the growth in credit and not the general price level. However, Myrdal rejected any notion of equilibrating tendencies, one of the central components of economic theory since Ricardo, arguing that an economy was in a constant state of dynamic disequilibrium. In the 1970s with the development of Chaos Theory, the natural sciences discarded the idea that the natural world oscillated around a state of equilibrium, focussing instead on the analysis of streams of data to make sense of the world. The same needs to happen in financial economics if pension schemes are to generate the necessary returns.

Historical empirical analysis using Wicksell's credit-based, data-intensive approach across several countries highlights that an investment process grounded in this credit-based view of an economy generates superior investment signals to those emanating from central banks based on the Great Myth. It is in fact possible to analyse where an economy is in relation to the business cycle, with the data showing that an economy hardly ever operates at equilibrium. Indeed, during the period of the Great Moderation, the economy was consistently operating at levels significantly above equilibrium, highlighting that the growth in asset prices was not in fact sustainable. Such an approach to investment will allow portfolio managers to avoid the pitfalls of catastrophic drops in the value of capital by following the business cycle, thus ensuring that the returns on pension fund assets are not impacted by extreme volatility.

As the demand grows from pension schemes to improve returns with lower volatility, the investment management sector will need to fundamentally change its approach to investment. This will require the industry to reject the current monetary framework based on price stability and general equilibrium, and embrace a credit-based dynamic disequilibrium framework instead. Credit-based frameworks can signal the trend of the business cycle which current monetary frameworks have failed to do. By avoiding the downturns of the business cycle with the associated destruction of capital, investors can provide the pensions industry with the returns it needs. This will surely go some way to help prevent intergenerational warfare breaking out, including the destruction of more than just golf courses.

Chapter 1

The Great Moderation and the unravelling of a Great Myth

Whenever a theory appears to you as the only possible one, take this as a sign that you have neither understood the theory nor the problem which it was intended to solve.

Karl Popper[1]

In June 2007, investors' aggregated view of the value of financial assets in both equity and credit markets demonstrated little sign that the economy was about to collapse, resulting in massive capital destruction. Economic forecasts across the board remained robust, from central banks through to financial market practitioners in the banking and fund management sectors. Equity valuations were forecasting strong profit growth with the S&P 500 in July 2007 above the dot com boom levels of July 2000. Moreover, the market's perception of credit risk was at an all-time low, with countries like Greece considered not much riskier than Germany (Figure 1.1).

For those commentators who believed that the housing market bubble and excessive levels of debt were about to send the economy into an abyss, years of academic research and several Nobel Prize winners suggested otherwise. Indeed, there were many good reasons for the market to think that the global economy would be able to maintain its robust trajectory of growth. In particular, the revolution in monetary policy since the high inflation of the 1970s had resulted in low unemployment, low inflation and economic growth – three of the vital ingredients required for rising corporate earnings and lower default rates. Moreover central bankers, who had taken on a more prominent role as the guardians of economic stability, appeared to be in control of any future fluctuations of the economy by their ability to manage expectations.

The unmasking of the Great Moderation

The scourge of inflation during the 1970s led to one of the few occasions in economic history when a consensus within the profession

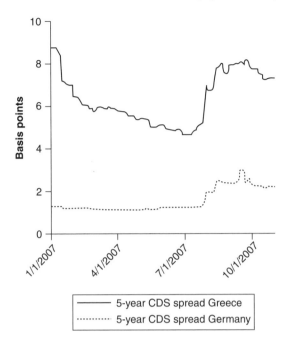

Figure 1.1   Five-year credit default swap (CDS) spread – Germany vs Greece
Source: Fitch Solutions.

developed. Keeping inflation expectations low and therefore inflation muted was considered crucial to maintaining economic stability, which in turn would optimise the level of output and employment. This would also ensure that asset prices fluctuated around their historical average. These ideas became central to the new neo-classical synthesis, which largely underpins monetary policy today. Indeed, this consensus is the main reason why most of the world's central banks over the last 20 years have pursued some form of inflation targeting, whether it be formal or informal. That means if prices fall, policy makers will be inclined to ease monetary policy to stimulate aggregate demand. In contrast, if inflation pressures are building, monetary policy will be tightened using short-term interest rates.

The net result of this development in monetary policy is that the general price level has come to be seen as *the* critical factor indicating the health of an economy. It suggests that lower prices equate to an economy that is operating at under-capacity and higher prices mean that the economy is operating at over-capacity, allowing the central bank to move interest rates to readjust the economy back towards a notion of equilibrium. For passive investors this signal has provided comfort that returns can be maintained close to their historical average. Active investors using real GDP forecasts have also been able to adjust their asset allocation by underweighting economies with rising prices, given that rising interest rates would reduce output. Economies with spare capacity and falling prices, leading to increased growth as interest rates fall, would be overweighted. The net result of this policy from the early 1980s to 2007 was a period of excellent returns, accompanied by low unemployment, low inflation and generally robust economic growth, otherwise known as the Great Moderation.

Figure 1.2 suggests that the ability of central banks to manage inflation may well have been one of the drivers of the Great Moderation. The first trend from the 1950s shows a general upward movement in inflation which peaked around 1980, accompanied by a lagging but generally comparable interest rate. This trend was highlighted by Milton Friedman in his seminal 1968 paper, where he argued that the adoption of cheap money policies after the war led to rising inflation.[2] The runaway inflation of the 1970s demanded a change in policy and when Paul Volcker was appointed

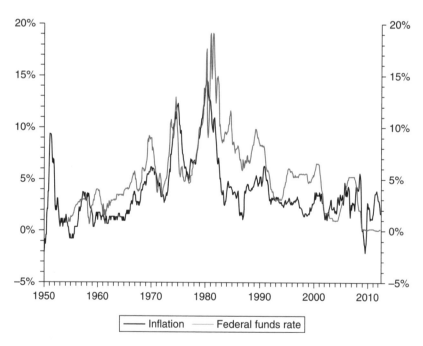

Figure 1.2   US inflation vs Fed funds rate
Source: Thomson Reuters Datastream.

as chairman of the Federal Reserve in 1979, he used the policy of raising the Fed Funds rate to choke off excess demand by increasing the cost of money, and more importantly dampening rising inflationary expectations.

The second trend from 1980 shows an initial dramatic fall-off in inflation as a result of Volcker's policies, but this time accompanied by a substantially higher interest rate until the early 2000s when it became more comparable again. As a result inflation since the early 1980s has remained low and stable except for a limited period in 2009 when prices started to fall. In summary, the chart shows that although monetary policy was ineffective in the pre-1980 period in managing inflation, post 1980 it can be considered a roaring success. Hence, central bankers have come to be well pleased with their performance in the last 30 years.[3]

The successful management of inflation since the early 1980s led to the idea that central bankers could steer the economy through the business cycle, which convinced most investors that they could use the signals emanating from central banks as core drivers in their investment process. Unfortunately for the theory, and more importantly for pensioners and tax payers, Figure 1.3 shows that managing the general price level does not necessarily lead to an optimum level of output and employment, highlighting one of the Greatest Myths in the history of economics and finance.

As Friedman predicted, the early 1960s era of low inflation, falling unemployment and robust growth gave rise to increasing inflation, rising unemployment and falling real GDP growth which continued throughout the 1970s. After the US economy came out of the early 1980s recession, real GDP growth remained reasonably robust and less volatile than at any time since 1950. This growth was accompanied by low inflation and low unemployment. However, the onset of the recent credit crisis has caused real GDP to dip to its lowest level in 50 years, and unemployment to rise to its highest level since the recession of the early 1980s.

The failure of the economy to maintain its non-inflationary growth rate has left a vacuum for investors, given that one of their most important signals has ceased to function as expected. This suggests that the macroeconomic consensus behind the Great Moderation may well be flawed. The 50-year time series in Figure 1.3 highlights the post-war macroeconomic debate particularly well with respect to output and inflation; which has been labelled as the Phillips Curve debate. The Phillips Curve attempted to explain the relationship between inflation and unemployment with the

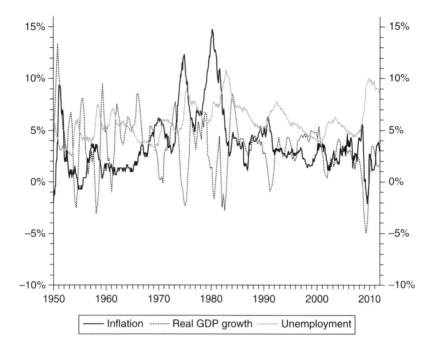

Figure 1.3   US unemployment, inflation and real GDP growth
Source: Thomson Reuters Datastream.

view that unemployment could be reduced at the expense of a bit
more inflation. When this policy was implemented in the 1960s
and unemployment fell, inflation picked up. As Friedman correctly
argued, this policy was inherently unstable as it would only lead
to rising inflation expectations and hence inflation spiralling out of
control with no long-term reduction in unemployment or growth in
output. The period from the mid-1980s up until the credit crisis corresponds particularly well to Friedman's extended Phillips Curve
where the policy of maintaining price stability led to stable growth.

However, the data since 2008 shows a relationship of low prices,
low output and high unemployment that was neither anticipated
by Phillips nor Friedman. This was why the real GDP forecasts in
the summer of 2007 turned out to be so wildly wrong. Once the
scale of the crisis was realised by the market, asset prices dropped
in value in order to reflect the new economic paradigm, resulting
in trillions being wiped off the value of pension schemes. Investors,
it seems, had been duped by a Great Myth which was based on a
series of invalid assumptions about the behaviour of the relationship
between inflation and output.

Although it may seem surprising that almost an entire industry was duped by the ideas of central bankers and academics, the origins of this myth has a rich intellectual heritage going back centuries to the beginning of theorising about the nature of money. Moreover, the idea of controlling inflation, which is at the core of the Great Myth, is highly relevant for investors, given that high levels of inflation are bad for pension fund returns. Indeed, the economic history of the 20th century demonstrates why investors and economists have become so obsessed with price stability.

Reinhart and Rogoff's study on the median inflation rate from 1500 to 2007 highlights a massive jump in inflation in the 20th century.[4] Destruction of the value of money by governments is much easier to do with printed notes than with coins. Although examples of coinage debasement driving inflation have been relatively ubiquitous throughout earlier periods of history, the level of inflation that can be reached with printed money is in a class of its own. Examples of hyperinflation (annual price increases of over 1,000 per cent) from the 1920s (Germany, Russia, Poland and Austria), to the 1940s (Hungary and China), 1980s (Bolivia, Brazil and Argentina) and finally to modern-day Zimbabwe, causing great misery and distress, are well documented. As wages tend to lag price rises, consumers soon find themselves poorer. Savings get wiped out driving levels of poverty even higher, which in turn causes investment to plummet due to falling levels of capital, and a catastrophic fall in the value of financial assets. Lower levels of investment lead to fewer jobs and so the cycle deteriorates. These levels of wealth destruction tend to generate widespread social and political dislocation too.

Fortunately these instances are less common, however even moderate levels of inflation have significant negative economic impacts. At its most basic level, rising inflation increases the cost of living as the value of money falls against a specific basket of goods. If wages are growing at a slower rate than inflation, then in aggregate, consumers are getting poorer. For instance, food prices rose 25 per cent in 2010 to all-time highs, which in turn fuelled popular protests against the incumbent governments in Tunisia and Egypt. Inflation also erodes the profits of businesses, whereby increased commodity and labour costs cannot always be passed on to consumers, resulting in falling profits and as a consequence, reduced investment. Finally, expectations of future levels of inflation can also have a significant impact on the rate of inflation itself. During the 1970s as inflation was rising, partially driven by exogenous commodity price shocks and unusual money supply experiments, expectations of inflation led to a wage price spiral and higher actual inflation. Given that wages were unable to keep up with the rising cost of living, this brought living standards down further, with the lower level of consumption driving the value of financial assets down, too. Moreover, breaking this cycle requires both determination and significant economic pain as policy makers and central bankers showed in the late 1970s and early 1980s.

Besides these negative consequences, another key reason for maintaining price stability is that it can provide clearer signals to stakeholders in the economy. The Fed's rationale behind this idea is worth quoting.

> When prices are stable and believed likely to remain so, the prices of goods, services, materials, and labour are undistorted by inflation and serve as clearer signals and guides to the efficient allocation of resources and thus contribute to higher standards of living. Moreover, stable prices foster saving and capital formation, because when the risk of erosion of asset values resulting from inflation – and the need to guard against such losses – are minimized, households are encouraged to save more and businesses are encouraged to invest more.[5]

Although inflation remains a key concern for investors as it impacts returns, the scale of capital destruction that has resulted from investment strategies based on the Great Myth, which prioritised price stability above all other factors, has been absolutely devastating for pension funds. As a consequence, passive investment strategies which depend on notions of equilibrium to maintain historical market returns, as well as active investment strategies that use real GDP forecasts to allocate assets cannot provide pension schemes with the returns that they need. The fund management industry, in order to generate improved returns for their pension fund clients, will therefore need to base their investment process on a different economic paradigm which minimises capital destruction. Before attempting to construct a new economic framework from which investors can profit, it is imperative to firstly understand why the Great Moderation, with its impressive intellectual history, turned out to be little more than a Great Myth.

Most of the research related to money and inflation that contributed to the Great Myth tended to develop as a result of economic disruptions at a particular point in history. Although theories written at the time appeared to solve the specific issue at hand, unfortunately they more often than not were unable to explain economic behaviour at a later point in time. Two themes that have generally been present in the historical development of these ideas include the idea of the equilibrating tendencies of the market and the notion that the quantity of money available in an economy has an impact on prices. The Quantity Theory of Money was formed mainly as a result of the influx of silver from the new world which appeared to drive price increases. In general this relationship was considered to be proportional, whereby a doubling of money would lead to a doubling of prices. Subsequent debates then attempted to understand how such a shift in the money supply might impact unemployment and growth in relation to the general equilibrium of the economy. Hence monetary policy became central to the Great Moderation which generated misleading signals for investors. However without understanding why these signals failed so catastrophically, it will be far more challenging to construct a new economic paradigm. Thus it is to the origins of these ideas that we now turn.

Historical underpinnings of the Great Myth

John Locke was one of the earliest theorists to use the so called Quantity Theory of Money argument. Locke was a practising medical doctor who turned to political philosophy later in his life. His writings were mostly published after returning from political exile in the Netherlands, after Britain had agreed to limit the power of the king. His ideas related to the Quantity Theory of Money were set out in a letter to Parliament in 1691, arguing against a reduction in the rate of interest from 6 per cent to 4 per cent.[6] The demand for money, he argued, ought to regulate its price. He stated that the value of money depended only on the plenty or scarcity of money in proportion to the plenty and scarcity of commodities. In essence, a change in the quantity of money had no bearing on the price, which is determined by the proportion of the number of buyers and sellers. Thus a doubling of the money supply would double prices. Although the theory seemed be logical in itself, it was neither tested nor observed empirically. Thus Locke set the scene for several hundred years of economists describing logical theories without testing or observing them.

Less than 15 years after Locke's letter to Parliament, another economic thinker and notorious gambler, John Law, came up with a rather different view of the impact the money supply might have on an economy. Law famously argued in *Money and Trade Considered*, published in 1705, that, 'domestic trade depends on money. A greater quantity employs more people than a lesser quantity. Good laws bring money to full circulation forcing it to those employments that are most profitable to the country'.[7] In essence, increasing the money supply would lead to higher output without any impact on price, thus generating a productivity gain. The idea, although unorthodox, seemed plausible to many and in particular to the heavily indebted French government. The French government granted a license to Law to set up a private bank, Banque Royale, to issue large amounts of paper money. Suffice it to say that the asset bubble that ensued in combination with high levels of inflation soon ended this economic experiment. This incident did provide a useful stream of data demonstrating that there clearly was some sort of relationship between an increase in the quantity of money, inflation and asset price bubbles. Unfortunately, the incident also set a precedent for governments to scour the intellectual landscape for new ideas that might help them get out of the various economic predicaments they often find themselves in. Law was forced to flee France in 1720 and died in poverty in Venice some years later.

Ironically, it was one of Law's associates who provided one of the first useful theories of the relationship between the money supply and output based on actual observations of the economy. Richard Cantillon left Ireland at the turn of the 18th century, becoming involved in the French banking sector from around 1715. He became a French citizen and through banking became acquainted with John Law. It is a testament to Cantillon's understanding of the nature of the economy that he invested heavily in the Mississippi Company as shares were rising, but sold out before the collapse. The Mississippi Company, run by John Law, monopolised trade in the West Indies and North America. In 1720 the Company was united with the Banque Royale to attract more capital. Within months the asset bubble burst, and Law's business collapsed. Asset price bubbles always offer opportunities to smart investors to make money, although in reality there are very few who have both the insight and the nerve to make these decisions. Investing whilst in the throes of an asset bubble would thus appear to be a completely rational undertaking – the key is knowing when to get out. With his fortune amassed, Cantillon travelled around Europe and eventually settled in London, where he wrote an essay entitled *On the Nature of Trade in General* in 1730. This essay was one of the few references used by Adam Smith in *The Wealth of Nations* that was written over 40 years later.

Cantillon argued that there was a relationship between an increase in the quantity of money and prices. According to Cantillon, 'everybody agrees that the abundance of money or its increase in exchange, raises the price of everything. The quantity of money brought from America to Europe for the last two centuries justifies this truth by experience.'[8] He then described the process whereby prices gradually increase as the money supply increases, and went into some detail to illustrate the transmission mechanism. These observations caused him to fundamentally disagree with Locke's notion of proportionality, concluding with:

> An increase of money circulating in a State always causes there an increase of consumption and a higher standard of expenses. But the dearness caused by this money does not affect equally all the kinds of products and merchandise proportionably to the quantity of money, unless what is added continues in the same circulation as the money before, that is to say unless those who offered in the Market one ounce of silver be the same and only ones who now offer two ounces when the amount of money in circulation is doubled in quantity, and that is hardly ever the case. I conceive that when a large surplus of money is brought into a State the new money gives a new turn to consumption and even a new speed to circulation. But it is not possible to say exactly to what extent.[9]

Cantillon's honesty in believing that it is actually quite difficult to model the circulation of money around an economy and the impact it has is not only refreshing, but centuries ahead of his time. However, it was not long before these kind of helpful observations were soon ignored in favour of logical models. This backward step in thinking about the relationship between the money supply and prices was definitively made almost 90 years later, when David Ricardo published *On the Principles of Political Economy and Taxation* in 1817. Like Cantillon, Ricardo made a great deal of money from investing before turning to economic theory, although Ricardo's wealth seems to have come to him more by luck than by design. From 1811, Ricardo's stockbroking firm was one of the loan contractors for the government of Great Britain and Ireland. The final war loan raised on 14 June 1815 had priced at a discount to previous loans, given the state of the war with Napoleon.[10] Several days later, when news reached London that Wellington had been victorious, Ricardo found himself sitting on assets that had increased almost fivefold.

Ricardo's long-run equilibrium framework makes Cantillon's observations of what happens in the real world largely irrelevant. Ricardo's model of how an economy functioned was based on the notion that markets will always clear, given any change in the price level. 'With the rise or fall of price, profits are elevated above, or depressed below their general level, and capital is either discouraged to enter into, or is warned to depart from the particular employment.'[11] His example of an increase in demand for silks at the expense of woollens due to a change in fashion initially generates higher profits for silks and lower profits for woollens. However, the consequent transfer of capital and labour from woollens to silks eliminates this short-term deviation. This framework means that money is essentially neutral in the process. Ricardo continued the argument with regard to food stating that,

> a fall in the value of money...is another cause for the rise in the price of food, but will make no alteration in the quantity produced. Money wages will rise, but they will only enable him [labourer] to furnish himself with the same quantity of necessaries as before...so if corn and all the necessaries of labour be doubled in price also, and while there is no interruption to the usual demand and supply of necessaries and of labour, there can be no reason why they should not preserve their relative value.[12]

Thus all long-run price rises are driven by an increasing quantity of money, and any initial deviations from equilibrium cannot be caused by changes in the money supply.

Since Ricardo's book was published it has unfortunately had a profound impact on the consequent development of economic thought to this day. For example, Ricardo's influence on Karl Marx was such that the great Austrian economist Joseph Schumpeter called Marx Ricardo's only great follower. Marx was attracted to his logical method and of course his Labour Theory of Value. Throughout the 19th century, as Marx's influence grew, a reaction developed to counter Marx's revolutionary ideas and in particular, to attack his (and Ricardo's) Theory of Value. However, in doing so, many thinkers went back to Ricardo's general framework as a reference point. The most important of these economists is without doubt Leon Walras.

Walras had an eclectic career in Paris, including a stint as a journalist, novelist and failed banker, before moving to Lausanne and becoming an economics professor at the age of 36 in 1870. He attacked Ricardo's Theory of Value that was based on labour and instigated the neoclassical revolution of value determined by marginal utility simultaneously with the English economist William Stanley Jevons and the Austrian Carl Menger. Marginal Utility argued that value was determined by the importance attributed to the good by the consumer and not by production costs or labour input. His highly influential *Elements of Pure Economics* also advanced the importance of mathematics for economic analysis. Walras even went so far to argue that 'economics, like astronomy and mechanics is both an empirical and a rational science.'[13]

Walras argued that there were a set of prices that could explain the supply and demand across *all* markets, resulting in an overall economic equilibrium of that economy. Price inflation, as Ricardo had argued, is thus only a temporary phenomenon, with equilibrium being restored through the self-adjusting market mechanism. Walras's model assumed that each consumer acts to maximise utility, each producer to maximise profits and above all, that perfect competition prevails. Walras did concede that 'equilibrium in production like equilibrium in exchange is an ideal and not a real state. It never happens in the real world that the selling price of any given product is absolutely equal to the cost of productive services that enter into that product.'[14] Walras qualifies his model further by stating that equilibrium is constantly being disturbed and re-established through a process defined as 'groping'. This process is where market participants learn of the relationship between prices and supply and demand, which then moves the system towards a general equilibrium because of the assumptions around utility and profit maximisation.

Walras's model made a couple of other important assumptions. Firstly, there will also be an equilibrium between capital formation and saving, thus ensuring that structural imbalances are unable to distort the system in the long run. Any instance of over-investment will lead to falling prices and a consequent withdrawal of capital, resulting in increasing consumption and a fall in savings, thus rebalancing the system. Secondly, money is external to general equilibrium. The price of money, Walras argued, is 'established through its rise or fall according as the desired cash balance is greater or less than the quantity of money.'[15] In essence, that the value of money is inversely proportional with its quantity is just a restatement of the Quantity Theory of Money. The world of economics had begun to set a higher priority on the logic of internal models than on the real-world observations of the likes of Cantillon. Given that the aim was to establish economics as a science, this shift is perhaps unsurprising.

The internal logic of general equilibrium was powerful for a number of reasons: firstly, the notion that one can sum up all economic activity taking place at the micro level, thus providing a clear insight into what is happening at the macro level, is intuitive, and secondly, the view that if a general equilibrium exists, then it ought to be possible to ascertain whether an economy is at its equilibrium level, and if not, what policy might be required to move it to the equilibrium level. Walras's ideas soon spread, including to the United States via the first rock-star economist, Irving Fisher of Yale University. Fisher met Walras in Lausanne and became profoundly influenced by Walras in terms of general equilibrium as well as the use of mathematics.

Fisher, in his seminal work *The Purchasing Power of Money*, published in 1911, argued that the price level depended on three factors, which were the quantity of money, the velocity of its circulation and the volume of trade. Fisher stated that the quantity theory of money had often been incorrectly formulated, given that only when the velocity of circulation and the volume of trade are static do prices vary proportionally with the quantity of money. However, he argued that as a doubling in the quantity of money will not 'appreciably affect either the velocity of circulation of money or of deposits or the volume of trade, it follows necessarily and mathematically that the level of prices must double.'[16] Using Walras's idea of general equilibrium, he argued that any disturbance in the price level coming from a change in any one of the three factors means that 'equilibrium will eventually be restored through an international or interlocal redistribution of money and goods.'[17] The notion of equilibrium led to Fisher stating that a change in the quantity of money can therefore have no impact on the volume of trade as 'the stream of business depends on natural resources and technical conditions, not on the quantity of money.'[18]

Although Fisher argued that other factors influenced the price level indirectly through imported price movements due to favourable conditions for producers, including natural resources, the division of labour, and the knowledge of the technique of production, any change in prices can only be temporary. If prices fall, the increase in demand for the product will result in, prices being pushed back up. Conversely imported inflation would lead to falling demand, which in turn would lead to lower investment, and thus prices would fall back to their equilibrium level.

Although equilibrium theory guides Fisher in his analysis, he does describe a transition process whereby 'if the quantity of money were suddenly doubled, the effect of the change would not be the same at first as later,'[19] or once equilibrium has been restored. Fisher describes this process in some detail, highlighting a rise in prices will initially lead to a rise in profits due to the lag in the rate of interest. The rise in profits leads to an expansion of economic activity. However, eventually the rise in the rate of interest overtakes the rise in prices as the banks need to rebalance their loans relative to reserves. Higher rates of interest cause a fall in investment due to an increase in the cost of capital. Moreover, higher interest rates on existing loans lead to falling profits and, in some cases, businesses to fail. This in turn leads to falling prices, with the consequent adjustment back towards equilibrium.

Fisher's description of the business cycle has over time become central to modern monetary theory. Firstly, he highlights the notion of using interest rates as a key tool to maintain equilibrium, although the lagging effect that Fisher described implies they might be too crude for the job at hand. Secondly, and more importantly is the notion that by maintaining price stability it will stave off any cyclical movements, thus conquering the business cycle itself. During the 1920s, Fisher's research into prices, output and unemployment led him to conclude that because prices had remained stable with higher profits due to technical progress, 'stock prices have reached what looks like a permanently high plateau'. Unfortunately he made this statement just a few days before the stock market crash of 1929, which may have had some bearing on why his ideas had little impact on policy whilst he was alive. Despite the fact that the stock market crash smashed a gaping hole in his theory, Fisher's ideas were eventually resurrected to support the triumph of the Great Moderation.

The onset of the Great Depression and rising mass unemployment, in conjunction with a book by a Cambridge University economist, led to a shift away from the idea that markets automatically cleared and that the Quantity Theory of Money was of use to policy makers and investors. John Maynard Keynes was the bursar of King's College and responsible for investing its assets, which he did so very successfully. His interaction with financial markets gave him a different perspective on the functioning of the economy than many of his academic peers. When he published his *General Theory* in 1936 he attacked the prevailing view that markets cleared providing full employment, arguing that a general equilibrium could be reached with high unemployment due to lower aggregate demand. Keynes's observations that markets did not clear automatically were well made, although his policy advice on government intervention to bring full employment back has remained controversial as well as poorly understood. Besides arguing that markets didn't always clear, Keynes started to pick holes in the traditional Quantity Theory of Money, and therefore the relationship between the quantity of money and output.

Keynes argued that 'true inflation' would only take place once full employment had been reached. Hence at full employment any increase in the money supply would drive up wages due to increased demand and hence prices. However, he goes on to state that most of the assumptions around, trying to enunciate a quantity theory of money, are in fact, not close to what happens in practice. He is clear that effective demand will not change in proportion to the money supply because resources are not homogeneous, nor interchangeable and that wages can rise because of these factors before full employment has been reached. Keynes also makes it clear that an increase in the quantity of money where there are available unemployed resources will not have much impact on prices.[20] Keynes's observations are in many respects similar to Cantillon's, highlighting that an increase in the quantity of money in certain circumstances can have an impact on increasing prices, although it depends on the equilibrium of employment for each commodity.

He then goes on to attack the prevailing orthodoxy à la Fisher on the relationship between the money supply and prices, stating that 'the view that any increase in the quantity of money is inflationary is bound up with the underlying assumption of classical theory that we are always in a condition where a reduction in the real rewards of the factors of production will lead to a curtailment of supply.'[21] The idea that markets always clear as per Walras's general equilibrium had little bearing on reality. Keynes sums up the issue, asserting that attempting to ascertain the relationship between the quantity of money and price increases is of limited value because of the 'extreme complexity of the relationship between prices and the quantity of money'.[22] Indeed, Keynes goes on to state that 'in exceptional circumstances an increase in the quantity of money will be associated with a decrease in the quantity of effective demand.'[23] A decrease in effective demand of course may result in falling prices, something that central bankers during the credit crisis ought to have been more aware of, given the trillions of dollars that have been injected into the global financial system in an attempt to kick-start the economy. This part of Keynes's theory is related to his idea of a liquidity preference. In a crisis period, although governments may decide to inject large amounts of money into the economy in an attempt to reflate it, however, 'a large increase in the quantity of money may cause so much uncertainty about the future that liquidity preferences due to the precautionary motive may be strengthened.'[24]

In essence, the government's intervention sparks a flight away from risk assets to cash or today's cash equivalents which include high quality and, more importantly, liquid government bonds. This in turn causes the cost of capital to rise because of increased perceived risks. Increased risks will of course *reduce* the propensity to consume and hence to invest, thus compounding the economy to remain in the doldrums. Moreover, even reducing interest rates may have a limited impact on increasing the quantity of money in an economy, particularly if the rate of return on capital is such that it makes little sense to undertake investment. Keynes's argument remains rather prescient. However, it was of course his fiscal policy that was central to his theory, and after the Second World War it did take centre stage as a result of research by the New Zealander Bill Phillips at the London School of Economics.

In 1958 Phillips published a paper on the relationship between wages and unemployment. The initial relationship was striking in its simplicity in that the lower the rate of unemployment the higher the rate of inflation. It appeared that the government could now bring down unemployment at the expense of a bit more inflation. This seemed to support Keynes's argument that fiscal stimulus could help reduce unemployment. One aspect of Phillips's paper that remains largely ignored was related to where the relationship didn't appear to work, which was in two specific cases. Firstly, Phillips states that when an economy is shocked by rising import prices, the relationship breaks down. Secondly, Phillips struggled to explain the period between 1879 and 1886, putting the issue down to some peculiarity used to construct the index during these

years.[25] However, this was right in the middle of a period of deflation. As industrialisation spread to other European economies and
the United States, competition drove prices down.[26] Import prices
can of course fall as well as rise. In essence, the Philips Curve only
appears to explain the relationship where price is endogenously
driven, or in a closed economy.

However, even the relationship that ignored exogenous price
changes began to break down in the mid-1960s and as a consequence, so did the theoretical idea that unemployment could be
reduced by accepting a bit more inflation. The attack on the Phillips
Curve and the Keynesian model of government demand management came from a group of economists led by Milton Friedman at
the University of Chicago. Friedman spent most of his life as an
academic economist; however, his role working for the FDR administration between 1935 and 1937 is worth noting, where he worked
on the job creation programmes and was also exposed to the wage
and price-fixing measures of the Administration. Throughout the
1960s he challenged the prevailing orthodox view by reinstating
Fisher's ideas. In 1963 he published a *Monetary History of the United
States* with Anna Schwarz, providing a detailed empirical analysis
supporting his restatement of the Quantity Theory of Money. The
premise of the tome was that business cycles, including the Great
Depression, were caused by erroneous monetary policy. Friedman
highlighted how the Fed had taken a significant amount of money
out of the economy in the 1930s, causing the Great Depression.
By 1968, when he published his landmark paper *The Role of Monetary Policy*, Friedman proposed the notion that the goal of monetary
policy was to prevent itself from being a major source of economic
disturbance. This paper also played a key role in ensuring the attack
on Keynes and the Phillips Curve remained in the ascendancy.

Friedman argued that in the long run, higher levels of inflation
would generate higher wages, which in turn would have limited
impact on unemployment, only at a higher rate of inflation. He
surmised that in the long run only a single rate of unemployment
could lead to a stable rate of inflation. This level of unemployment
became known as the Natural Rate of Unemployment. If unemployment falls below the natural rate then inflation will accelerate.
In the late 1960s as inflation began to bite, it became clear that trying to manage expectations of inflation was extremely challenging
and policy makers turned to Friedman for help. Based on the

idea that the Quantity Theory of Money was central to Monetary Theory, Friedman recommended that central bankers target the growth in the money supply. Friedman had previously argued that interest rates were too crude to stabilise inflation, as Fisher had alluded to. Inflation, according to Friedman, was purely a monetary phenomenon, and therefore the response was simple: take money out of the economy using money growth indicators as benchmarks. This policy was pursued in both the United Kingdom and the United States in the 1970s and 1980s; however, it soon became clear that the relationship between the money supply and inflation was not as consistent as Friedman and his fellow monetarists had thought. Indeed, even Friedman expressed surprise at the way some monetary indicators performed. It is perhaps a testament to Friedman's ability to communicate his ideas that the European Central Bank and the People's Bank of China still maintain money supply growth aggregates as key indicators of monetary policy, despite the evidence suggesting that they are not particularly helpful.

The demise of monetarism in the 1980s was subsequently filled by a loose conglomeration of ideas which eventually developed into the new Neo-classical Synthesis forming the backbone of monetary theory today. These ideas borrow substantially from the general equilibrium framework of Walras, through to the ideas on money from Fisher and Friedman and with a little bit of Keynesian realism about how markets do not function thrown in for good measure. In addition to this body of thought, a number of ideas that were developed in the 1970s by Robert Lucas Junior were added. Lucas, another University of Chicago economist and influenced by Friedman, argued that economic agents were rational and thus could not be systematically wrong in their predictions of the path of economic variables such as inflation and output. By implication this means that the errors made by economic agents are random in nature, fluctuating around equilibrium, as the forecasts of rational agents do not differ systematically from equilibrium results. The idea of fluctuations around general equilibrium was enhanced in the 1980s by Real Business Cycle Theory, which highlighted that in downturns, potential GDP can fall due to negative external shocks. Real Business Cycle Theory argues that exogenous shocks to an economy lead to changes in output which cause the oscillation around equilibrium, with the corresponding changes in output being an efficient response to the shock.

Lucas's other major contribution was the idea that macroeconomic models should be built on microeconomic foundations. These ideas were further enhanced by the development of mainly neo-Keynesian economists who argued that such models ought to be more realistic and include assumptions of imperfect competition and the stickiness in the movement of prices and wages when adjusting to new economic conditions. This led to the development of Dynamic Stochastic General Equilibrium (DSGE) models that broke down an economy into a series of economic agents interacting with each other to help understand the behaviour of households and firms related to changes in consumption, savings, labour supply, wage setting, investment and capital accumulation. At the heart of DSGE models was the assumption that the supply and demand between producers and consumers based on profit optimisation and utility maximisation leads to a general equilibrium. By the late 1990s DSGE models began to complement the Keynesian large macroeconomic models used by central banks to forecast key economic variables.

The most important component of modern macroeconomic theory is however the notion that central banks are able to control inflation via monetary policy. The implicit assumption being that an economy can be maintained close to its equilibrium level by adjusting the nominal rate of interest in response to changes in key economic variables. These ideas, which originated from Irving Fisher, were further developed by the work of John B. Taylor at Stanford University. What came to be known as the Taylor Rule was developed as a practical tool for central banks to maintain actual inflation close to target inflation and actual output close to potential output by using the nominal rate of interest. Taylor used this theoretical background to generate a simple rule which stated by how much a central bank should move the nominal interest rate in response to changes in inflation or output. Implicit in the Taylor Rule was Friedman's idea that inflation was an endogenous variable. Using the Quantity Theory of Money equation, Taylor argued that as velocity was a function of interest rates and output, the rate of interest could be expressed as a function of prices and output. Thus, Friedman's money growth targets were substituted by interest rates. Taylor also argued that nominal interest rates should be raised by more than a change in the rate of inflation to manage expectations and reduce the size and duration of the fluctuations of output, employment and inflation, which were Taylor's ultimate objectives. Thus a zero-output gap target, where actual GDP is equivalent to potential GDP, would bring stability to an economy.

The Great Myth comes under attack

By the summer of 2007, after 25 years of low inflation, low unemployment and robust growth, not to mention the thousands of research papers and the millions of hours that had gone into improving our understanding of the economy, the Great Myth had reached its pinnacle. The core ideas of general equilibrium, rational expectations and inflation targeting, it seemed, had conquered the business cycle, providing producers and consumers with the ideal environment for the market to function as it was supposed to. Moreover, the idea that it was the wisdom of the central bankers and economists that had brought this scenario about was, unsurprisingly, extremely well received by the leading players.

The fact that almost an entire industry was duped, resulting in investors losing trillions of dollars of their clients' money should therefore not be as surprising as one might think. The theory seemed logical and it took inflation into account, which is bad for investors. The fact that some data discrepancies in the theory were ignored was unfortunate as data discrepancies play a crucial role in invalidating theories of all kinds in the social as well as the natural sciences. For example Newtonian mechanics could not explain the trajectory of Mercury's orbit around the sun. It wasn't until Einstein's theory of relativity that Mercury's orbit could be forecast accurately. However failures in economics impact the daily lives of people, including through unemployment and falling living conditions. Thus it is even more important that data discrepancies are taken into account in economic models, rather than being conveniently ignored.

As the financial crisis deteriorated, the chorus of attacks on the Great Myth began to get louder from former central bankers and economists. In 2008 Joseph Stiglitz wrote a short article for the Project Syndicate blog attacking inflation-targeting as being based on little economic theory or empirical evidence.[27] Some economists have taken a different approach and in fact questioned whether central bankers' policies of inflation-targeting had much to do with the reduced inflation volatility of the last 25 or so years, or whether broader macroeconomic trends were responsible for this reduction in volatility. Mankiw, a Harvard economics professor, stated before the Crisis that 'monetary policy has improved both in those countries that have adopted inflation targets and in those that have not',[28] the implication being that perhaps it wasn't due to the wisdom of central bankers and modern monetary theory after all. Mankiw concludes his paper on a similar note to Buiter, stating that from the 'standpoint of macroeconomic engineering, the work of the past several decades looks like an unfortunate wrong turn.'[29] Other economists have also argued that inflation-targeting has in fact had little impact on the Great Moderation with its low inflation volatility.[30]

The Nobel Laureate Robert Solow has also criticised the current approach to macroeconomic modelling in elite universities and central banks as having 'absolutely nothing to say about the problem'.[31] Buiter's comments in his *Financial Times* blog echo this, highlighting that the economics profession was caught unprepared when the crisis struck, due to the focus of economic research on the internal logic of established research programmes rather than on a desire to understand how the economy works. Furthermore, a paper by two economists at the Bank of England in 2009 accepted that recent events were hard to reconcile with existing economic theory, stating that 'the coexistence of stable growth and inflation and a long lasting credit and financial cycle brought to an end by a global financial crisis *challenges* the macroeconomic consensus that has grown up since the emergence of inflation as a major economic policy problem in the late 1960s and early 1970s. That consensus stressed the importance of controlling inflation as an essential underpinning for broader economic stability.'[32] More recently the Bank of International Settlements highlighted that central banks are now making decisions, 'in full knowledge that their benchmark macroeconomic paradigms have failed them.'[33]

Although this ever-growing band of commentators is highlighting that the current approach to monetary policy is flawed, in the absence of anything else to fill the vacuum, many economists are still focused on how to improve the existing framework. Central banks retain a large amount of staff to maintain complex statistical models in an attempt to try and make them perform better in relation to recent data sets. Investors are trying to make sense of these signals; however, the volatility of financial assets since the onset of the financial crisis highlights the uncertainty of many investors related to which signals they should now be using. However, the fact that some hedge fund managers have been able to generate excellent returns through time by ignoring the framework of general equilibrium, rational expectations and inflation-targeting suggests that investors would be better off rejecting the system that has led to such catastrophic falls in returns. This puts the onus on constructing a new theory that can provide investors with a more consistent signalling framework to chart the ups and downs of the business cycle. Monetary policy has clearly failed in its attempt to conquer the business cycle, thus rendering modern macroeconomic theory as mostly unhelpful for investors.

Chapter 2

From model failures to streams of data

Professional economists, after Malthus, were apparently unmoved by the lack of correspondence between the results of their theory and the facts of observation. A discrepancy the ordinary man has not failed to observe.

John Maynard Keynes[1]

The negative performance of pension funds since the Financial Crisis started in 2007 has provided the market with a new stream of data that exposes the Great Moderation as nothing more than a Great Myth. This Myth, with its impeccable intellectual background, became the framework for an entire generation of financial market practitioners, resulting in the fall of future retirement income for savers as well as increasing unfunded liabilities for tax payers. In conjunction with this new stream of data, a groundswell of opinion has begun to attack the very foundations of the Myth as it no longer fits the facts. Indeed, some economists and successful investors have argued that it never fitted the facts and that economic modelling is incapable of providing any useful predictions about the future anyway. An economy is a highly complex system and the simple assumptions made that are supposed to help predict the trajectory of an economy are highly dubious. However, like any idea that has had some longevity, it is unlikely to go down without a fight.

A number of arguments have been put forward supporting the current macroeconomic framework, stating that there is nothing fundamentally flawed with the current theory. Hence blame has been lumped on exogenous factors, such as the ineffective implementation of policy, lax regulation of the banking sector, OTC derivatives, poor structured finance credit ratings and fraud in the mortgage market. Clearly all these factors played a role in the lead-up to the Crisis, and new regulation will help prevent some of these specific issues from occurring again. However, there is no substantive reason why the current macroeconomic framework will generate useful investment signals, even if some of the described exogenous factors are neutralised. This is because the simplistic assumptions about the nature of equilibrium as it pertains to the relationship between inflation and output are inherently flawed.

It just needs tweaking

One of the more lucid arguments that support the current macroeconomic framework is from Chairman Bernanke of the Federal Reserve. In March 2005, Bernanke gave a lecture to the Virginia Association of Economists.[2] His remarks focused on the issue of the growing US current account deficit, raising the question why the world's largest economy was, 'borrowing heavily on international capital markets – rather than lending, as would seem more natural?'[3] His answer to this question was that during the Great Moderation a global savings glut developed, which in turn had pushed long-term US interest rates down.

Bernanke recognised that part of the problem was because the savings rate in the United States had fallen considerably over the period. Hence, there was a need to finance the deficit using external capital. However, he also highlighted the fact that an 'excess' of capital due to higher savings rates from the emerging markets was looking for assets to invest in. He noted that this savings glut was perhaps unsurprising, given that crises in both Latin America and Asia in the 1980s and 1990s highlighted the dangers of borrowing on the international capital market. The rise in the price of oil also increased surpluses in oil exporting countries. Bernanke sums up the issue succinctly. 'This increased supply of saving boosted US equity values during the period of the stock market boom and helped increase US home values during the more recent period, as a consequence lowering US national saving and contributing to the nation's rising current account deficit.'

Given Bernanke's role as Chairman of the Fed, this statement is somewhat puzzling as it gives the impression that there was little the Fed could have done about it. Indeed, he concluded by stating that 'inward looking policies are unlikely to resolve the issue. Thus a more direct approach is to help and encourage developing countries to re-enter international capital markets in their more natural role as borrowers rather than as lenders.' Bernanke consequently restated this conclusion post-Crisis in March 2009.[4] Moreover, this view has a number of other influential adherents.[5] However, as highlighted in an excellent paper from the BIS, this view needs to be reconsidered, particularly given that that the United Kingdom (a deficit country) in conjunction with the eurozone (in balance) were the largest buyers of US securities, largely undermining Bernanke's assertions.[6]

Thus Bernanke's conclusion that the system just needs a few tweaks is problematic. Firstly, the implication of policies to encourage foreign governments to dictate to their populations how much to spend and how much to save looks like a victory for centralised planning. Centralised planning does not feature in the assumptions in macroeconomic models based on micro foundations. Centralised planning, and its attempt to force economic behaviour on populations, was a bad idea in the 20th century and it is still a bad idea today. Secondly, is why the Fed did not raise interest rates to stop money flowing into housing assets given its ability to influence the cost of credit. Higher rates would have reduced borrowing for consumption and buying houses, as well as improving the outlook for savings. Indeed, higher borrowing costs would have acted as a restraint, bringing the housing bubble to an end. Perhaps Bernanke's response would have been that raising interest rates may have generated deflation, which, given his knowledge of the Great Depression by definition, meant economic contraction.

However, the criticism of the Fed for not raising interest rates fast enough was indeed the view of John Taylor. In 2007 he presented an interesting paper at Jackson Hole, arguing that the Taylor Rule still worked.[7] The problem, he argued, was that interest rates were held too low for too long between the second quarter of 2002 and the third quarter of 2006, causing the housing boom that turned to bust at the onset of the Crisis. Indeed, Taylor's model suggests that had the Fed followed the Taylor Rule, much of the housing boom would have been avoided. However, Taylor's paper does not state what might have happened to inflation had rates been raised as he had suggested. If inflation had fallen to zero, what would Taylor's rule then have recommended? Rate cut? Another aspect of Taylor's analysis that is also problematic is during the 1990s when foreign capital flows were fuelling US equity values, according to Taylor, the Fed set interest rates in accordance with the Taylor Rule. The influx of foreign capital in the 1990s according to Bernanke was similar to the housing boom in the early 2000s suggesting rates were too low during both periods. Thus the Taylor Rule appears to be unable to consistently explain deviations from an optimum level of growth. The reality is that the more economists have looked at elements of the current macroeconomic framework the more problems are found. One of the most important assumptions in the theory is related to how the central bank can maintain an economy close to equilibrium by minimising fluctuations in inflation and output. This necessitates central banks to be able to accurately measure the difference between actual GDP and potential GDP. The measurement process is however ad hoc at best generating dubious results, which is another reason why investors should refrain from using signals emanating from central banks in an investment process.

Problems in measuring equilibrium

The first of the issues in measuring equilibrium is that actual output data are continually revised, meaning that the known variable is not in fact as well-known as one would hope. Secondly, the calculation of potential GDP is fraught with difficulties which the Fed itself has highlighted as being problematic. The Fed stated that 'the current rate of inflation and position of the economy in relation to full employment are not known because of data lags and difficulties in estimating the full-employment level of output'.[8] The measurement of potential output is problematic as two of the key inputs that feed into the calculation are pure estimates: the growth in the labour force and the underlying growth in labour productivity. Changes in the size of the labour force can vary greatly over time due to immigration, both legal and illegal, and emigration. Moreover, social changes have resulted in shifts in working patterns, such as more women entering the work force or changing retirement patterns, thus making estimates of the size of the labour force more difficult. The measurement of underlying productivity growth is even more challenging and has varied considerably over recent decades. Indeed, the subsequent evolution of data, particularly for labour productivity, may indicate that the economy has undergone a structural change. According to the Fed, these differences can be considerable, moving from 'approximately 1 per cent or so per year to somewhere in the neighborhood of 3 per cent or even higher, getting a major boost during the mid- and late 1990s from applications of information technology and advanced management systems'.[9]

Finally, estimates of potential output differ significantly depending on the statistical approach used to generate the estimates. The scale of misleading signals because of these issues can be considerable according to two leading economists. 'Ex post revisions of the output gap are of the same order of magnitude as the output gap itself.... Moreover, these revisions are highly persistent and tend to be severely biased around business cycle turning points, when the cost of policy induced errors due to incorrect measurement are at their greatest.'[10]

Perhaps somewhat surprisingly central bankers have been quite candid about this problem. The Central Bank of Iceland highlighted that calculating the output gap raises problems because there are numerous statistical approaches that can be used to generate estimates. The problem is that all approaches 'yield different outcomes, often with marked divergences'.[11] The Central Bank of New Zealand also highlights the problem of potential output measurement, concluding that using a single measure of potential output is not acceptable for policy purposes because of the bias it causes in inflation forecasting.[12] Indeed, the scepticism of being able to provide any useful estimates on the output gap goes back to Milton Friedman himself. Friedman argued that the central bankers should focus on aggregates they can control, hence his recommendation to target monetary growth aggregates. However, given that monetary targets proved an abject failure, it has been left to central bankers to at least take a stab at what potential output might be. Taylor argued that this issue should not be of major concern for central bankers as errors in stimulating potential GDP will eventually reveal themselves in rising or falling inflation.[13] The central bank would then see the undesirable change in price levels and correct the level with the appropriate shift in interest rates. The data leading up and into the credit Crisis shows this guide did not work.

This leads on to the second major problem related to measuring equilibrium, which is the relationship of inflation to potential output. The output gap in Taylor's formula and in many central banking models is defined as the component of real output that is associated with changes in inflation. This implies that inflation is endogenous and also that inflation itself is the yardstick with which to measure deviations from an optimum level of output. If an economy is overheating, it will reveal itself in higher inflation, and if it is underperforming, inflation will fall. This would appear to be a reasonable assumption for a closed economy. However, this is clearly not a particularly useful approach given the current interdependency of the world economy. Interestingly, Irving Fisher did argue that exogenous shocks will impact prices in the short run but that general equilibrium will ensure these increased costs are transient rather than permanent. However, as was observed in Bill Phillips' data set, there is no relationship between employment and inflation when there is imported inflation and deflation, a fact that seems to have been consistently ignored by monetary economists such as Friedman and his followers.

Today, most central banks make a distinction between endogenously driven inflation and imported inflation, and as a result have divided up their inflation measures into two different data sets labelled as core and non-core. The idea being that core inflation excludes 'imported prices' whereas headline inflation or non-core includes it. As commodity prices have risen since 2009, central bankers are beginning to focus on this distinction more; however, it is unclear whether this distinction has any real meaning when it comes to expectations of inflation. Indeed, rising import prices have historically had a devastating impact on expectations and inflation. Meghnad Desai in his excellent book *Testing Monetarism* highlighted two examples where dramatic falls in output impacted prices, leading to hyperinflation. The French occupation of the Ruhr in 1923, which produced a third of Germany's output, accelerated, if not initiated, Germany's hyper-inflation. As Desai argues, 'an exogenous reduction of one third in output cannot easily be said to have no effect on prices'.[14] Furthermore the loss of output for the Chinese economy, according to Desai, 'could not have been negligible', after the Japanese occupation of Manchuria impacted China's hyper-inflation in the 1940s.

More recently, central banks in emerging markets have also felt the importance of exogenous factors with regard to inflation. Both the Central Bank of Chile and the South African Reserve Bank have highlighted these issues, particularly related to oil and food prices.[15] It is hard to imagine a Walrasian situation where rising food prices means consumers eat less, resulting in falling demand, and so prices fall. Rising food prices tend to cause social unrest in emerging markets as the recent Arab Spring uprising demonstrated. It can take a considerable amount of time for new supply to make it on to the international market to bring prices down – which is why there has been a steady growth in food commodity prices over the last decade. Hence, it was all the more important when a recent paper by two economists at the ECB highlighted that commodity price shocks that increase headline inflation do feed through to core inflation. In essence, exogenous factors do have an impact on inflation.[16] Research by Borio at the BIS has also highlighted the importance of the global determinants of domestic inflation as did the IMF to an extent.[17]

This fact is crucial because from time to time significant structural shifts take place that impact the global economy. One such structural shift that occurred during the 1990s and early 2000s was when China, and to a lesser extent India, exported deflation to Europe and the United States.[18] Several hundred million people who were previously part of closed, domestic economies entered the global labour market. The challenge with these shifts is that it is not always obvious at the time that the shift is indeed occurring. Secondly, even if the shift is recognised, it is not clear what impact it will have on the economy. Most economists, central bankers and hence investors it seemed thought this was beneficial. Europe and the United States could maintain their growth rates in conjunction with low interest rates without seeing the spectre of inflation rearing its ugly head. There was very little questioning that this might have had a negative impact; it appears to have been just accepted as a fact of the new global economy.

Just after the launch of the Euro at a conference in Frankfurt, a senior central banker from the Bundesbank was sitting on panel discussing macroeconomic shifts in the global economy. A member of the audience smugly asked him what he was going to do now that the ECB was set up. 'Actually I wasn't doing anything before the ECB was setup,' was his reply, 'we outsourced monetary policy to China several years ago.' The response was greeted with hoots of laughter with the questioner abruptly sitting down with a rather embarrassed look on his face.

The response highlights why investors should reject their current signalling framework. The implications are that as long as inflation is kept low, it is theoretically impossible for an economy to be growing above its long-term trend. Current monetary theory suggests that it is inflation itself that indicates whether or not an economy is operating above its long-term potential, and yet in this instance, it was China (and India) deflating the general price level. This raises the possibility that the whole Western economy may have been growing above its optimum level, with interest rates held consistently too low for over 20 years. If that was the case then the Financial Crisis ought to have been predictable. Indeed those investors who did ignore the current macroeconomic consensus and went against the trend made an absolute fortune.

Given the challenges of measuring equilibrium as well as the fact that the relationship between inflation and output stopped behaving as expected, predictions of asset price movements based on economic forecasts have lost any credibility they may have once had, and rightly so. The view that by reducing a highly complex system with millions of interacting agents into a series of simplistic assumptions about human behaviour and then expect the outputs to have value as part of an investment process is naïve at best. This view is becoming increasingly accepted, which is another reason for investors to reject the existing monetary policy framework as a source of investment signals.

The failure of economic modelling

In 2011, the Federal Reserve published a paper that compared economic forecasts based on micro foundations with more standard macroeconomic models. The conclusion was rather bleak for economists and potentially for investors. It stated that 'DSGE models are very poor in forecasting, but so are all other approaches'.[19] However, this has not stopped the wide use of econometric models by investors in an attempt to identify factors which can provide leading indicators of asset value trends. The reality is that these models are far too simple to capture the dynamism of an economy, and given the unexpected fall in pension assets have not turned out to have been particularly useful. When models are set up, they are generally built to fit past data as a way of testing the model's validity, which clearly becomes self-referential. Although out of sample tests are a useful validation technique, the calibration process is generally fitted to observed historical data sets and the apparent stability of those relationships over time. The reflexivity or expectations aspect of such models are also crucial, given this acts to reinforce the relationship in stable conditions. However, once the relationship becomes unstable and breaks down, the relationship can become non-linear and difficult to model. This is exactly what happened during the Crisis when the relationship between low inflation, rising asset prices and sustainable output broke down. However, this does call into question what the actual relationship between these variables was.

Indeed, an analysis of the constant streams of data gives a different perspective to an econometric analysis of the data. For instance, when Phillips plotted his curve, statistically it looked robust enough from which to develop broad statements about how an economy behaved. These insights could then be translated into investment signals with regard to forecasting real GDP growth and asset allocation strategies. The relationship between unemployment and inflation appeared to hold statistically only because the observations that disproved the relationship were conveniently ignored.

Friedman's argument which undermined the Phillips Curve focused almost entirely on expectations, thus ignoring the statistical anomalies in Phillips' analysis. Indeed, in constructing his own argument to demonstrate that it was the rate of money growth that caused an economy to move in and out of equilibrium, Friedman committed the same errors by conveniently ignoring data anomalies.

In *A Monetary History of the United States* co-authored with Anna Schwarz, Friedman demonstrated a broad relationship between the growth of the money supply, economic activity and inflation. However, the relationship did not always hold, and there are many instances of charts in his book which highlight these deviations.[20] This 'stable relationship' led Friedman in conjunction with his adherence to the quantity theory of money to conclude that stable growth in monetary stock equated to stable inflation and stable output. He also argued that 'these common elements of monetary experience can be expected to characterise our future as they have the past'.[21]

The period of the Great Moderation which was distinguished by its non-inflationary expansion was in many respects similar to the period of the 1920s. Although the Fed in the 1930s was guilty of certain policy failures, Friedman's argument that the economy was in fact doing just fine in 1929 because inflation was low and the money supply was 'stable' is reminiscent of the Great Moderation argument. Friedman's policy recommendation of an injection of money to maintain the level of output has been disproven by the data, further undermining the credibility of his entire argument. Indeed, between 2008 and 2011, central bankers returned to monetarism and embarked upon a massive monetary stimulus plan, with little sign of an economic renaissance. This is not to dispute that an increase in money does not have a general tendency under certain conditions to increase inflation, only to demonstrate that the relationship cannot be used as a fundamental building block in order to generate useful investment signals because under certain conditions the data shows it does not hold.

Econometric models have been used for decades to demonstrate how relationships do or do not exist between variables. This is not to deny the importance and utility of econometrics in attempting to explain historical patterns; it is just that it needs to be accepted that they have limited predictive power. However, even attempting to explain the historical relationships can be challenging, with economists sometimes focussing on the results as the deciding factor, when they should only be seen as helpful supporting evidence.

My econometrics teacher warned me of this when he described a former colleague and professor of economics who was paid by the tobacco lobby to demonstrate statistically that there was no link between smoking and lung cancer. The results were compelling enough to prevent governments from intervening in the market for many years. Unfortunately the professor fared less well. A heavy smoker, he died of lung cancer.

Other aspects of modelling have also caused investment signals to fail, in particular this relates to the assumptions made by the models themselves. For example, most macroeconomic models that are used to forecast output and inflation assume that consumers and producers are intent on maximising utility and profits. Clearly the real-world experience of consumers and producers is rather different. Firstly, time horizons for consumers and producers to maximise their utility and profits will be different. Hence, an economy is infinitely more complex with different decisions being taken by different agents at different time frames. The second problem relates to the questioning of the motives themselves. The explosion of social enterprises and altruistic consumer behaviour are the often-cited examples where these assumptions are flawed, although the assumptions may well hold in certain circumstances for certain people. However, the behaviour within the so-called profit maximising producer set is also, often, far from being what the neo-classical economists call 'rational'.

According to the management theorist Peter Drucker, companies rarely pursue profit maximising behaviour as, if they did, they would most likely lose their client base and go out of business in the medium term. Hence he argued that corporations ought to pursue a policy of a required minimum profit to cover their own future risks and maintain intact the wealth-producing capacity of their resources.[22] Indeed Drucker lambasts the assumption by the neoclassical economists of profit maximisation, particularly given their limited experience in running companies. Moreover, many decisions made within companies are often more closely aligned to the utility of individuals rather than the company itself, such as executive remuneration. Decisions about which suppliers to choose may also have strands of individual utility creeping in for senior executives. One specific example I came across early in my career was a North American company which was buying expensive product components made in France, which could have been bought from a supplier 50 miles away at a lower price. The initial reason given by the manager in concern was quality. However, it seemed that the annual trip to visit the company in Paris had other benefits, particularly shopping for luxury goods.

Profit maximising behaviour also assumes that executives have sufficient information about their own businesses with which to make these decisions. Indeed, the ability of companies to take bad decisions because they have bad data is highly plausible, which may partly explain the unpredictability of company-specific risk. This is why it is hard for investors to maintain a consistent track record of selecting good stocks. There are just too many unknowns. However such potentially random-like outcomes do appear to be explained by one of the most controversial assumptions in finan- cial economics – that of the efficient market hypothesis (EMH). Robert Lucas, one of the intellectual founders of the current macroeconomic paradigm has stressed our inability to forecast sud- den falls in the value of financial assets because of the assumptions of EMH.[23] Lucas uses EMH, where the price of a financial asset reflects all relevant, generally available, information to show this. If prices were able to be forecast, then this information itself would become reflected in the price. Indeed, the nature of randomness in EMH and in Rational Expectations Theory is a very powerful argument that forecasts of the future are fundamentally unsound. If that is the case then the investment management sector cannot add much value to the investment process, and ought to just inform their clients that nothing could have been done to stop the fall in the value of assets.

However, this does not explain how some investors, by ignoring the current economic paradigm, have been able to invest through the cycle. Moreover, one of Lucas' central premises is that the out- come of rational expectations cannot lead to outcomes that are systematically different to equilibrium. The data since 2008 shows that the expectations of the market in 2007 were wildly wrong. Indeed, it is striking that the investors who were never taken in by the Great Myth generally used data intensive methods to form trading decisions rather than using modelling techniques based on simplified assumptions of human behaviour.

Efficient markets?

EMH expounds the view that all relevant information is already priced into a security today, and that the information from yes- terday's price has no impact on today's price. This requires that each price in a time series are independent of each other, and that prices only change with respect to changes in underlying fundamentals. Moreover, it asserts that it is not possible to predict future returns and thus returns, both positive and negative (losses), are distributed normally. These ideas have always remained traditionally contested by market participants who felt that EMH was contradicting the fact that they were smart enough to beat the market. Despite this fact EMH still became a central plank of derivative pricing. Other opponents included a small band of behavioural economists, who in particular have cautioned against some of EMH's wilder claims and the fact that it ignores human behaviour. For instance, in October 1987 when the stock market crashed, an economist posed the question as to whether 'the present value of the US economy really fell more than 20 per cent on that Monday and then rose over 9 per cent on Wednesday?'[24] Robert Shiller in his excellent book *Irrational Exuberance* also attacked the ideas around efficient markets arguing that 'investors, their confidence and expectations buoyed by past price increases, bid up stock prices further, thereby enticing more investors to do the same, so that the cycle repeats again and again, resulting in an amplified response to the original precipitating factors'.[25]

Since the onset of the recent Financial Crisis, the level of criticism of EMH has gone up several notches, particularly given that such dramatic changes in asset prices in 2008 suggest that there was indeed a period of mispricing before the Crisis, rather than a sudden jump in fundamentals within such a short space of time. Moreover, the idea that there was a credit bubble leading up to the Crisis is widely accepted, which is of course contrary to EMH and rational expectations which argues that asset bubbles cannot exist. Finally, assumptions of the normal distributions of returns meant that investors remained generally unconcerned about large unexpected events, as from a probabilistic perspective such events were so remote that they could be discounted. To a large extent most of the criticisms of EMH have been made against the simplest model of EMH which assumes independence of observations and normal distributions. However, it is worth pointing out that most recent testing for EMH has been done on a weaker version of the random walk where the condition for price independence and normal distributions is relaxed.[26]

The results in general are mixed with no real consensus developing, with perhaps one exception as highlighted by the great economist Paul Samuelson. Samuelson believed that markets are generally micro-efficient but certainly not macro-efficient.[27] At the micro level, EMH argues that there is no point in constructing sophisticated models to project an individual company's future valuation, as markets do a reasonably good job at synthesizing the information relevant to that company. It is only when insider information is disclosed that prices move, and this can move in both ways. The fact that it is very hard for stock pickers to consistently beat the market suggests that this is potentially a good proxy. However, the idea that EMH is useful at the market level is clearly counterintuitive given there is a great deal of evidence that asset bubbles do exist. Moreover, in general the investors who have been able to consistently beat the market have been global macro investors and not stock pickers.

The problem with EMH at the macro level is that it makes the huge assumption that investors are able to digest all the relevant information available to make sense of the trajectory of an economy. Given the complexity of the system, this is an almost impossible task; hence, most investors have been using the assumptions filtered by the intellectual background of general equilibrium. In reality, this amounts to assessing the relationship between output and inflation and what it can tell us about the future direction of these variables. If the relationship between output and inflation did hold through time as Fisher, Friedman and the new neoclassical synthesis have led us to believe, then EMH at the macro level would be more plausible.

This issue challenges the nature of rational expectations when it comes to macroeconomics, as it assumes investors know what information is the right information to be looking at. If that information has been sending misleading signals to investors, then we should have expected to have seen periodically large unexpected losses, which we clearly did in 2000 and 2008. This also suggests that at the macro level, data series are less likely to be independent of each other, with yesterday's price having more in common with today's price and tomorrow's price, a process described as long-term memory. This is in keeping with Shiller's analysis of human behaviour and of course explains asset bubbles too. Such an approach to analysing macro data also suggests that the behaviour of markets changes through time. It is perfectly possible for markets to display linear and random behaviour for a time generating a stream of data validating EMH. However, there are also likely to be periods when markets display a non-linear and deterministic trajectory which refutes EMH. Indeed, such a trajectory is more in line with the nature of complex, dynamical systems and an economy is one of the most complex systems that can be analysed.

The implication that the streams of data through time at the macro level are constantly changing has a bearing on the distribution of returns. If the streams of data are generated from a simple, linear and random process, then a normal distribution (Gaussian) is appropriate. However, if the process is non-linear and displays long-term memory, then a different distribution of returns can be expected. Any process with an extended long-term memory is likely to have an increasing probability of extreme values. Indeed, the idea that the probability of heavy losses can increase and decrease through time depending on the extent of long-term memory is critical for investors to take note of. These ideas are however not new; they were introduced into financial theory decades ago by the mathematician Benoit Mandelbrot.

In the early 1960s Mandelbrot, in an analysis of cotton prices, found that values might persist for some time and then suddenly change, but that there were also periods where sudden discontinuous changes can occur. This insight can be broadly applied to financial data, whereby in an asset boom, the way in which markets develop owes more to the reflexive or self-referential information of investors believing in the boom as described by Shiller. Thus tomorrow's value is more related to today's value. Given that asset price bubbles are unsustainable, at some stage this leads to a sudden jump or fall. This in turn induces a period of volatility where prices jump around violently. Mandelbrot labelled these two effects as Noah and Joseph.[28] The Joseph effect describes the upward movement of an asset bubble or general trend akin to the Biblical story about seven continuous years of abundant harvests. The Noah effect describes sudden discontinuous changes which generally describe a highly volatile period with a great deal of uncertainty, akin to God's attempt in Genesis to purify the world with a catastrophic flood.

For an asset bubble to exist, the market would by definition be increasing along a predictable trend line, which implies stored long-term memory. This of course means that signals emanating from current monetary policy as deployed by central banks are not efficient and therefore investors should stop using them. Interestingly, Shiller and Jung have empirically looked at Samuelson's famous statement and provided a strong argument to support it.[29] Such an approach also means that non-linear trajectories are far more likely to explain an economy than a linear one. As John Kay argued in the FT, 'economic systems are typically dynamic and non-linear. This means that outcomes are likely to be very sensitive to small changes in the parameters that determine their evolution. These systems are also reflexive in the sense that beliefs about what will happen influence what does happen.'[30] Buiter also highlighted the reality of the non-linear relationships in an economy which are complex to model and which resulted in the new neoclassical contingent, 'stripping the model of its non-linearities and by achieving the trans-substantiation of complex convolutions of random variables and non-linear mappings into well-behaved additive stochastic disturbances'.[31]

Modelling non-linear systems is hard in the natural sciences as well, as they generally have multiple solutions, many of which are impossible to calculate. Linearising any non-linearities eliminates any understanding of the dynamism of the non-linear system. Hence it is interesting to note that the natural sciences have been moving away from attempting to model complex systems towards looking at streams of data as being the most effective way of understanding the nature of a complex, dynamical system. For example, the way in which a drop of water drips from a tap highlights not only the challenge of modelling non-linear systems but also the way scientists have fundamentally changed the way they now approach these kind of problems. Science has increasingly moved away from attempting to construct complex models towards analysing streams of data. This change came about in the 1970s and was the result of the development of Chaos Theory. James Gleick's book on Chaos recalls the research by Robert Shaw, one of the pioneers of Chaos Theory that is worth repeating. The ability to predict when the drop might actually drip would require a very complicated model of the physical processes. After identifying the main variables including the flow of water, the viscosity of the fluid and the surface tension, the challenge comes with predicting the behaviour of the process. As the drop fills with water oscillating in multiple directions, it eventually reaches a critical point and snaps off. As Gleick writes: 'A physicist trying to model the drip problem completely – writing down sets of coupled non-linear partial differential equations with appropriate boundary conditions and then trying to solve them – would find himself lost in a deep, deep thicket.'[32]

The solution was of course to abandon the modelling and analyse the output of streams of data instead. This is no different to the handful of investors who were able to make sense of the direction of an economy by ignoring the current economic modelling paradigm, analysing streams of data instead. So how can the collected and on-going data be used to understand the behaviour of a system? Shaw in the late 1970s used his data from the dripping tap to plot a graph of the relationship between a single drop and its subsequent drop. If the dripping was regular and predictable it would always fall on the same spot. If it was random, dots would be scattered all over the graph. What Shaw found was that there was a deterministic pattern to the dripping that resembled a chaotic attractor, including elements of unpredictability. The challenge was then how to generate simple equations that would explain the chaotic system through time.

Chaotic attractors were first discovered by the meteorologist Edward Lorenz back in 1962. Lorenz found that by inputting the same data into a weather prediction computer programme at different stages of the programme led to different outcomes. This formed the basis of the now well-known concept in Chaos Theory of the sensitivity to initial conditions or the Butterfly Effect. The flapping wing represents a small change in the initial condition of the system, which then causes a chain of events leading to large-scale phenomena. Had the butterfly not flapped its wings, the trajectory of the system might have been significantly different. Such an approach however rejects the notion of any natural tendency towards equilibrium. Indeed, as biologists have begun to study the brain in more detail, they have found it is one of the most chaotic organs in existence. This has led the scientific community away from the traditional view of equilibrium as being a natural state. According to one leading neuroscientist, 'when you reach an equilibrium in biology, you're dead'.[33] Given that an economy is a function of the decisions that millions of chaotic brains make, it should not be surprising that an economy does not naturally tend towards an equilibrium state. Moreover, the idea that an economy might follow a deterministic but unpredictable trajectory is also highly plausible given the arguments of Shiller and the behavioural psychology school.

This begins to resemble our problem with economic modelling and to an extent validates the Fed's paper on forecasting and Lucas' views on EMH. Given that there is determinism in the system, short-term forecasts in economics are still valid; however, any medium-term predictions become redundant due to the sensitivity of the system to any changes in initial conditions. This suggests that investors need to stop modelling and focus on the analysis of streams of data if they are to generate returns for their clients. This approach is supported by Mandelbrot who stated that 'we cannot know everything. Physicists abandoned that pipedream during the twentieth century after quantum theory and in a different way after Chaos Theory. Instead they learned to think of the world in the second way as a black box. We can see what goes into the box and what comes out but not what is happening inside.'[34]

An economy does not function in a random way at all, but is rather the outcome of the individual decisions made by the hundreds of millions of economic agents across the globe. Research has highlighted that deterministic non-linear systems can generate apparent random behaviour, which is why empirical studies of the random walk, even at the macro level, can hold in certain periods of time.[35] This determinism is complemented by unexpected outcomes supporting the notion that observing inputs and outcomes is more likely to be of use than trying to understand what is going on inside the system. In a recent paper two economists highlight much of this thinking, posing the question that if 'business cycles are caused by non-linear dynamics, how appropriate a scientific approach is to base our analysis on linear considerations?'[36]

The analysis of streams of data, instead of depending on the signals of real GDP forecasts emanating from the general equilibrium framework, can provide a new structure for investors to avoid the pitfalls of large and unexpected losses. However, investors need to understand the nature of the determinism in the system in order to make the appropriate investments. This can be reduced to understanding the general economic trend, and more importantly, how far away from equilibrium an economy is trending. The key stream of data that can help understand this determinism is related to the growth in credit, something that was largely ignored by the new neoclassical synthesis. Indeed, the existing set of macroeconomic models that underpin monetary policy assumed that credit markets would maintain some form of equilibrium, thus preventing credit bubbles developing.

The omission of credit from macroeconomic models is both unsurprising, given the intellectual heritage of the new neoclassical synthesis, and shocking, given credit is the life blood of modern capitalism. As two leading monetary economists have pointed out, 'there are by construction no banks, no borrowing constraints, and no risks of default, the risk free short term interest suffices to model the monetary side of the economy. As a consequence money or credit aggregates and asset prices play no role in standard versions of these models.'[37] Not surprisingly, these omissions are beginning to be heavily criticised with the BIS stating that 'the role of monetary and financial factors is too peripheral in today's macroeconomic models. In particular the paradigms do not capture the essence of what Wicksell called pure credit economies. This is the true essence of current fiat money arrangements in which the creation of credit and hence of purchasing power is only constrained by the central banks' control over short term rates. The models are in effect real models disguised as monetary ones'.[38]

Money is a crime?

According to Friedman, the credit market was merely a supporting player to the central role of money.[39] This followed on from Fisher's description of business cycles as being the dance of the dollar. Unfortunately the influence of Fisher and Friedman on today's monetary theory has largely been responsible for the fact that money remains in the ascendency with credit an aside. It is no accident that we refer to central bank policy as monetary policy rather than credit policy. One reason why credit has often been ignored is that it is more difficult to model than money. Money is anonymous and therefore is not impacted by the agents who use money to buy/sell goods. Credit is based on whether an agent can be expected to pay money back at a point in the future, and thus is totally dependent on the individual agents themselves. As information specific to every individual agent is crucial in determining the credit worthiness of every individual, any attempt to model credit at the macro level has been ignored due its complexity.

However, the ascendency of money over credit is particularly odd given that money is a function of credit. Indeed, the existence of credit precedes money by over 2000 years. Although coinage is dated from the first millennium BC, Sumerian documents from 3000 BC reveal a systematic use of credit based on loans of grain by volume and loans of metal by weight. Some of these loans carried interest.[40]

The recent stream of data from the Financial Crisis suggests that the market economy does not have any tendency to move towards equilibrium. Moreover, given the prolonged nature of the downturn, it also highlights that the economy does not have the ability to self-correct excesses of supply and demand either. That is why asset prices fell so catastrophically. Investors attempting to understand the general direction of asset prices need to ignore signals emanating from fitted models of the way humans and money should behave and focus on analysing continuous streams of credit-related information instead. Over the last few decades as the new neoclassical synthesis took a stranglehold on the profession, a minority of economists and financiers maintained their stance and argued that credit was far more important to understand. They argued that general equilibrium models were pointless because they did not take credit into account, and it is credit that is the cause of an economy's instability. Investors who followed this approach were able to continue to generate strong returns right through the business cycle. Hence it is to these investors and thinkers who prioritised credit above money that we now turn.

Chapter 3
The problem of credit

Modern man drives a mortgaged car over a bond-financed highway on credit-card gas.

Unknown

During the Great Moderation investors became dependent on the signals emanating from central banks as up until 2007 the signals worked well in generating robust returns. The signals were of course predicated on the view that as long as inflation remained under control, the economy was not over-heating and thus assets could continue their growth in value. However, there is now a great deal of evidence that the Great Moderation was distinguished by a substantial growth in credit which drove asset prices higher, creating an unsustainable boom. This boom in asset prices was perceived by many market participants as being sustainable, because the underlying macroeconomic models assumed that credit markets were efficient and cleared. Any excess release of credit into the economy would naturally lead to higher inflation, thus causing interest rates to rise to choke off the excess expansion. According to this model, unsustainable credit booms could not exist. Credit was therefore largely ignored by the investment community as well as the central banks.

A handful of investors who were busily analysing streams of credit-related data and looking for patterns believed they had stumbled across an unsustainable boom in credit creation which would eventually lead to a bust. Their challenge was which trade to put on to profit from it, and how long could they hold on until the market turned. They did not believe that credit markets could be in equilibrium, as it was becoming increasingly clear that the expansion in credit was going to borrowers who plainly were unable to pay it back, and therefore defaults were going to rise substantially. Credit bubbles therefore did exist and they were potentially very profitable, or very dangerous if you believed they did not exist.

Credit booms and busts

Since the collapse of the Japanese, UK and Nordic property bubbles in the late 1980s and early 1990s, a great deal of empirical research has gone into analysing credit booms and busts. In particular, the focus has been on the relationship between credit, asset prices and economic activity. One of the first major studies was conducted by a team of economists at the BIS in 1994 which focused on the Nordic countries, Japan, the United Kingdom and Australia. Their summary is worth quoting. 'A distinguishing feature of the pronounced medium term asset price fluctuations observed since the early 1980s has been the role of credit. The major expansion of credit in the wake of a substantial heightening of competitive pressure in the financial industry appears to have been a significant factor in facilitating and sustaining the upswing.'[1]

The team also highlighted that future credit/asset price spirals should not be underestimated. Detailed analysis of housing markets, credit and economic activity conducted over the last two decades has consistently highlighted the issues of credit, raising concerns about how credit is treated within current monetary theory.[2] However, there does not appear to be any consistent conclusion with regard to how monetary policy ought to react to credit booms, and therefore how investors ought to change their asset allocation as a result. For example the 1994 study by Borio et al. argued that 'historically the best safeguard against instability in asset prices has been a firm long term commitment to fighting inflation'. Most evidence, however, suggests the contrary. The Japanese property boom in the 1980s and the 1920s US equity boom were both accompanied by low inflation, as was the most recent house price boom in the United States. Indeed recent research published by the Fed firmly supports these observations stating that 'credit booms are generally not associated with surges in inflation in either industrial or emerging economies'.[3]

The authors emphasised the importance of attempting to identify credit booms given the economic carnage they cause using a variety of statistical techniques. However, one challenge with such attempts is that it requires an estimation of the long-run trend of real credit per capita, which raises similar estimation issues that policy makers found trying to implement the Taylor Rule. Moreover, the modelling is also based on stylised facts, such as specific lengths of a business cycle which may or may not hold in the future. However, the authors did use data from firms and banks in an attempt to identify the microeconomic drivers of historical credit booms. This approach is a welcome change in direction, as developing aggregates from summing up the outputs of what is happening at the micro level is likely to provide much better economic indicators than using standard macroeconomic indicators.

In particular, this analysis has provided an insight into the different possible causes of *prior* credit booms, including total factor productivity (TFP) increases, financial liberalisation and large capital inflows. In each of these cases, according to the authors, credit expands at a faster rate than its long-term trend rate, causing asset prices to boom and the upswing of the business cycle. The results show that in developed economies '40 per cent of the credit booms followed large TFP gains and 33 per cent followed significant financial reforms. In contrast, in emerging economies we find that over 50 per cent of credit booms were preceded by large capital inflows, while TFP gains and financial reforms play a small role.'[4] Although the exact results are debatable, it is clear that the increased liberalisation of a financial system plays a critical role in credit booms. Moreover, the liberalisation of credit markets, which generates a growth in credit, tends to increase collateral values and reduce expected default rates, which in turn feeds back into the credit decision-making process. Research by Goodhart and Hofman demonstrated not only links between credit, housing, economic activity and broad money but also that the relationships between the factors are multidirectional, implying an element of feedback, thus potentially giving rise to non-linear relationships.[5]

This evidence supports the views and theories of many active and successful investors in the credit markets who have had little time for equilibrium theory and linear models. Indeed, anyone who has attempted to model credit risk using structural[6] or reduced form[7] approaches will have experienced the non-linear nature of credit. Both approaches demonstrate that the perception of credit risk during boom times reduces significantly. Besides market participants believing that actual risks are considerably lower than they are, those who manage risks in boom times often make claims that risk has reduced due to superior risk management techniques. Unfortunately this is rarely the case. The reality of course is that rising collateral values in a boom feed back into the credit risk management process, generating an improved outlook for credit. As the recent crisis unfolded, most risk managers were still conned into thinking that the economy remained at equilibrium due to subdued inflation. Hence the idea in the summer of 2007 that large and unexpected losses were about to hit them was largely discounted.

The historical data of course suggests that the world of finance does not generate normal returns, and that large unexpected losses are far more common, as Taleb has demonstrated. This adds further evidence to the notion that credit markets are rarely in equilibrium.[8]

Given the volatile nature of credit, the longer a time series displays long-term memory, the higher the probability of a Noah effect taking place. In the summer of 2007, the credit bubble had almost reached its peak after a Joseph-style period in the preceding years; thus the probability of extreme losses had increased substantially. In a credit boom collateral values are not sustainable, and when they begin to fall, default risk suddenly jumps – a process akin to Mandelbrot's Noah effect. Figure 3.1 highlights the default of Lehman Brothers causing a severe dislocation in credit risk, with the one-year probability of default index for North America, based on a barrier option model, jumping substantially before falling again a year later.

The onset of the credit crisis has led to increasing scepticism from market participants that credit markets tend towards equilibrium.

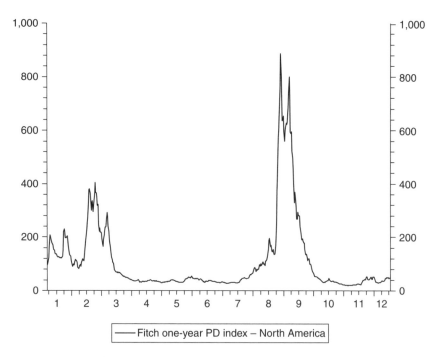

Figure 3.1   North America one-year probability of default index
Source: Thomson Reuters Datastream.

However, such views had been held by a minority of economists and financiers before the crisis too. Indeed, these critics believed that the notion that credit markets cleared and were in equilibrium was one of the daftest assumptions of modern economic theory.

The outsiders

One of the loudest critics from the investment community about credit markets being in equilibrium has been George Soros. Soros has consistently argued that credit markets are in a constant dynamic disequilibrium due to the reflexive nature of credit. This is because of the asymmetrical way in which credit markets develop where the value of collateral determines the credit worthiness of the borrower which in boom times increases substantially. Soros also highlighted that in order to avoid the complexity of adding unstable credit markets to economic models, economists generally ignored credit and concentrated on the money supply instead, which is of course determined by credit. This substitution of money as a proxy for credit is of course fatally flawed as money is anonymous and fungible, whereas credit is fundamentally localised and unique to a specific entity. Thus it should not be surprising for investors to be misled by monetary policy signals as they are missing out on what is happening in the world of credit. Soros' rather negative view of modern economic theory is based on his conclusion that if you follow it you tend to lose money, but if you ignore it you can profit. As Soros stated in 1998:

> I have to confess that I am not familiar with the prevailing theories about efficient markets and rational expectations. I consider them irrelevant and I never bothered to study them because I seemed to get along well without them, which was perhaps just as well judging by the recent collapse of Long Term Capital Management, a hedge fund whose managers aimed to profit from the application of modern equilibrium theory.[9]

Investors with a deep knowledge of credit it seems do far better by ignoring signals emanating from central banks which assume we live in a wonderful world of equilibrium. The challenge for most savers is that fund managers like Soros, Dalio, Howard are few and far between. Besides the absolute return hedge funds, a handful of fund managers have consistently outperformed market benchmarks with a large amount of assets under management. In particular, Bill Gross's (PIMCO) total return fund with $250 billion in assets and significantly larger than the other successful global macro-hedge funds grouped together has maintained an outstanding performance since inception due to a deep knowledge of credit. Unfortunately for pension investors, there are trillions of dollars of pension assets in the market; thus, most savers miss out as they deposit their savings in standard equity or fixed income trackers which go up and down with the cycle, generating highly volatile returns with periods of substantial losses. It is clearly not possible for everyone to beat the market, but if the benchmark of the market were defined by a knowledge of the business cycle, then returns would be far less volatile than they currently are.

One reason why there are so few financial products that can provide investors with returns over the business cycle is that there appears to be so little debate and disagreement by those who theorise about financial markets. As can be surmised from Soros' statements, it is common for there to be quite fundamental disagreements between practitioners and academic theorists, but in general it is rare for there to be such an agreement amongst the theorists themselves. Indeed, during the Great Moderation such dissent when it came to monetary theory was not particularly common given that monetary policy appeared to be working rather well. Thus the criticism from practitioners such as Soros was generally ignored. However, the recent crisis has highlighted that these issues can no longer be swept under the carpet by assuming that the existing models just need to be tweaked. The investment signals emanating from central banks are fundamentally flawed and are generating unacceptable returns for pension schemes.

Interestingly, during the 1920s and 1930s, when the global economy followed a not too dissimilar pattern from today, there was a great academic debate taking place on the underlying problems of the economy. Moreover, that debate focussed on credit instead of money, which remains central to today's debate. Many of those economists including Keynes and Hayek believed that the Walrasian framework was not particularly helpful for understanding the underlying nature of money and credit. Since the development of the new neoclassical synthesis, there have been far fewer dissenters, with such dissent being pushed out of the mainstream debate. However, two dissenters of repute are worth discussing in some detail, particularly because their views on credit are at odds with general equilibrium. These two are Hyman Minsky and Joseph Stiglitz.

Stiglitz, a professor at Columbia University and Nobel Laureate, has been questioning some of the core principles of the neoclassical structure since the 1970s. This has included research on asymmetric information for which he was awarded the Nobel Prize, as well as on market failure and the behaviour of credit markets in general. Many of these ideas were summed up in a book on monetary economics co-authored with Bruce Greenwald, also at Columbia, which detailed why the credit system driven by the banking sector does not sit well in a standard general equilibrium model.[10] Given the implications of credit not fitting into a general equilibrium model, it will pay dividends to spend some time understanding the arguments as to why credit is so inherently unstable.

The authors argue that it is the quantity of credit and not the quantity of money that determines economic activity. Money is a second-order variable, being largely determined by the movement in credit. Therefore, the focus of monetary policy 'should shift from the role of money in transactions to the role of monetary policy affecting the supply of credit'.[11] This point is emphasised by arguing that although there is some relationship between money and credit, credit should always take precedent. In particular the focus on money in a crisis, 'is foolish and dangerous',[12] which Friedman's disciples in the central banking community are slowly beginning to realise. Critical to the determination of the release of credit into an economy is of course the banking sector. Therefore a much better understanding of the nature of banking behaviour is required in order to comprehend macroeconomic trends, given the expansion and contraction of the availability of credit through the business cycle.

Reinhart and Rogoff's detailed study of the failure of banking systems through time highlights that failures are rather more common than we might think.[13] At the root of banking failures are generally bad lending practices, in particular real estate loans, which have been a force of economic volatility and dislocation.[14] Moreover, in recent years, banking behaviour has been substantially affected by deregulation which encouraged a significant expansion in credit growth fuelled by low interest rates. In boom times, as bank lending grows with rising collateral values and falling expected default rates, banks begin to take on larger risks. The promise of higher profits without any apparent significant increase in risk makes this an easy decision for many. However, such behaviour becomes systemic with the banks that decide not to partake in reckless lending, potentially being driven out of business despite the fact that they are the banks capable of withstanding a downturn.[15]

Another factor highlighted by the authors that causes banking instability is the notion that equity and debt financing are not risk neutral,[16] which undermines another one of the central pillars of modern financial theory.[17] Equity capital is not widely used by companies for expansion purposes as it dilutes the value of the company,[18] and as a consequence, the management's compensation. Hence, compensation schemes create an incentive to leverage up using debt, which increases the risk of default. Therefore in an upswing, economic agents become highly leveraged with the banking sector obliging in the provision of credit. However, increasing the rate of leverage is not sustainable in the long run, causing the demand for loanable funds to dry up, leading to a downswing.

In the downturn, interest rates will generally rise to stem losses due to increased risk exposure to the banking sector. This credit withdrawal in turn impacts the economy, potentially leading to bankruptcies. Importantly, a higher level of bankruptcy reduces supply,[19] thus in downturns deflationary pressures can be overstated. This contradicts the standard approach to monetary theory which argues that a fall-off in output leads to less pricing pressure. Economies that fail to adjust to lower levels of aggregate demand by reducing aggregate supply from bankruptcies such as Japan are more likely therefore to experience deflation. It is noteworthy that the credit default swap market trades at a substantial discount in Japan compared to the United States because of fewer expected defaults. In essence, the Japanese banking system has been willing to continue to provide funds to firms that in the United States would probably have been forced to file for bankruptcy. Given corporate America's willingness to restructure after the 2008 downturn by reducing aggregate supply, deflationary pressures in the US economy have been consistently overstated, with comparisons to Japan's lost decade naïve at best.[20]

One further issue that can also impact output in a downturn is the withdrawal of credit during a crisis by the banking sector when the authorities demand that banks rebuild their balance sheets. As the authors argue, 'a recession is hardly the best time to raise new capital'.[21] As a consequence, those firms who require credit to expand their operations may find that credit is just not available, something that regulators and governments are just beginning to realise. It is however worth pointing out that given expectations are low during a crisis the demand for credit would have fallen considerably too.

The impact of this boom and bust process due to credit creation and withdrawal over time generates a non-linear and unpredictable outcome.[22] Despite the nature of the relationship, it is still possible to identify the general direction of the economy using the cost of capital as an indicator. This is because a key decision-making signal for individual economic agents is the cost of capital related to any expenditure – whether it be for consumption or investment pur-poses. As the authors emphasise, when the cost of capital is low, cheap credit can drive an increase in expenditure, and as the cost of capital increases it is likely to prevent some of these decisions from going ahead.[23] Hence the cost of credit through time is fundamental in understanding the nature of credit booms.

One final point of their analysis worth highlighting is a reference to Keynes' liquidity trap. They repeat his mantra that no matter how much money is thrown into the economy – it may well have no impact on output.[24] The difference between this analysis and Keynes' is that large shocks to the banking system cause market fail-ure rather than a new equilibrium at a lower level. This is a major departure from Keynes himself, but it is a crucial one. Market fail-ures imply that standard policy initiatives embedded in a general equilibrium framework are largely irrelevant. Indeed, market fail-ure has a substantial impact on the expectations of future demand which is why, when the banking sector fails, it has such a devastating impact on the real economy as the 1930s highlighted. Bank failures destroy informational and organisational capital required to man-age credit.[25] This informational capital on loans/assets is critical to the functioning of an economy and takes a great deal of time to rebuild, which along with the debt overhang is one of the reasons why it takes so long for economies to pick up speed after a credit bubble has burst. In summing up, the authors' description of credit and banking crises is striking in its predictive quality of what has happened since 2008.

> Mounting non-performing loans result in liabilities in excess of assets; banks cannot fulfill their promise to depositors, let alone continue to perform their central role in providing credit. Inevitably the recriminations against politicians who have allowed lax regulation, possibly under the influence of corruption and pursued misguided macroeconomic and structural policies are followed by bail outs and bank closures accompanied by high minded speeches about never allowing such a state of affairs to arise again . . . . Unfortunately many of the doctors that have been

called in to nurse the banking sector back to health have too little understanding either of the role of finance and credit in the economy or of the micro foundation of banking.[26]

Certain things about our economy and society, it appears, do not seem to change. Tweaking the same old models is no longer an option. Moreover, the issues raised by Stiglitz and Greenwald about debt and the banking sector were exactly the same issues raised some 30 years before in the mid-1970s by Hyman Minsky. These ideas were incorporated into a stimulating book in the mid-1980s, *Stabilising an Unstable Economy*. Minsky was an academic economist at Washington University, St Louis, who was very much outside the mainstream of academic thought. However, his interest in credit booms and busts meant that many practitioners were interested in his work in order to work out how to profit from it.

'The major flaw of our type of economy,' Minsky argued, 'is that it is unstable. Instability is due to the internal processes of our type of economy. There is now ample evidence to indicate that almost all systems which are multi-dimensional, nonlinear and time dependent are endogenously unstable.'[27] Minsky had little time for Neoclassical Equilibrium Theory. Indeed, Minsky is very clear that it is an economy's intrinsic instability that leads to business cycles. The neoclassical synthesis of course did not have any real concept of the business cycle given the nature of equilibrium and the fact that it ignores financial institutions, capital and the uncertainty of investment, all of which are external to general equilibrium.[28]

Minsky's notion of a business cycle is however rather simplistic in terms of its initial cause where he uses a Fisherian view of an increase in the quantity of money as being the initial driver.[29] Indeed, he does not explore the initial reasons that might lead to a bubble being created. However, he is clear that once a bubble starts, the profitability of an enterprise is critical in determining how well a capitalist economy works. Thus, 'policy to control the aggregate performance of the economy needs a handle by which it can affect profits. One such handle is monetary policy.'[30] During a credit bubble as business profits are increasing, the cost of capital tends to fall as Stiglitz noted. This fall in the cost of funding reinforces the growth in profits, driving the credit bubble up to ever higher levels. The bubble is further maintained by the wide availability of credit, allowing for increased expansion. In essence, higher profits are fundamentally linked to increased credit expansion.

Once profits increase, it leads to an increase in investment. According to Minsky, 'investment is the essential determinant of the path of a capitalist economy . . . . Although the behaviour of money wages and government budgets can amplify or dampen economic stability the fundamental cyclical properties of our type of economy are determined by relations among profits, capital assets, financial market conditions and investment.'[31] Minsky is clear that no matter what, instability cannot be fully eradicated from an economy. Even if a situation arose where an economy had full employment, this would also be destabilised through increased investment, leading to rising debt financing and new forms of money being created, generating inflation. There is clearly no room for an equilibrium of any sort.

As the profits of companies increase, so do the price of capital assets traded in the market, which increase at a faster rate due to the rising expectations of future profits. This expectation of rising profit in turn drives companies to expand using external debt financing which in turn drives inflation, as profits and expected profits increase.[32] This process sets in train an asset bubble.

Clearly this boom is unstable due to the run up in leverage and the only way for the boom to continue is for ever increasing amounts of leverage – hence the comparison of credit booms to Ponzi schemes. A capitalist economy eventually runs into problems when profit maximising behaviour does not generate sufficient cash to service debt and therefore sustain asset values. Moreover, the increase in output due to the boom, Minsky argued, will lead to inflation and thus higher interest rates. These higher rates lead to a fall in demand for capital assets and may lead to the present value of the investment good as a capital asset falling below the supply price, generating a negative return on investment and ultimately capital destruction.[33] Minsky's view of inflation is thus akin to Fisher's, arguing that inflation is endogenously determined and the money supply is a response to increased demand.[34] However, he does clarify his stance by disassociating himself from Friedman arguing that clearly 'inflation is not everywhere a monetary phenomena'.[35] Controlling the money supply only addresses the symptoms, not the causes.

Once an economy has fallen victim to an asset price crash, Minsky repeats Keynes' views on government intervention – although he highlights the inflationary bias of going down this route with public sector wage increases driving productivity down. More importantly, Minksy highlights the fact that governments cannot just keep raising debt to get themselves out of their predicament. Markets need to believe in the story that the borrower can generate sufficient cash flows to pay back the lenders. This means that the deficit has to be a transient phenomenon. Unfortunately for many eurozone countries during 2011, the capital market did not perceive that any such raising of capital would be transient, hence the record levels of bond yields.

Minsky focuses most of his attention on the banking sector itself, which makes the system inherently unstable. An increase in leverage increases the money supply – indeed, the liabilities of large commercial banks constitute a large portion of the money supply.[36] However money, according to Minsky, 'is difficult to identify and is created and destroyed by banks'.[37] This is why Friedman's money growth aggregates have not proven to have been particularly successful. The cumulative effect of increasing bank credit leads to a fragile financial system, which is made more difficult with the banks innovating to circumvent the authorities. In general they almost always win with a resulting destabilising economy. The losers of course are those hit by unemployment and inflation. The logic of Minsky's argument is that credit markets are fundamentally unstable and therefore there can be no equilibrium.[38]

Minsky and Stiglitz both provide important insights into the instability of credit markets and how general equilibrium theory is unhelpful for the modelling of credit. Although both economists did put forward some policy recommendations, they did not provide an alternative framework that investors could use. Indeed, using Minsky's theory would have led to massive losses because the bubble was not inflationary. The challenge that remains for investors is what signals should they use to monitor the business cycle so they can avoid being hit by large unexpected losses? Both Minsky and Stiglitz were heavily influenced by Keynes' views that markets are prone to excess and instability, which were central to Keynes' views on the nature of the business cycle. Keynes argued that business cycles are driven by changes in the marginal efficiency of capital which in an economic crisis can suddenly collapse when the cost of capital rises due to increased risk. Keynes' views on how a bubble collapses are worth quoting in light of Minksy and Stiglitz's comments on business profits and the cost of capital.

The latter stages of the boom are characterised by optimistic expectations as to the future yield of capital goods sufficiently strong to offset their growing abundance and their rising costs of production and probably a rise in the rate of interest also. It is of the nature of organised investment markets under the influence of purchasers largely ignorant of what they are buying and of speculators who are more concerned with forecasting the next shift in market sentiment than with a reasonable estimate of the future yield of capital assets, that when disillusion falls upon an over optimistic and over bought market it should fall with sudden and even catastrophic force.[39]

Keynes' main focus was, of course, on how it might be feasible to lift an economy out of the doldrums. He states that once an economic crisis has begun, 'a decline in the rate of interest will be a great aid to a recovery and probably a necessary condition of it'. However he warned that 'the collapse in the marginal efficiency of capital may be so complete that no practicable reduction in the rate of interest will be enough'.[40] Keynes is quite clear that the only factor that will bring about normal conditions is the return of confidence. That means the confidence to consume more and therefore the confidence of businesses to increase investment. So how does that help investors today make sensible decisions during the crisis?

Keynes is clear that monetary policy cannot resolve these issues, but that rates should be kept low to ensure that the cost of capital does not exacerbate the situation. Keynes is also clear that until confidence has returned investors will park their money in cash or cash-like equivalents, which means US treasuries and other liquid, highly rated government bonds, which is what has happened in the recent Crisis. Keynes' solution in terms of ensuring consumer confidence returns to the economy is twofold. Firstly, he argues that interest rates should be kept low during booms in order to stimulate the boom even more. This equates to the view that only by constant stimulation can slumps be avoided. In practical terms, this means that the system must be based on an infinite Ponzi scheme that can continually provide credit to consumers, allowing them to spend more of their income and save less.[41] The second and of course central idea of the General Theory is to use fiscal stimulus to maintain consumer confidence by job creation programmes. This would require heavily indebted consumers to keep on spending as they were doing in the boom.

On both accounts, as Minsky highlighted, these policies are not sustainable. At some stage the lenders want to know that they will get their money back. The valuation of their assets is dependent on an actual future stream of cash flows coming back. Moreover as Minksy argued, continuing to leverage up as the route out of a recession must be seen to be a purely transient phenomenon. Indeed, it would be hard to argue that Greece could have borrowed its way out of the predicament it found itself in 2011. This would have required creditors to have provided the Greek government, consumers and banks with lines of credit based on the assumption that the money would be paid back. The same issue of ensuring adequate funding applies to all economic agents attempting to invest their way out of a slump.

However, this has been one of the key policies pursued by Japan since the equity and property crash of the early 1990s. The Japanese government increased investment in an attempt to stimulate demand. This has led to a jump in Japan's general government debt as a per cent of GDP, from 67 per cent in 1991 to 230 per cent in 2011. Yields on Japanese bonds remain low due to continuing demand from willing Japanese investors to finance the debt. However, to assume that Japanese investors will be willing to finance ever-increasing amounts of debt without expecting a return for the increased risk would be a dangerous assumption given the nature of credit, particularly if this debt was not being used to generate wealth in the economy. Indeed, Keynes was rather clear on the point that investment is a 'sheer waste of resources' if the investment is unable to generate a positive return over its lifetime. This means that any investment *needs* to generate a positive return on investment.[42]

From this brief analysis of Minsky and Stiglitz's antipathy towards credit and general equilibrium, it is now clearer that the neoclassical synthesis, as Buiter and Mankiw highlighted, has clearly ended up in a cul-de-sac. The question for investors is how do we get out of the cul-de-sac and ensure that such misleading signals will not cause a catastrophic destruction in wealth again? One place to start this search is to return to the debate of the 1930s where credit was seen as being more important than money. The two main protagonists, Keynes and Hayek, disagreed on many aspects of policy; however, there were also many similarities related to an understanding of the nature of credit economies. That influence came from the Swedish economist Knut Wicksell. Keynes' views on trade cycles where he discusses the ideas of the interest rate and the marginal efficiency of capital were influenced by Wicksell. Hayek also notes in his two most important books, *Prices and Production* and *Monetary Theory of the Trade Cycle*, the importance of Wicksell's ideas. Wicksell also influenced a loose grouping of Swedish economists in the 1930s, including Gunnar Myrdal the joint Nobel Prize winner with Hayek, whose ideas are also relevant to the issue at hand. However, knowledge of Wicksell's credit-based theory remains less well known in the Anglo-Saxon dominated profession.

In 1898, Knut Wicksell in his book *Interest and Prices* proposed the idea of looking at the relationship between the interest rate, or cost of capital, and the marginal efficiency of capital, or return on capital, in order to define equilibrium in a credit economy. Wicksell's pure credit-based concept of an economy was a radical change in the direction of monetary economics at the time, something that Hayek appreciated more than Keynes. Unfortunately, credit-based theories of economics were largely ignored in the post-1945 Keynesian and monetarist revolutions which largely influences today's discourse. Given the central role that credit has in the modern economy, this is a rather astonishing omission. Hence it is to the ideas behind credit-based theories of economics that we must now turn to.

Chapter 4

The Vienna and Stockholm schools: A dynamic disequilibrium approach

Theories that explain the trade cycle in terms of fluctuations in the general price level must be rejected not only because they fail to show why the monetary factor disturbs the general equilibrium, but also because their fundamental hypothesis is, from a theoretical standpoint, every bit as naive as that of those theories which entirely neglect the influence of money.

Friedrich Hayek[1]

The neoclassical synthesis' inability to explain the behaviour of credit resulted in monetary policy generating false signals for investors. These false signals led to large and unexpected losses for the world's pension schemes. As Stiglitz and Minsky argued, credit is external to general equilibrium because credit markets do not clear and are inherently unstable. Moreover, their analysis highlighted two of the characteristics of credit bubbles that drive this instability. Excess business profits are a critical factor in driving increased credit expansion as investors look to continue to increase the rate of profit growth. This increased level of business profits then helps to drive down the cost of capital due to lower expected default rates, thus providing the fuel for further credit expansion. However, the models that have been constructed to identify credit bubbles have generally relied on price stability to provide the framework for such an identification. Indeed, Minsky based his model on Fisher, thus requiring a rise in the general price level and deviation from equilibrium to signal the existence of a credit bubble. Furthermore, this model has been widely popularised via Kindleberger in his groundbreaking book on business cycles and bubbles.[2] Hence it is perhaps unsurprising that the majority of investors and central bankers in the summer of 2007 did not believe that the rise in asset prices was unsustainable as inflation remained subdued. However, as has been argued, this approach is fundamentally flawed. Credit bubbles are not generally accompanied by high inflation.[3] Moreover, inflation is also determined by exogenous factors which may or may not be correlated to endogenous factors at a given point in time. Finally, measurement issues with regard to an economy operating at its potential level put further doubt on the ability of inflation targeting to provide a sound signalling framework for investors.

Although a strong case, both empirically and theoretically, has been made that monetary policy generated false signals losing investors trillions, the absence of a competing theory to replace it highlights that such criticism is of little practical use for investors. The exception being that every so often investors might lose a significant amount of money which is not a particularly insightful or helpful comment. Thus, it is imperative that a new framework is developed that can provide an improved signalling framework. Such a model would need to not only be able to identify credit bubbles but also explain the broader macroeconomic relationships between money, investment and output. This is why Hayek's statement above is rather promising, given he attacks the notion of using the general price level as an indicator. Hayek's ambition throughout the 1920s and 1930s had been to integrate money and capital in order to explain business cycles. Hayek's controversial approach, often referred to as Capital Theory, attempted to analyse whether excess credit growth led to over-investment across the various stages of production. The net effect of this over-investment was an unsustainable level of growth, or boom phase, followed by a bust because the incremental investment that had taken place at the expense of consumption began to generate negative returns. Although these ideas were widely discussed in the 1930s, Hayek's star pupil Kaldor, in an article penned in 1939, successfully put an end to this line of thought. According to a leading monetary economist, 'Kaldor's attack was crucial in the abandonment of Hayek and capital theory after the 1930s, but in my view this was to cost the economics profession dearly.'[4] Desai remained one of the few dissenters to current monetary theory, prior to and during the Great Moderation. The ideas inherent in Capital Theory were subsequently omitted from most post-war economic theory, including Neo-Keynesian, neoclassical as well as monetarist thought.

Thus a further exploration of Hayekian ideas and Capital Theory may well provide the foundation for a new signalling framework which can prevent investors from periodically losing a substantial part of their portfolio. To fully appreciate Hayek's contribution it will be necessary to explore the development of his ideas from Carl Menger and the origins of the Austrian School of Economics. This body of thought influenced the great Swedish economist Knut Wicksell, who developed the first credit-based economic theory which became central to Hayek's framework. However, there were a number of issues with Hayek's theory that remained problematic and which were not resolved until the Stockholm School took the final step in ditching equilibrium analysis. It is upon this foundation that a robust theory can be constructed to replace the new neoclassical synthesis in order to generate superior investment signals.

Revolution in Vienna

The marginal utility revolution came about independently through the work of three economists: Walras, Jevons and Menger, where price became a subjective value based on individual utility as opposed to being based on the cost of production. In many respects there is little to differentiate between the three of them. However, there were two key differences between Menger and his two rivals which had a considerable influence on the development of economics in Vienna and to an extent in Stockholm. More importantly, these differences facilitated the development of a competing monetary theory to Walrasian General Equilibrium.

Carl Menger started out his career as a journalist writing daily reports on the capital markets. As he wrote these reports Menger became struck by the 'contrast between the traditional theories of price and the facts which experienced practical men considered as decisive for the determination of prices'.[5] These deliberations led Menger to spend four years writing *Principles of Economics*, which was published in 1871. One of the key differences between Jevons and Walras was Menger's belief in cause and effect. Indeed, *Principles of Economics* opens with the following statement: 'All things are subject to cause and effect'.[6] Jevons and Walras largely rejected this approach, favouring the use of simultaneous determination, or the technique of modelling complex relations as a system of simultaneous equations. This difference becomes critical when one tries to understand the nature of the production process as it attempts to predict the needs and desires of individuals to acquire individual final consumption goods.

This is important because in reality each part of the production process has limited control over decisions made along the supply chain, which are ultimately made in response to changes in consumer preferences. This level of uncertainty means that decisions made along the chain will not be homogenous with any simultaneous determination of outcomes, but will instead impact the production process, often resulting in a mismatch between consumer preferences and final consumption goods. Menger stressed the importance of how time can impact production processes where often decisions have to be made in advance to meet consumer preferences.[7] Given that to manufacture just one final consumption good a multitude of decisions need to be taken over a considerable period of time, it is hardly surprising that mismatches and errors are made. When this process is scaled up globally, the complexity of the mechanics for the delivery of all final consumption goods in relation to consumer preferences is clearly quite extraordinary. These quite basic notions have unfortunately been largely underestimated by most modern economic theory, particularly given that decisions may cause the economy to shift in unpredictable ways.

The second major difference between Menger and his two rivals was related to his views on money. He argued that money per se was not the measure of exchange value, but rather a medium in which buyers and sellers are able to calculate relative price movements.[8] This becomes important in attempting to understand how one might create stable currencies that are not governed by the cost of production or scarcity, such as gold or precious metals which was the norm at the time. Moreover, the elimination of a currency based on its own intrinsic value has implications for the way in which price increases are understood. Indeed, such a shift would move an economy away from a general concept of price moves towards an economy where relative price differences are more relevant. Finally, this idea is crucial when one begins to deal with a pure credit economy where physical money has less relevance in day-to-day transactions due to the clearing systems of banks.

For the most part, economists and social scientists focussed on the marginal utility ideas of Menger as part of the broader revolution in the Theory of Value, and as such the differences in Menger's thought have often been ignored. However, Menger's writings did go on to inspire a separate branch of economics, now generally known as Austrian Economic Theory, where the differences to Jevons and Walras became central to its outlook. One of Menger's most important disciples was a young law student at the University of Vienna called Eugen von Bohm-Bawerk. As a result of reading Menger's *Principles*, Bohm-Bawerk decided to leave law and study political economy instead. After making this switch, Bohm-Bawerk's career was interspersed between his time as an academic at the universities of Vienna and Innsbruck and working in the

Ministry of Finance – including three stints as finance minister of the Austro-Hungarian Empire. From 1884 he began to publish his ideas on economics which became part of his monumental work *Capital and Interest*.

The capital in capitalism

Despite the marginal utility revolution replacing classical theories of value in most university faculties, the rise of Marxism proved less straightforward to counter. In pure economic terms, the debate focussed on the relationship between the rewards of capital and the wages of labour. Marx, taking a lead from Ricardo's Labour Theory of Value, argued that the returns to capital (variable capital) were in fact the wages of labour that the capitalist had exploited, otherwise known as surplus value. Bohm-Bawerk dedicated a significant portion of his work to point out the flaws in this argument attacking the views of Marx and Rodbertus.[9] Part and parcel of this attack was to develop a theory of capital and its rewards based on the marginal utility revolution. Hence the first task for Bohm-Bawerk was to provide a definition of capital.

According to Bohm-Bawerk, capital is the sum total of intermediate products which come into existence at each stage of the production process. The owners of capital are able to derive a permanent income from it, which is often known as interest.[10] The rate of interest or revenue stream that filters back to the owners of the capital is therefore the return on the capital invested. Each individual product has a rate of return or rate of interest peculiar to itself which is determined by the return on the last fraction of invested capital which will tend to diminish in a stationary economy. Thus he emphasises the importance of productivity growth which generates lower costs per output in order to maintain the rate of interest or return on capital. The wealth of a nation is therefore related to the extent of its capital stock which is continually driven by the desire to invent and improve.

These definitions are central to his argument throughout his three volumes, which leads Bohm-Bawerk to criticise the way other economists have defined capital. He attacks the idea from Adam Smith that capital is an input into the production function. He understands why Smith may have argued this because capital was initially an interest-bearing sum of money that was also loaned out to entrepreneurs in order to generate revenue. The important point here is that an interest-bearing loan will be used to either buy capital goods or labour and consequently is not a factor in itself. This highlights the importance of Menger's idea of money as being a reference tool to explain the relative prices of different kinds of goods.[11]

Bohm-Bawerk's definition of the nature of capital itself is further clarified as being the product of nature and labour where any capital good is defined as previously applied productive force. However, Bohm-Bawerk is insistent that labour cannot be defined as capital per se, although he is unable to explain why this cannot be the case, arguing that it can only result in 'perpetuating the present confusion in nomenclature'.[12] After having defined capital, Bohm-Bawerk proceeds to explain the nature of the production process in relation to savings and consumption. All human production has its object of the acquisition of consumption goods, so the cause of the process of production is the perceived desire that in the future the product will be consumed. This ability for producers to anticipate future consumption given the uncertainty of outcomes becomes the reward for the entrepreneur willing to take on the risk of production in the first place.

An increase in savings (fall in consumption) requires that the production process must become more productive in order to sustain the level of interest (profit) due to lower aggregate demand. Savings are of course used to invest in the production process, leading to capital accumulation, thus providing the necessary productivity increase. For a production process to become more productive, Bohm-Bawerk uses the concept of the lengthening of the production process. This concept is generally taken to mean an increase in the division of labour as part of the supply chain of a production process, which in turn leads to an increase in the capital stock due to higher productivity. This conclusion of Bohm-Bawerk is logical, given he argues that labour cannot equal capital. Bohm-Bawerk also postulates what happens should individuals consume more of their income instead of saving. The net result of this is a lower rate of investment and lower capital accumulation, where an increase in demand will not be met with increased productivity but instead with the exploitation of the existing production capability.[13] These ideas on the nature of capital clearly provide a theoretical backdrop in order to explain business profits or the return on capital. However, the cost of capital was also something that Bohm-Bawerk understood was crucial to the process too.

According to Bohm-Bawerk the money rate of interest (or cost of capital) has its origins in the difference between the current and future value of goods. For example, 10 tons of grain in year two is worth only 9.5 tons of grain in the current year. This difference in subjective use value equates to a premium for current consumption which in this case is 5 per cent. This 5 per cent premium would therefore also be the value of the loan made to the producer to be paid back in year two. Bohm-Bawerk assumes that the loan market functions along the same lines as perceived use values of the output of goods of the production process over time.[14] One of Bohm-Bawerk's conclusions from this theory is that given a one-year production process, the value of labour must therefore be lower today than the value of labour at the end of the period, highlighting the wage differential between the two periods. This argument was used to attack the Marxian perspective of the exploitation of labour generating surplus value.

Although this is an interesting model, there are two obvious flaws in it. Firstly, Bohm-Bawerk's definition that labour cannot be defined as capital because it might cause confusion is hardly a compelling reason, particularly as he contradicts himself by stating that when labour manufactures a capital good, this stored labour is capital but in a current production process labour cannot be considered as capital. Moreover, his argument makes little sense where labour is heterogeneous. If capital is an income-bearing asset where one unit of labour can be substituted for another without any change in the rate of interest, then clearly his argument holds. It is of course possible that very simple production processes do not require any stored knowledge and therefore there will be no immediate impact on output. However, in today's economy if the workforce of a company were swapped for a different one overnight, it would be hard to argue that the company would function effectively, thus the rate of interest would fall. In essence, the accumulated knowledge by a workforce over time needs to be considered as part of the definition of capital which generates a return in the way the workforce interacts with the tools that are acquired. The tools of course being a function of applied knowledge further up the supply chain.

Bohm-Bawerk's definition that labour cannot equal capital has another logical conclusion that has caused a great deal of confusion in the way that Capital Theory has been misunderstood. This is that the only way of increasing productivity is to invest more in capital. In reality, productivity improvements in a production process can come about through improved process and accumulated knowledge. Thus capital investment or a lengthening of the production process as such is not necessarily required to boost productivity.

The second major flaw in the theory is that the money rate of interest in reality is determined by the financial sector providing the loan, which in turn depends on the credit worthiness of the borrower and the probability that the producer can return the money loaned based on its business case. The existence of other revenue streams and assets that might be used for repayment purposes in the event of a default also plays a role in pricing the risk of the loan. Bohm-Bawerk's theory was however recognised as being important should any attempt be made to understand the nature of credit economies. It was this issue that the Swedish economist Knut Wicksell took up a few years later as the basis of trying to understand the optimum output level of an economy in relation to the general price level.

A Swedish felon

Knut Wicksell initially trained as a mathematician, getting his doctorate from the University of Uppsala before travelling to Vienna and hearing Carl Menger lecture. He turned his focus immediately towards economics but found he was unable to get a job as a professor in economics without a law degree. This did not stop him however from writing one of the most important books in the history of economic theory published in 1898, *Interest and Prices*. Unfortunately for Wicksell, his own life story is perhaps more well known than this important work. His provocative public lectures on the causes of prostitution, drunkenness, poverty and over-population (he was a big advocate of birth control) seemed to have cast a shadow over his academic contribution. Moreover, he is one of the only economists to have ever been to jail for his opinions. In a lecture in 1908, he satirised the Immaculate Conception and was sentenced to prison for two months in 1910.

Interest and Prices was an attempt to explain the issue of price stability which had troubled him because of the phenomena of falling prices during the 1880s. Wicksell was rather sceptical of the Quantity Theory of Money, which he argued did not explain what had happened during that period. He criticised the assumption of a constant velocity of circulation which made little sense in a credit economy. 'The quantity theory of money states that rising prices are due to an excess of money, falling prices to a scarcity – does not accord with actually observed movements in the rate of interest. Abundance or scarcity of money is now imbued with a merely secondary importance.'[15] Thus he argued that the impact of credit is much more pronounced for an economy that is wealthy enough to have a substantial amount of credit in circulation. Credit allows payments to be completed without the employment of money which is what the interbank payments systems was developed for, thus highlighting the increasing irrelevance of the Quantity Theory of Money.

One other important observation made by Wicksell was that as the banking industry developed towards the end of the 19th century, banks became ever more adept at taking in customer deposits and lending out sums of money, extending far beyond their deposit base. Thus banking became not only a vehicle for channelling savings back into the economy, but also an agent of credit creation itself. Thus Wicksell noted the expansionary and contractuary nature of credit, and the impact credit has on an economy. This led Wicksell on to the question of how one might be able to maintain some sort of equilibrium in a credit economy that in turn would generate stable prices which was his ultimate aim. His idea of such an equilibrium was the following:

> There is a certain rate of interest on loans which is neutral in respect to (commodity) prices and tends neither to raise nor to lower them. This is necessarily the same as the rate of interest which would be determined by supply and demand if no use were made of money and all lending were effected in the form of real capital goods. It all comes to much the same thing to describe it as the current value of the natural rate of interest on capital.[16]

Wicksell argues here that there are two rates of interest. There is a money rate of interest or the rate of interest on loans. And there is also a natural rate of interest, which is based on Bohm-Bawerk's definition of capital and originary interest which is determined by the efficiency of production or the marginal productivity of capital. When these two rates are equal, he argued that an economy was in equilibrium, which in turn would result in stable prices. Thus in Wicksell's barter economy, the entrepreneur borrows goods in kind and pays back in consumption goods. If loans are made this way, the conditions of economic equilibrium are also met and there will be no price movements. The implication of this is that if the money rate is higher or lower than the natural rate, equilibrium is disturbed. If the money rate is lower, then the entrepreneur generates surplus profits at the expense of the capitalist, leading to the expansion of production. When the money rate is higher then the returns are unprofitable, leading to bankruptcy and contraction, or companies closing down unprofitable lines.

Wicksell believed an exact coincidence of the two rates was unlikely, but he deduced that the money rate of interest in combination with price information would allow this to be of use from a policy perspective.[17] In a credit economy, Wicksell argued, there will be a natural tendency for the economy to move back towards equilibrium. Thus if the bank rate is too low and expansion ensues, increasing prices would force banks to push their lending rates up, resulting in a lower demand for credit and thus pushing prices back down. If the money rates are too high, then prices will fall, leading banks to lower interest rates to stimulate demand. Hence the money rate of interest will always coincide eventually with the natural rate because of the tendency towards equilibrium.[18]

Given these broad-brushed definitions, Wicksell accepted that his two rates of interest were rather vague conceptions, but he argued that understanding the broad trend of the relative position of the rates was more important than some exact measurement. Moreover, instances where the two rates were different over an extended period of time had a cumulative effect on the economy, which could be either inflationary or deflationary depending on which rate was higher.

The logic of the argument shows that banks can have a significant impact on determining the trajectory of an economy through the money rate of interest which they control. Thus low money rates of interest relative to the natural rate leads to higher levels of production, rising labour costs and inflation, as well as increasing asset prices. Conversely, higher money rates of interest relative to the natural rate lead to deflation and falling asset prices.[19] Thus Wicksell sums up his ideas in relation to price stability. 'So long as prices remain unaltered the bank's rate of interest is to remain unaltered. If prices rise, the rate of interest is to be raised, and if prices fall the rate of interest is to be lowered, and the rate of interest is henceforth to be maintained at its new level until a further movement of prices calls for a further change in one direction or the other.'[20] Wicksell's notions of price stability are in many respects aligned with the Fisher–Friedman–Taylor approach and the idea that interest rates can be used to manage price stability as part of an inflation-targeting approach to monetary policy. Indeed, Michael Woodford, a leading proponent of the new neoclassical synthesis, used Wicksell's framework to substantiate the argument that the nominal rate of interest in a credit economy could be used to maintain price stability. Woodford entitled his book *Interest and Prices* in homage to the Swede.[21]

With his theory constructed, Wicksell then attempts to explain the deflationary impact of the 1880s by arguing that the money rate during this period was above the natural rate.[22] Such a tendency of course was not sustainable in the long run because of a natural shift back towards equilibrium. Although this conclusion was logical it did not fit the facts, because if the money rate was higher than the natural rate, output would also have fallen, which was not in fact the case.[23]

Wicksell's attempt to understand an economy as a pure credit economy without the use of money was extremely far-sighted, given that all economies were still based on some metallic standard, whether it was gold or silver. Although there were a number of problems with Wicksell's theory, particularly with regard to the aim of price stability, it remains important for being the first coherent economic theory based on credit. What was more relevant was that his framework influenced Von Mises and Hayek in their attempt to explain the business cycle and the unstable nature of credit by using the two rates of interest that Wicksell described.

Austrian theory of the trade cycle

Ludwig Von Mises attended the University of Vienna from 1900, becoming acquainted with the work of both Menger and Bohm-Bawerk. His route into economics was as required via the law faculty, which he graduated from in 1906. By then he was already attending Bohm-Bawerk's post-doctoral seminar in economics and teaching at the Viennese Commercial Academy, as well as being the secretary of the Vienna Chamber of Commerce. During this period he was not only influenced by Bohm-Bawerk and Menger but also by Wicksell's theory of interest. Indeed, he sought to explain the business cycle using Wicksell's framework, leading him to write the *Theory of Money and Credit* that was published in 1912.

Von Mises like Wicksell did not believe the Quantity Theory of Money had much to offer monetary economics, and in particular attacked Irving Fisher's notion of proportionality as pure nonsense.[24] Von Mises argued that an increase in the quantity of money alters the distribution of economic goods among agents, but the impact of these increases is uncertain, although it cannot increase the total amount of goods. It may have limited impact, or if it increases demand, it may well be inflationary. These ideas were harking back to Cantillon and the notion of the complexity of an economy. Like Wicksell, he believed that the cause of upward and downward movement of prices was related to the relationship between the natural and money rates of interest. Thus the stability of money ought to be a policy objective, given inflation erodes incomes, making the population poorer. Where Von Mises added to the debate was in his analysis of the banking sector and how the release of credit causes business cycles.

Entrepreneurs get loans from banks of capital in the form of money to pay for the production process. His interest in the problem lay in how the money rates of interest might be determined. He argued that if the banking sector deliberately depressed the money rate of interest, it will increase the natural rate of interest or the income stream from capital. This will stimulate demand for loans given the increased profitability of production. The surge in investment due to the lower rate of money causes an economic expansion which generates inflation. Inflation ends up eroding the profits of the banks and so they end up raising rates, which in turn causes business failures. This is the downward swing of the cycle where there is an economic contraction which in turn causes credit to be withdrawn and capital destruction.

As a business cycle theory it certainly seems to explain how banks might induce a credit expansion. Furthermore, Von Mises highlighted an important trend related to the behaviour of the banking system. If one bank reduces the money rate to get more business, other banks will follow due to competition, thus causing an industry-wide injection of credit into an economy. This he pointed out was the problem of the 'gratuitous nature of bank credit'.[25] Stiglitz and Greenwald also picked up on this point in their analysis of the modern banking system in terms of risk-taking behaviour.

However, Von Mises' theory was lacking in a number of places. Firstly, it assumed that the marginal efficiency of capital remained constant, and therefore the only variable worth looking at was the money rate of interest. The marginal efficiency of capital is dynamic and can vary quite dramatically. Indeed, Keynes argued it was the major cause of slumps. Secondly, like Wicksell, Von Mises argued that price stability ought to remain central to monetary policy. Such a policy as was seen during the Great Moderation generated false signals resulting in large unexpected losses for investors. Despite these problems, his theory was important because it influenced

Hayek who was able to develop these ideas into a more coherent business cycle theory linking capital and money.

Friedrich Hayek enrolled in the University of Vienna after returning from the Italian front in 1918 gaining a doctorate in law, and then a further one in political science. It was only after he read Menger's *Principles of Economics* that he became hooked on economics and soon made contact with Von Mises, attending his private seminars. In 1923 he set off for New York for just over a year, where he became deeply interested in monetary theory and business cycles. In the late 1920s he co-founded and served as director of the Austrian Institute for Business Cycle Research which took Von Mises' initial ideas to a new level. His work attracted the attention of Lionel Robbins who invited him to join the London School of Economics. In 1930–1931 he gave a series of lectures at the LSE which came to be known as *Prices and Production*. These ideas were an elaboration of his earlier work published only in German which came to be known as the *Monetary Theory and the Trade Cycle*. Hayek's ideas were both difficult and novel for the audience at the LSE who had been submerged in Marshall and the 'Cambridge School'. His assault on many traditionally held views on economic theory in his lectures caused a sensation, according to Robbins.[26]

In *Prices and Production*, Hayek attacked Fisher and the Quantity Theory of Money arguing that it had not only usurped the central place in monetary theory but had hindered progress in the field by isolating the theory of money from the main body of general economic theory.[27] Hayek also rejected the notion of attempting to establish causal relations between macro aggregates, such as the general level of prices and the total quantity of production, which blatantly ignores the individuals whose daily choices drive economic activity. Following on from Cantillon, Hayek described how money impacts prices, which necessitates an understanding of where the additional money is injected into circulation. Indeed the effects of such an injection may be quite opposite according to whether the money goes into the hands of traders and manufacturers or salaried people employed by the state.[28] Hayek disputed the ideas of Fisher and his followers that money acts upon prices and production only if the general price level changes. Other erroneous assumptions he argued included the notion that a rising price level causes an increase in production and vice versa, and lastly that monetary theory was based on how the value of money is determined. 'It is such delusions,' argued Hayek, 'which make it possible to assume that we can neglect the influence of money so long as the value of money is assumed to be stable.'[29] Hayek's attack on these assumptions remains valid today.

Hayek summed up his views on the irrelevance of general price levels in relation to the business cycle stating that 'they are not only unessential [general price levels] but they would be completely irrelevant if only they were completely general – that is if they affected all prices at the same time and in the same proportion.... Every disturbance of the equilibrium of prices leads necessarily to shifts in the structure of production which must therefore be regarded as consequences of monetary change.'[30]

After destroying the foundations of the Quantity Theory of Money and its focus on the general price level which formed the basis of 1920s and current monetary theory, Hayek turned to construct an alternative approach. The basis for his framework was Wicksell's breakthrough in taking Bohm-Bawerk's theory of interest and setting it against the money rate in an attempt to explain the dynamics of a credit economy. This is nothing more than the relationship between the return of capital and the cost of capital – the very issues raised by Minsky and Stiglitz. Hayek does however point out a number of issues with Wicksell's argument.

He criticises Wicksell for asserting that when the money rate of interest coincides with the natural rate, money bears a completely neutral relationship to the price of goods and tends neither to raise nor lower it. Wicksell believed that in the absence of a disturbing monetary influence, the average price level must remain unchanged, which also assumes that the supply of savings and demand for investment is equal. According to Hayek, in this situation a contradiction would arise, where 'on the one hand we are told that the price level remains unaltered when the money rate of interest is the same as the natural rate and on the other, that the production of capital goods is at the same time kept within the limits imposed by the supply of real savings'.[31] According to Hayek, in an expanding economy, if the two rates of interest are equal and the supply of real savings equates to the demand for capital, prices cannot be stable as well.

Stability of the price level presupposes changes in the volume of money; but these changes must always lead to a discrepancy between the amount of real savings and the volume of investment. The rate of interest at which in an expanding economy the amount of new money entering circulation is just sufficient to keep the price-level stable, is always lower than the rate which would keep the amount of available loan-capital equal to the amount simultaneously saved by the public and thus despite the stability of the price level it makes possible a development leading away from the equilibrium position.[32]

Hence, if an expansion of production leads to a fall in price levels, to ensure a steady price level the money rate of interest will need to be lowered below the equilibrium rate. Thus the equilibrium rate will not maintain price stability. Indeed, any change in the amount of money must always influence relative prices but not necessarily the general level of prices. As relative prices determine production, a change in the amount of money must influence production. Thus even if a stable price level could be successfully imposed on the capitalist economy, the causes making for cyclical fluctuations would not be removed. Hayek concludes his attack on price stability stating that 'this doctrine which has been accepted dogmatically by almost all monetary theorists seems to me to lie at the root of most shortcomings of present-day monetary theory and to be a bar to almost all further progress'.[33] This statement is rather prescient given the lack of credibility that current monetary theory has, which resulted in investors being misled and pension schemes remaining badly underfunded.

Hayek continues by arguing that monetary theory needs to shift away from a theory of the value of money in general towards a theory of the influence of money on the different ratios of exchange between goods of all kinds. 'What we are interested in is only how the relative values of goods as sources of income or as means of satisfaction of wants are affected by money.' Hence the notion of neutral money is introduced where money has no impact on the prices of relative goods. Hayek takes this idea further by introducing a notion of equilibrium which would correspond to this idea. This requires the proportion of money spent on consumer and intermediate goods to equal the demand for both, which in turn must correspond to the output of intermediate and consumer goods in the same period.[34]

This definition is important because from a practical perspective it is highly unlikely ever to exist because of the nature of time and the complexity of the production process that Hayek describes. Demand by consumers is not constant, which means consumer goods producers need to forecast what this demand might be. However, decisions made by intermediate goods producers often have to be made much in advance depending on the complexity of the supply chain. For example, the time lag from identifying an upward trend in demand for a product, say iron ore, to locating a source, acquiring a license to mine, digging the shaft and building the necessary infrastructure can take over a decade. This is where the uncertainty comes into an economy. If half way through the process the price of iron ore collapses, the producer may well be left with a loss-making asset. The result of any process of investment to expand production is that the amount of money spent on producer goods during any period of time may be far greater than the amount spent on consumer goods in the same time. The traditional Walrasian approach where markets automatically clear, as opposed to the cause and effect of decisions made along the supply chain, can therefore generate radically different outcomes. Indeed, the automatic clearing of markets reduces much of the uncertainty which is far from reality. The management of this uncertainty of course generates a reward for the successful entrepreneur. Hayek's great insight is that the complexity of lags in the production process impacts prices in different ways.

Hayek then proceeds to apply his theory to explain the business cycle. He first rejects monetary theories of the trade cycle based on price levels as they fail to show why the monetary factor disturbs the general equilibrium. He concludes by stating that the only proper starting point for any explanation based on equilibrium theory must be the effect of a change in the volume of money.[35] He argues that 'changes in the volume of money which, in an expanding economy, are necessary to maintain price stability lead to a new state of affairs foreign to static analysis so that the development which occurs under a stable price level cannot be regarded as consonant with static laws'.[36] Hence changes in the volume of money may often exist without changes in the value of money.

With his framework in place, Hayek goes on to describe the drivers of the business cycle. Following on from Von Mises, Hayek accepts that the banking sector may indeed deliberately lower the rate of interest below the natural rate. This reduces the cost of capital for enterprises, thereby increasing their profits. However, he also states that the same effect can be also produced by an improvement in the expectations of profit, which may drive the natural rate above its previous level. Hayek describes the variety of reasons why the natural rate may increase, which may be due to 'new inventions or discoveries, the opening up of new markets, or even bad harvests, the appearance of entrepreneurs of genius who originate new combinations, a fall in wage rates due to heavy immigration and the destruction of great blocks of capital by a natural catastrophe'.[37] In essence anything that increases the profitability of any group of enterprises causes the natural rate to rise.

As the two rates of interest diverge, they impact relative prices across the production process. If the money rate falls below the natural rate (or the natural rate rises above the money rate), investment increases to take advantage of the new increase in profitability, driving a credit expansion above an equilibrium level. This causes businesses to lengthen the production process, thus increasing its capital intensity and productivity. This means consumption falls, driving down the value of consumer goods, whereas producer goods increase in value because of the incremental investment. According to Hayek, this requires savings to be channelled, or forced, into investment in capital goods production. However, as investment continues over time, the returns will begin to fall for producer goods, but the new higher levels of income lead to increased consumption and lower savings. Hence profit margins will begin to increase further down the production process towards consumer goods.

Whatever the cause of the initial divergence between the two rates, once an economy starts on an upward trajectory due to a mismatch between the two rates, it is generally accompanied by an extension of bank credit. As some banks begin to respond to the demand for credit, the whole sector acts to ensure their own profitability is maintained and follow suit. As investment increases, the perceived risks of borrowing are less, which induces the banking system to take on more leverage, as a smaller reserve is perceived as sufficient to provide the same degree of security.[38]

As the boom progresses, at some stage the over-investment process may not result in sufficient cash flows to sustain the bank and/or increased default risk, and therefore interest rates will have to rise. This may have already been preceded by an increase in the central bank rate if the boom leads to rising inflation. As interest rates start to increase, it may cause certain production processes to cease, particularly where excess capital accumulation has taken place. This of course results in the destruction of capital and the downward phase of the business cycle. The extent of the boom and therefore the subsequent destruction of capital are largely determined by the rate of divergence of the two rates (assuming the natural rate is higher than the money rate). This difference dictates the incremental volume of money being created which seeks higher rates of return.

Moreover, as this process is cumulative, the volume of incremental money being produced can impact the economy in multiple ways.

In the case of excess capital intensity, interest rates of course need to rise to rebalance the economy where excess consumption has led to savings being depleted. As a result, aggregate supply needs to decrease in order to reach a new lower level of equilibrium given the lower level of demand. The result of this of course is that output will fall until such time that the excess capacity has been eliminated from the system, thus driving up profit margins once more and the cycle begins again.

In summing up his ideas, Hayek approaches how such a monetary theory might be implemented, although he is generally negative about the practicality of implementation. This was considered a huge anti-climax by his students who invested a lot of time in trying to understand this novel approach to economic analysis. Indeed Hayek's negativity about how one might measure the natural rate of interest was probably one of the main reasons why his ideas did not become more widely followed.

> An adequate explanation of that 'natural rate' is the indispensable starting point for any realization of the conditions necessary to the achievement of equilibrium, and for an understanding of the effects which every rate of interest actually in force exerts on the economic system.... For the most part however no solution has been found to the wider problem of building up on the basis of the theory of an equilibrium rate of interest which can be deduced from the credit less economy, the structure of different rates which be simultaneously observed in a modern economy. The solution of this particular problem should provide a most valuable contribution to a deeper insight into cyclical fluctuations.[39]

Hayek's conclusions thus seem to ignore the possibility that monetary policy could ever be effective and that business cycles are here to stay. Indeed, Hayek almost seems to support the very nature of the volatility of the cycle as being critical to rising prosperity over time. 'So long as we make use of bank credit as a means of furthering economic development we shall have to put up with the resulting trade cycles. They are in a sense the price we pay for a speed of development exceeding that which people would voluntarily make possible through their savings.'[40]

The problem with Hayek's theory

Hayek's theory is compelling for a variety of reasons. Firstly it provides an explanation for the causes of business cycles which are related to excess business profits and/or a falling cost of capital. This argument is based on a solid economic theory of a credit economy as expounded by Wicksell, whereby the main cause of a boom is a cumulative increase in the volume of money due to excess credit expansion. However, unlike Wicksell, Hayek argues that an increase in the volume of money has different impacts on prices across the supply chain, thus ignoring the notion of price stability which provides misleading signals to investors. Hayek also argues that an economy is a highly complex system with inter-temporal decisions causing mismatches leading to imbalances, particularly in relation to capital. Hence one needs to think of the economy as being dynamic rather than stationary,[41] unlike the work of his great rival Keynes. Moreover, examples of Hayek's notion of capital destruction due to over-investment can often be seen around the world, particularly when it comes to real estate. The sight of half completed and derelict buildings in Spain and Ireland in 2010 was all too common.

Hayek's view of expectations is also of interest. For Hayek's model to work, it is clear that investors need to be continually wrong about their plans. Modern theories of rational expectations suggest this is not plausible as investors should realise this fact and adapt. However, the period of the Great Moderation highlights that most market participants were indeed fooled for a very long time given the false signal emanating from the price system.

The excitement that Hayek's theory generated in the 1930s amongst the economics profession all but dried up by the Second World War. Kaldor's attack on Hayek – despite its incredibly basic premise that his theory was flawed because capital was homogenous – seems to have been largely accepted by the profession. More importantly though was that Keynes's theory provided the framework for a simple stationary model that could be used by economists for policy. In conjunction with the view that most economists believed in their ability to make a difference (preferably a positive one), whereas Hayek's approach pushed them out of the limelight, the initial enthusiasm soon fizzled out. Finally, Hayek himself gave up the challenge, turning back towards political science by the end of the Second World War. In recent years, a small following of Hayek's has developed following on from the work of Murray Rothbard and more recently Roger Garrison.[42] However, their attempts have had little impact in terms of rehabilitating Hayek back to mainstream economics. This is largely because there were a number of problems with Hayek's model.

One of the most important issues with Hayek's model is that it ignores the ability of the banking system to use financial innovation to leverage up. Despite basing his model on Wicksell, Hayek seems to ignore the role of the banking sector in money creation, focusing instead on the sector as being the channel for savings and investment. The creation of new money of course allows investors to get increased purchasing power, but without the need to necessarily increase savings. This means that his whole premise of forced savings, which in turn reduces consumption, completely ignores the existence of leverage. The banking sector's ability to innovate should not be underestimated as the recent subprime crisis has shown. Banks were able to create money for consumers to buy houses, despite the savings rate being depleted during the period of the Great Moderation. Thus his argument of forced saving becomes largely irrelevant. Moreover, the ability of leverage to create money totally undermines Hayek's argument on why production and consumption must move in contrary motion. Empirical analyses show that production and consumption increase in a boom as do investment and employment.[43]

The second major problem with his model is the way he understands the economy will behave in terms of investment. He assumes that forced savings will increase the amount of credit available for investment in producer goods, thus lengthening the capital structure of the supply chain. Moreover, there is an implicit assumption that any observed capital destruction is a function of over-investment. Poor management of companies can be just as destructive of capital, which may have little to do with macroeconomic factors. However, Hayek assumed that all businesses would naturally deepen the capital structure, and in his later work, he went to unusual depths to describe the industrial stages of production, superimposing on industry the decisions that entrepreneurs might make.[44] This is an oddly prescriptive approach for Hayek which contradicts Carl Menger's views that an economy is made up of individuals who make their own decisions. Although some entrepreneurs may indeed decide to increase capital intensity, others might not want to expand at all and others may look towards human capital to drive productivity growth which leads on to the third issue with his model, which is related to labour.

Although Hayek in general argues that labour is heterogeneous and not easily substituted,[45] his use of Bohm-Bawerk's definition of capital ignores the ability of labour to drive productivity increases. This means in Hayek's world it is impossible to 'intensify' the capital structure by using human capital. Thus Hayek's simplistic notion of capital ignores a rather important point in the way firms actually work. Some data points will help to highlight the problem at hand. One study highlighted that it takes on average 30 months from the decision by a firm to lengthen its capital structure using physical capital to completion. Moreover, the durability of that capital is between 18 and 30 years.[46] The idea that a firm cannot improve its productivity outside of those 30 months is clearly nonsensical. Moreover, if capital lasts for so long, these decisions are rather rare which does not seem to fit well with business cycle data. My own experiences of running credit and economic analytics businesses highlight these issues. From time to time technology investments are necessary, but the drive in productivity has to be constant even when there is no new capital investment. This comes from the team of employees working with the existing technology combined with their shared, accumulated knowledge. Indeed, a large body of management writing influenced by Peter Drucker's ideas of the knowledge worker has emerged highlighting this point.

In his later writings Hayek totally ignores this point, arguing that there is a 'Ricardo effect' whereby as interest rates fall there is a labour substitution by capital.[47] Clearly there is a possibility that this may happen; however, it assumes that a sector is set up in such a way that it can or ought to happen. For instance, this was indeed the case in the French restaurant industry, which instead of buying labour to wash up bought industrial washing machines instead. However, there are many instances where a firm when faced with rising labour costs may focus on reducing headcount in tandem with core productivity objectives for the remaining workforce. Or firms may just decide to move labour to a cheaper location, which can be quicker and more profitable than large-scale capital projects, particularly given the time lags of being able to reduce costs.

However, the biggest issue in Hayek's model is his attitude towards equilibrium, where he describes a disequilibrium phenomenon which inevitably reverses to equilibrium. Moreover, the process of the inevitable return to equilibrium seemed to justify his fatalistic approach towards policy. His arguments on why the business cycle turns rely on ad-hoc assumptions of bank behaviour, including the banks' increasing interest rates as the default risk rises in a boom.[48] Interest rates tend to rise once defaults or expected defaults increase, which generally happens after the boom and are generally driven by asset price falls. Moreover, his argument that the boom drives inflation, which in turn pushes interest rates up, is a contradiction of his criticism of general price movements of Wicksell and Fisher. Although this may well happen, there is nothing inevitable about inflation coexisting in a boom as the Great Moderation and the 1920s demonstrated. According to the economist Tyler Cowen, inflation may distort resource allocation, but it does so in a variety of ways, and in ways which are hard to predict.[49] His final argument that a demand for cash will force interest rates up is also rather odd given his theory is based on Wicksell's credit economy, where demand for cash is less of an issue.

It is feasible that Hayek just was not able to completely ditch the notion of equilibrium and therefore he was unable to 'admit of disequilibrium as a persistent tendency'.[50] That is not to say that the notion of equilibrium is unnecessary, indeed without it, it would be impossible to measure the business cycle. However, the logic of the complex economy that Hayek describes is that it must be in a continuous state of disequilibrium, which moves up and down in relation to a notional equilibrium position. It has been argued that in 1938 Hayek accepted that any attempt to integrate general equilibrium and business cycle theory had failed because there was no way of constructing a general theory of the business cycle within the premises of the Walrasian tradition. This led Hayek to doubt the existence of a single theory for business cycles, given that the cycles all seemed to be different, which in turn introduced a great deal of scepticism on his previous decade or so of work.[51] This is perhaps why he gave up his investigation turning back towards political science. Despite this decision, Hayek's work remains invaluable in understanding the nature of business cycles and in attempting to ascertain why the new neoclassical synthesis failed investors so badly, resulting in massive losses.

In recent years, other economists have taken a look at Austrian theory as a potential foundation for business cycle analysis. Tyler Cowen's work on cycles is of particular interest as he argued that Austrian theory cannot be ruled out if there has been an increase in the money supply growth, and if we are willing to reject the rational expectations assumption. It is worth highlighting that trying to make sense of money supply data is extremely challenging as central bankers found out when they tried to implement monetarism. Moreover, a great deal of credit creation during the

Great Moderation took place in the shadow banking sector, making money flows much more difficult to detect. Hence, money signals could easily have duped investors for an extended period of time, leading to a rejection of Rational Expectations Theory.

According to Cowen, Hayek's view of cycles is a conceivable but incomplete scenario.[52] Cowen put forward a different view based on risk-based cycles, where an increased perception in risk leads to a downturn as investors move away from risky, capital-intensive and high-yielding investments. Interestingly Cowen's conclusion highlights that the empirical data 'neither discriminates decisively in favour of risk based nor traditional Austrian theories as opposed to other potential business cycle mechanisms'.[53] So where does this leave the quest for an alternative to the new neoclassical synthesis?

In 1974 the Nobel Prize for Economics was awarded to two economists for their work on monetary theory in the 1930s. Hayek was one of the economists; the other was the Swede, Gunnar Myrdal. Amusingly, both economists apparently expressed extreme annoyance of having being paired with the other. Myrdal was a social democrat and Hayek a libertarian. Unfortunately very little attention was paid to Myrdal's monetary theory outside of Sweden during the 1930s. Furthermore, the Keynesian revolution after the Second World War has meant that Myrdal's work remains largely ignored.

Dead foxes and the Finnish divorce rate

Myrdal gained his doctorate in economics in 1927 from Stockholm University after taking the normal route via a law degree. He is probably best known for his study *An American Dilemma: The Negro Problem and Modern Democracy*, which attempted to explain how racial issues were viewed in the United States. During the 1930s however, he was focussed largely on monetary economics using Wicksell as a framework, as well as some Austrian ideas of the trade cycle. In the late 1920s after stints in Germany, the United States and the United Kingdom, he helped found the Econometric Society in London. However, he was renowned for questioning the results of regressions due to their spurious nature, highlighting that correlations are not explanations which can be as spurious as the high correlation in Finland between foxes killed and divorces. In 1931 he published in Swedish a series of lectures on Wicksell's framework. In 1933 Hayek asked Myrdal to contribute to a book he was editing and Myrdal added a few more chapters on top of the Wicksell lectures. This book, which was in German, formed the basis of the English translation which was published in 1939 entitled *Monetary Equilibrium*.

When it came to monetary theory, Myrdal set to work on the notion of disequilibrium which was clearly the direction Hayek had been headed in. General Equilibrium Theory refers to a point in time and thus excludes the time factor of credit. This renders general equilibrium mostly irrelevant as an economic framework with shifts in bank credit having a significant effect on an economy.[54] In a stationary state there is no need for a monetary theory as 'everything there is in equilibrium by definition'.[55] Wicksell's system however is designed to cope with a dynamic economy, where equilibrium is defined at the point where the natural rate of interest equals the money rate of interest.

Myrdal's notion of equilibrium in a dynamic economy is purely a conceptual one rather than an attainable one as it can only be maintained by incessantly counteracting influences.[56] His argument that an economy is in a state of continuous disequilibrium was a radical departure from the traditional way of analysing an economy. This departure was as radical as the chaos revolution of the 1970s, when scientists discarded the traditional view that the physical world was naturally in a state of equilibrium. From an economic perspective the extent of disequilibrium was a function of the dynamic cumulative process from the notional equilibrium of the two rates of interest. Wicksell's other notions of equilibrium were, according to Myrdal, less convincing.

Myrdal dismissed the idea of price stability as pertaining to equilibrium in the tradition of Hayek and Davidson, a Swedish contemporary and friend of Wicksell's. 'An increased productivity necessarily increases the "natural rate of interest" and, if the money rate of interest is not immediately increased correspondingly and a fall in the price level provoked, the monetary equilibrium is disturbed.'[57] Hence, the money rate of interest ought to be adjusted up and down with respect to productivity gains, which would impact the general price level, thus rendering Wicksell's notion of price equilibrium flawed. Myrdal provided further detail why price stability cannot equal monetary equilibrium. Firstly, agents in an economy often make use of multi-year fixed contracts. Secondly, there is an inertia to the adjustment of prices over time, and finally, there exists opportunities for price manipulation due to the lack of competition. These arguments hark back to Cantillon and the notion that changes in the money supply impact commodities in different ways. Myrdal concludes that price stabilisation cannot be attained without disturbing monetary equilibrium and hence 'price stabilisation and the elimination of the business cycle are thus to some extent competing and contrary objectives'.[58] However, Myrdal does accept that reducing large price swings which in turn can amplify the business cycle due to entrepreneurs shifting sentiment should be taken into consideration. In essence, dismissing price stability as the central plank of monetary policy does not mean that prices should be completely ignored.

Myrdal also attacked Wicksell's assumption of monetary equilibrium when savings equals investment. Like Hayek, he states that saving and investment are carried out by different individuals with different expectations over different time horizons.[59] Hence saving and capital formation are not identical but can be compared. However, he goes one step further, highlighting the differences between ex-ante and ex-post measures of saving and investment.[60] The important point is that entrepreneurs are continually surprised by the differences between actual returns compared to expected returns, which is the cause of the dynamic nature of the economy. An increase in savings generally leads to falling demand and therefore lower capital values and initially lower investment. However, increased savings reduces the cost of credit boosting investment, hence capital values will begin to increase. The critical component for any increase in investment is of course the expectation of an increase in future profits. Hence, in a depression, free capital disposal exceeds the volume of investment even before an increase in savings, which implies capital availability is not the issue, but future profit expectations are.[61] Myrdal also raises the important point about banking liquidity – that should there be a liquidity crisis – then the availability of capital will clearly fall impacting investment.

Myrdal attempts to replace Wicksell's savings and investment equilibrium with a notion of equilibrium on the capital market where free capital equals investment on an ex-post basis. Clearly ex-ante and ex-post differences are driven by whether the investment will actually realise a gain or a loss, or whether costs or revenues change over the period. With ex-post calculations one can ascertain whether monetary equilibrium in a past period has reigned, and to which side of equilibrium it has deviated and to what intensity.[62] This logic means that ex-post income is equal to ex-post saving but also that it is equal to investment, the volume of investment being determined by the rate of interest relative to profit expectations.

Myrdal's goal was an attempt to develop a series of tools that could be used by central banks to maintain economic stability. He argued that the equilibrium rate of profit was the rate of profit that maintained equilibrium in the capital market. Hence it ought to be the job of the central bank to move the money rate of interest in line with the changing natural rate of interest. Unlike Hayek, Myrdal had no concept of any necessary reversal, arguing that the cumulative process goes on as long as expectations are such that profits will meet expectations. As soon as the expectation of profits falls, investment drops. He thus recommended that an index be created of underlying constituents of the heterogeneous economy, which when weighted could provide an indication of the driver of capital values or an aggregated natural rate.[63] Myrdal also assumed that there was no single natural rate for an economy.[64] Piero Sraffa, one of Keynes' colleagues at the University of Cambridge, had roundly criticised Hayek's *Prices and Production* for assuming that an economy had a single natural rate of interest in 1932.[65]

Myrdal argued that policy should be directed towards achieving the most complete fulfilment possible of the equation, where the cost of production of new investment equals the amount of free capital available, compatible with the least possible movement of a price index.[66] This approximately equates to the natural rate of interest equalling the money rate of interest. Moreover, prices should move inversely to productivity as Davidson had argued. Myrdal accepts that the shift away from stabilising prices will require entrepreneurs now and then to suffer gains and losses that would not exist if price stability were the aim of monetary policy.[67] However, he cautioned that central bankers should not permit very large, uni-directional price movements.

Myrdal also warned of central bank complacency that if the capital market and prices were stable, this was all down to credit policy being able to maintain a monetary equilibrium. Myrdal stressed that credit policy alone was not enough to stabilise an economy. Maintaining a monetary equilibrium is a question of economic policy as a whole, including the impact that cartels and unions may have.[68] Indeed, if the economy is stabilised for a certain period then it is the result of a very complicated system of causes, and the ability of credit policy to attain the same result is certainly not proved by this stability.[69]

The release of the minutes of the Federal Reserve FOMC meeting from 31 January 2006 is perhaps the best illustration of Myrdal's warning having been largely ignored.

The economy looks pretty good to us, perhaps a bit better than it did at the last meeting. With the near-term monetary policy path that's now priced into the markets, we think the economy is likely to grow slightly above trend in '06 and close to trend in '07.[70]

Although Myrdal believed that monetary policy could not maintain any sort of equilibrium by itself, he still argued that central bankers needed to intervene to improve economic conditions, thus attacking Hayek's fatalistic approach. In a downward Wicksellian process, the policy response ought to be focussed on increasing capital values by increasing profit expectations.[71] In a downturn, an investment in public works can be of use, although it is a precondition that it generates a return on capital, driving further increases in the expectation of profit.[72] However unlike Keynes, Myrdal argued that attempting to maintain low unemployment would increase wages, generating an upward Wicksellian cumulative process and inflation, thus anticipating Friedman.[73] Myrdal firmly believed that credit policy could make a real difference to minimising fluctuations in the business cycle; however, due to the complexity of an economy they cannot be eliminated totally.[74]

Myrdal set out a series of improvements to Hayek's model, but there remained some outstanding issues. Myrdal like Hayek assumes that increased profitability (increased savings) leads to increased investment. However, it is future expected profit margins and not current margins that determine investment. As such, the notion of equilibrium between ex-post savings and investment makes little sense. Moreover, the ability of the banking sector to provide more capital for investment purposes than is saved suggests that such a pursuit for an identity between savings and investment is futile. In 2011 corporations hoarded cash like crazy despite the fact that they were making strong profits. Corporate executives just did not like what they saw ahead of them and they were right. Finally, the assumption that excess liquidity had to be invested in physical assets was not resolved until a few years later when one of Myrdal's colleagues, Bertie Ohlin, argued that excess liquidity could also be invested in financial assets.

As the Wicksellian model continued to be improved in Stockholm, it is perhaps odd that this great intellectual movement that was beginning to triumph over Walrasian General Equilibrium Theory came to an end so abruptly. Unfortunately for the economics profession it became eclipsed by the rise of Keynesian economics. As one monetary economist has put it, 'the contrast between the simplicity of the Keynesian message that movements in output and employment were themselves equilibrating mechanisms, a message readily summarised in a diagram that could be embossed on the cover of a text book', versus the Stockholm School's complex approach which demonstrated 'that almost anything could be the outcome of a dynamic sequence is a telling one'.[75] With the new neoclassical synthesis under attack for completely missing one of the largest credit bubbles in history, leading to a crash in asset values and rising unemployment, a resurgence of Keynesian ideas is sweeping the economics industry once more. Neo Keynesians would however do well to understand the Stockholm Keynes debate before embarking on any more crazy economic experiments, particularly in light of the fact that the Stockholm School were neither hard-line conservatives nor libertarians. They just thought Keynes' theory had missed the point.

When Mr Keynes came to Stockholm

In October 1936, Keynes gave a lecture to the Political Economy Club in Stockholm rather pompously entitled 'My grounds for departure from orthodox economic traditions'. Unexpectedly for Keynes it was not well received, mainly because the young Swedes thought he was too classical and had not departed much from orthodox economics at all. During the speech the audience struggled to understand what was in fact new, which made Keynes very irritable. According to one of the Swedish economists present:

> It was certainly a remarkable event when the great prophet came to Stockholm pretending that he had seen a new light only to be taken down by the Swedish youngsters – who told him that he was rather old fashioned, that Swedish economists had gone much further and that his, Keynes' very method, the equilibrium method was unsuitable for the treatment of dynamic problems.[76]

A year later, one of the young Swedes published two articles which were rather critical of the *General Theory*, arguing that parts of Keynes' book were 'simply the long-awaited conversion of a Cambridge economist to the almost generally accepted standpoint elsewhere'.[77] In particular, Bertie Ohlin highlighted Keynes' preference for a classical system, with a focus on equilibrium and the over-simplistic formula that the volume of employment depends on the volume of investment.[78] Ohlin continued his attack on Keynes' inability to differentiate between ex-ante and ex-post, stating that 'either Keynes' reasoning is ex-post and then it explains nothing, or it is ex-ante and then it is entirely wrong'.[79] Finally Ohlin was also rather dubious of Keynes' Multiplier Theory, arguing that it can tell us but little about the effects of a certain increase in investment. 'It leaves out of account... the general business situation on profit expectations and the willingness to invest.... At the bottom of a depression public works for a moderate sum may start a recovery.... In another situation an increase in public works may scare the business work to such an extent that private investment activity declines and total output increases by less than the sum allocated to public works.... Thus the multiplicatory effect may easily at one time be ten and at another time considerably less than one.'[80]

One other important step that the Stockholm School clarified was the relationship between labour and capital. Although workers receive a wage, they may also consist in part of the amortisation of the capital which the worker represents.[81] Hence, the notion of labour becoming part of the definition of capital is crucial, largely influencing Sweden's more interventionist policy. Indeed, it is noteworthy that the Swedish committee set up to look at unemployment were asked to understand the nature of the 'economics of unused resources', indicating both physical and human resources.[82]

Despite the Keynesian and Monetarist revolutions a handful of Swedish economists kept pushing these ideas forward, in particular Axel Leijonhufvud at UCLA. Leijonhufvud dismissed once and for all the notion of an equilibrium between savings and investment, stating that 'if household saving and business investment are necessarily and therefore continuously equal, then it would seem that the banking system cannot possibly be doing anything else but simply serving as an obedient go between. So we can just as well erase it.'[83] Hence, increased leverage – lending more to the business sector than flowing in as savings from the household sector – of the banking system will cause the circular flow to expand.[84]

Leijonhufvud's insights however go much deeper than this in the way he describes the various trends in monetary economics. His savings and investment diagram highlighted the various strands based on the assumptions that are made and the various subsequent logical outcomes of these assumptions. Such a simple overview of the profession is quite revealing, particularly given that it explains why, from time to time, economics ends up in a cul-de-sac because of the erroneous assumptions made upfront.[85] 'If you are in a subject,' he argued, 'that possesses tremendously effective methods for always eliminating them you get a tree with a very tall trunk – a

Californian Redwood.' The idea is that deviations from the proven body of knowledge that turn out to be false are just small branches that fall off. The way that physics has largely developed is a case in turn. Although Newton's theories have been found to have had flaws, they are not totally useless.

However, Leijonhufvud's conception of economics is 'some sort of untidy, ill-pruned bush with a lot of branches and with sap running in unlikely places'.[86] His point here is that when a new system of economics is set up, the trend appears to be that economists seem to follow these ideas in a herd-like fashion until they run into the wall. From Keynesianism to Monetarism and lastly the new neoclassical synthesis, all ended up going down the wrong path, creating large ugly branches that led nowhere. Leijonhufvud suggested that as these new branches of economics get set up, there are at the time other competing ideas that are subsequently ignored. Hence, it pays to return to those ideas in order to embark upon a trend that may provide a better foundation for a tall tree. The Stockholm School is indeed such a foundation.

The development of Hayek's theory through Myrdal and other members of the Stockholm School has provided monetary economics with a distinct alternative to the new neoclassical synthesis. Economic modelling has to be dynamic and continuous due to the dynamic nature of capital through time. Such a framework also provides a notion of equilibrium from Wicksell's first equation of parity between the two rates of interest. Moreover, this framework highlights that price stability ought to be secondary in terms of policy. Finally, it has to be accepted that leverage from the banking system is the driving force of an economy and that savings and investment cannot be an identity where banks exist.

During the 1930s, the ability to model such a framework was limited. However, the development of Chaos Theory to analyse complex non-linear systems provides a robust foundation to dynamic disequilibrium modelling. This approach to modelling observes streams of data coming out of the model and what goes in, but not what is happening inside. Given the sensitivity of a complex system to initial conditions, the patterns emanating from streams of credit-related data can change rapidly. Hence, investors embarking on new asset allocation strategies will need to think differently about their internal investment process, and it is to the challenge of building such a model that we now turn.

Chapter 5

The neo-Wicksellian framework

It can scarcely be denied that the supreme goal of all theory is to make the irreducible basic elements as simple and as few as possible.

Albert Einstein[1]

Chapter 4 developed an alternative framework of monetary theory to the new neoclassical synthesis. This new framework ostensibly argues that the objective of price stability can lead to economic instability. Empirical data backs this claim up as the recent financial crisis has shown. The neo-Wicksellian framework stipulates that economic instability cannot be eliminated but only minimised. What follows is an attempt to synthesise these ideas into a coherent theory that is able to explain the nature of the business cycle, providing investors with improved market signals in relation to the assets they own. In conjunction with this attempt to construct a macroeconomic theory it is imperative that the theory is general rather than specific to individual cases. As discussed in Chapter 1, many economic theories work well for a certain period of time until the behaviour of the variables change, rendering the theory useless. Such a theory would therefore need to explain the recent financial crisis in terms of why some countries had significant credit bubbles but others did not. It would need to explain the Japanese lost decade, the 1970s period of stagflation, the Great Depression and the deflation of the 1870s. Clearly the amount of data available pre-1980 does shrink considerably; however, there are proxies that can be used to test the validity of the theory.

A neo-Wicksellian theory of credit and business cycles

In order for investors to be able to profit from the misleading signals emanating from central banks, a theory of the business cycle needs to be constructed to act as a benchmark in order to ascertain whether asset values on an ex-ante basis are expected to increase or fall. Once such a theory has been established, it ought to be reasonably straightforward to develop investment products that track the business cycle – the idea being that such an investment product would be less volatile than equities but generate better returns than investing in government bonds. The following principles derived from the Vienna and Stockholm schools form the basis of a theory of business cycles permitting investors to profit from current monetary policy.

Firstly, for any theory to be able to explain business cycles, it needs to have at its core the notion of an equilibrium level from which one can measure movements in the cycle. This does not mean that the equilibrium level is ever attained or that there is a natural tendency towards equilibrium, but only that there is a point of reference for measurement purposes. Our neo-Wicksellian theory is based on Myrdal's concept of a dynamic disequilibrium. Given the complexity of the cause and effect of the billions of decisions made every day by economic agents, an economy is clearly in a state of continuous disequilibrium. This is diametrically opposed to the neoclassical synthesis and its Walrasian heritage which provides a stationary equilibrium framework for an economy. Recent attempts to create dynamic equilibrium models in the form of DSGE models have not met with much success. The notional equilibrium position is defined when the natural rate of interest equates to the money rate of interest for an economy. The natural rate of interest is equivalent to the return on capital, and the money rate of interest is the cost of funding for a firm based on long-term funding rates. However, this is the only definition of our equilibrium. As per Hayek's argument, there is no equilibrium when there is price stability, which during credit bubbles has generally provided misleading signals to market participants. Moreover, there is also no equilibrium between savings and investment in a credit economy. This is because the banking system is able to inject more money into an economy than the savings it receives. Finally, there is no necessary cause-and-effect chain whereby excess profits (increased savings) must necessarily be invested in physical assets. Firms' investment decisions are based on future expected profits rather than whether there is available cash to invest. Excess liquidity is therefore generally invested in financial assets whose value is defined by the expected rate of growth of excess profits, as highlighted by Minsky.

In terms of measurement, the natural rate of interest needs to be divided between ex-post measures, that is after the investment has taken place, and ex-ante measures, which means the expectations of investors looking forward. The fact that ex-ante and ex-post measures are highly unlikely to ever tie up provides the natural tendency of an economy to be in a continuous dynamic disequilibrium process. Ex-post measurement is a reasonably straight forward, although data-intensive, process and is likely to provide the strongest signals of the extent of any disequilibrium in an economy. When an economy moves away from equilibrium, it starts off a cumulative process of credit expansion or contraction which explains why asset booms and busts are linked with the volume of money. Clearly there is some sort of relationship between the volume of money and output that Friedman's econometric analysis of the United States picked up, with the incremental or reduced amount of money acting as a stimulant or restraint on economic activity. However, money is a function of credit, and although at times tracks credit, its behaviour can be inconsistent, and more importantly difficult to monitor. Indeed, the complexity of the modern banking system makes tracking the volume of money around an economy very challenging.

Informal discussions with ex-ECB employees have confirmed that this remains a key issue for central bankers due to the shadow banking and offshore sectors. For example, in order to track changes in the money supply, observers need to be able to track all forms of credit creation. Clearly there are certain metrics that do provide some insight into this problem, including bank leverage, refinancing rates and the cost of funding; however, there is currently no single available measure. Moreover, if a substantial part of credit creation remains hidden from central bankers, using a volume of money indicator to measure the distance from equilibrium is not particularly useful, which is one of the reasons why monetarism failed. This is why an ex-post comparison of the natural rate of interest and the money rate of interest provides a better indication of where an economy is in relation to equilibrium.

Although an ex-post analysis is more straightforward to measure, it does not help investors to take the right decisions due to the time lag in its calculation. From an asset allocation perspective, an ex-ante model also needs to be developed which would be based on monitoring continuous streams of credit-related data that explain the cumulative process of business cycle dynamics. Such a model would display both linear and non-linear relationships, as well as the fact that economic systems are deterministic and can produce unpredictable outcomes. Given the sensitivity of an economy to small changes in initial conditions, it requires constant monitoring to detect turning points in the cycle. The factors relevant to Wicksell's cumulative process relate to the leverage of economic units from corporations, through to banks, consumers and governments. Indeed, it is the leverage of each economic unit that can drive capital values up over time by improving the outlook for profits. However, at some stage the excess of leverage in conjunction with a changed outlook for profits causes expectations to shift and the deleveraging process amplifies a negative outlook for profits. Besides understanding the relative leverage of the economy, the productivity of investment also needs to be taken into account. In a stationary economy, investment increases GDP; however, if that investment generates a negative return on capital, this will impact future growth rates. In essence, there is a significant difference in leveraging up to generate higher returns on capital than lower returns on capital. Significant changes in the general price level can also have an impact on the expectations of future profits which needs to be taken into account.

Finally, in relation to understanding the nature of capital itself and the way in which returns are generated, it is imperative to ensure the definition of capital is refined. Standard definitions of capital in neoclassical theory focus on machinery, which in itself is the result of prior accumulated labour. This view was stated by Bohm-Bawerk and continued by Hayek right through to modern-day economics textbooks. This contradiction is neither helpful nor appropriate for an economy where labour is heterogeneous and when combined with knowledge is the main driver of economic growth.[2] Indeed, management writers such as Peter Drucker have argued that that it is the inter-relationship of knowledge workers with their tools that drives productivity growth and hence capital values.[3]

These series of assumptions form the basis of a neo-Wicksellian theory of the business cycle. However, for these set of assumptions to have any validity they need to be measured and tested in numerous cases, both past and present. Besides the need to develop a systematic approach to measurement and test the data to show that it provides reasonable economic explanations of events on an ex-post basis, a robust approach to modelling ex-ante expectations also needs to be validated.

It's all in the measurement

In 1919 Arthur Eddington, a British physicist, led an expedition to Sao Tome and Principe on the west coast of Africa in an attempt to measure the deflection of light by the sun's gravitational field, thus providing data to substantiate whether Einstein's theory held. The results did indeed support Einstein's theory, although what followed was a protracted disagreement about whether there was an inherent bias within the measurement process of Eddington's experiment. Measurement issues in economics present the same challenges as they do in physics, with rather dull and highly technical discussions. However, these discussions are unfortunately critical in the testing of any theory as the experiment with monetarism showed. Friedman's econometric analysis, which for many of his followers backed up his ideas on monetarism, was found to have had significant flaws in it, and therefore did not provide sufficient evidence to substantiate his theory.[4] The problem of course was that Friedman focussed on money and not on credit in terms of the data. The neo-Wicksellian approach focuses on the ex-post measurement of the cumulative process of credit expansion and contraction. This allows investors to ascertain how far and for how long an economy has moved away from equilibrium. Unfortunately, Wicksell only gave rather vague guidelines about how the two rates of interest could be measured.

Starting with the natural rate of interest, Wicksell was in fact dubious that data existed for it to be measured. Although, he did highlight that if one tried to measure the natural rate a good place to start was a company's reported accounts. Hayek highlighted that the measurement of the natural rate was in the realm of theory, although Sraffa's attack stating that every commodity had its own natural rate suggested Hayek was in fact looking in the wrong place. Myrdal proposed that an index could be developed to measure the natural rate of interest based on individual company returns, although he warned of the dangers of purely using listed companies which are not representative of an economy. However, the assumption of using the return on capital for each individual company which would be weighted in relation to its contribution to output is clearly spelt out in Myrdal's writings. The reality is that in the 1920s and 1930s there was not sufficient information on a broad range of companies over an extended period of time to even attempt to measure the various rates of interest.

Given there is a great deal more data around today which can be compared internationally, particularly for larger developed economies, it is more feasible to estimate the natural rate of interest for an economy utilising the individual returns on capital for each company. It is worth pointing out that this approach is more

problematic for emerging markets where lower corporate governance standards may exist, leading to potentially misleading company accounts figures. Moreover, attempting to measure the natural
rate of interest in smaller economies can also be problematic due to
increased volatility of the output from a smaller data set.

In terms of available company data, this largely excludes the
vast number of privately held companies, thus forcing a more nar-
row focus on listed companies. Although listed companies cannot
be used to represent the overall returns to an economy, average
returns on invested capital can be generated for each sector which
can be used as a proxy for all companies in that sector. The averages
of each sector then form inputs into the calculation weighted by the
contribution of that sector to the economy. For example, the aggregated return on capital for the US listed construction sector[5] in
2010 was 9.06 per cent, while construction only contributed around
5 per cent to gross value added. Thus the natural rate of interest is
purely a simple weighted average calculation of aggregated returns
on capital for each sector in relation to each sector's contribution to
an economy as defined by gross value added.

Up until now, the definition of the natural rate of interest
has been loosely defined as either the return on capital or the
marginal productivity of capital. These terms are interchangeable
and highlight the impact investment has on generating future
income streams, where capital investment is defined in money terms
which is then allocated to both people and tools. As such, deciding
on which data type to use from the Worldscope database will have
a material impact on the outcome. An analysis of the Worldscope
datatypes has highlighted the return on invested capital as being
the best proxy for the natural rate of interest for each company.

The return on invested capital is defined by Worldscope in the
following way:

(Net Income before Preferred Dividends + ((Interest Expense on

Debt − Interest Capitalised) * (1 − Tax Rate)))/Average of Last Year's

and Current Year's (Total Capital + Last Year's Short-Term Debt

and Current Portion of Long-Term Debt) * 100

This definition functions reasonably well for non-financial corporations; however, it is problematic for banks given that capital is
almost exclusively financed using equity rather than debt. Hence
for financial institutions the natural rate of interest is defined by the

return on equity. The return on equity is defined by Worldscope as being:

(Net Income before Preferred Dividends – Preferred Dividend

Requirement)/Last Year's Common Equity $*100$

After the returns on capital and equity were extracted for each company in the index, a series of data quality checks were run on the data sets to ensure its integrity. Besides using standard statistical tests to remove outliers, certain accounting treatments can also skew data requiring removal from the calculation. For example, in boom years companies on acquisition sprees historically built up a goodwill reserve. If valuations of those assets then fell, it caused the goodwill to be written off on the P&L, which in turn may cause equity to be issued impacting the return on invested capital calculation substantially. This happens where accumulated losses exceed shareholders' capital. With the data preparation complete, the calculation of the proxy natural rate of interest for each economy is then straightforward using the weighted average calculation approach.

The net income before dividends component will of course also capture returns to capital investment that have been made in prior periods and already paid off. Any ability to deploy people to extract more value from existing tools will increase the return on capital as the numerator increases without an increase in the denominator. This is important to note given that data compiled on physical capital investment suggests a longevity period of decades.

The final step in the process is then to determine the cost of capital or funding, otherwise known as the money rate of interest. The cost of capital for any company is determined by the cost of debt and of equity. According to one study that assessed the sources of funding, retained earnings account for the bulk of investment at 70 per cent, followed by debt at 20 per cent of the total amount, with the residual made up of equity and other sources.[6] However, for start-ups and SMEs who are unable to get bank loans, companies are often financed using personal credit cards, personal savings or personal loans backed by collateral such as a house. Given that there are thousands of companies in an economy with different funding sources at different costs due to different perceptions of credit risk, such a calculation will prove very difficult to ascertain. As a result some assumptions will need to be made.

Firstly, the cost of retained earnings in corporate finance equates to the cost of equity which is defined as a premium above the risk free rate that shareholders require to earn as a reward for holding the equity. Hence, the risk premium becomes dependent on the riskiness of the company itself – often described by its volatility. In terms of calculating the cost of equity, there is no standard approach to generating estimates. Although historical premiums are widely used, the objective in attempting to calculate the cost of equity of a firm when an investment decision is made is clearly done on a forward basis. Thus it would appear appropriate to use an implied equity risk premium, particularly as the premium is likely to be volatile as market conditions change.[7] However, there is no one approach that provides an estimate of the implied risk premium with any degree of certainty, with some studies arguing that all measures are either spurious or unstable.[8] There do appear to be some broad trends that are observable, where in times of economic stress the cost of investing in equities tends to rise due to increased perceived risk, and as the equity market booms the cost of equity tends to fall as perceived risk falls. Debt generally follows a similar pattern with the cost of debt rising with increasing perceived risks and falling as risks decline. Given the general correlation between the costs of equity and debt, an estimate of the cost of debt will give a reasonable proxy for the cost of funding as both require a premium above the risk free rate, although it is assumed that the cost of equity will be consistently higher than debt.

In terms of estimating the cost of debt, Wicksell notes that long-term bond market rates ought to be used as a proxy, although he is not specific on which maturity should be used. The challenge of trying to estimate which maturity to use is again highly complex given some companies have no debt, and many may only use short-term debt for working capital purposes. Moreover, there is little data available on the debt profile of SMEs. For the purposes of this analysis, a constant five-year maturity rate will be used as a proxy for a number of reasons. Firstly, the credit default swap market, which allows investors to buy insurance on the bonds they hold, trades most at the five-year maturity. This is largely related to the fact that the average maturity profile of bonds issued and therefore held by investors is around five years. More importantly, it means that price formation at the five-year point is also stronger due to increased liquidity. Liquidity is an important factor in determining the quality of information emanating from the bond market. This is also why CDS index providers generally calculate indices at the five-year maturity.[9]

The final step to calculate the money rate of interest is which price indicators ought to be used to provide a consistent estimate of the cost of funding through time. Country CDS indices that are calculated by aggregating individual company spread levels can be a useful way of generating a proxy for the cost of funding for all companies within an economy. The need to consistently calculate a five-year point for all companies on a daily basis largely precludes the use of company bond prices given the lack of liquidity in the bond market. However, CDS data in volatile market conditions is also problematic due to sudden increases in counterparty risk of the banking sector who are the underwriters of the CDS contracts. As such, CDS data in volatile conditions can provide misleading signals due to an increase in the perceived risk of bank failures. Therefore the most consistent and stable indicator to use is the five-year government bond yield for each country. Clearly the actual cost of funding for companies in the Datastream indices will differ from the five-year sovereign bond yield in that most companies will have to pay higher costs than the sovereign yield. However, it is worth noting that between 2010 and 2011, some European corporates saw their cost of debt funding fall relative to sovereign debt. One further adjustment needs to be made to the five-year government bond rate given that some investment has taken place up to five years prior to the return on capital being calculated. Hence the money rate of interest used is a five-year moving average of the five-year bond yield. From a measurement perspective there are clearly a number of issues with any attempt to estimate both the natural and money rates of interest. The approach taken I believe does provide reasonable proxies given the nature of the problem and lack of consistent data through time.

Thus we can now compare the two rates on an ex-post basis, which allows us to calculate the returns above the cost of capital, defined as the 'Wicksellian Differential'. Hence our notional equilibrium can now be defined where these two rates converge and the Wicksellian Differential is zero. From an investor perspective, this has a great deal of value because the rate of change of the Wicksellian Differential itself ought to provide an indication of the trend of equity price movements. The Wicksellian Differential is of course measuring the rate of profit driven by a cumulative process of credit creation or destruction. Hence, should the difference be positive and growing, then one can expect equity prices to rise due to rising leverage across the economy. Should the difference be falling, equity prices ought to fall, and should the rate be negative but stable, equity prices would be neutral. However, for investors the time delay in waiting for all annualised accounts to be reported is problematic to be used as an investment signal. Thus the task at hand is to develop an ex-ante model that allows investors to understand the underlying structural shifts that impact asset valuations which are related to leverage.

It's a complex dynamic world

Current monetary theory assumes that the economy tends towards equilibrium and that the nature of economic data is generally linear and random. Clearly, where Myrdal ended up after Hayek's work on the business cycle was somewhere quite far away from a linear equilibrium approach. Unfortunately the neo-Keynesian revolution after the war institutionalised simple, equilibrium models, with the more recent attempts at modelling dynamic equilibrium also failing to provide much insight into the nature of an economy. The development of Chaos Theory in the 1970s however provided a different perspective on the problem of economic analysis challenging the ideas of equilibrium, which was subsequently taken up by a handful of economists. Some neo-Keynesian economists attempted to demonstrate that endogenous chaotic cycles existed, thus justifying government intervention.[10] These arguments were summarily dismissed by the neoclassical contingent who posed the question as to why the government should be any wiser than market participants in its knowledge of how one might restore equilibrium. More interesting was the attempt by a libertarian economist, influenced by Hayek, who argued that chaos was central to the self-organisation of an economy, which in turn was crucial to the spontaneity that drives progress. Don Lavoie believed that it was this instability itself that in fact makes the system more resilient.[11] However, such approaches in the face of general equilibrium combined with the stability of the Great Moderation meant research in dynamic disequilibrium remained on the outside of the periphery.

The reality is that the economy is a dynamic, complex system and although the Walrasian system of multiple simultaneous equations and regression models may still have some value for economic analysis, it has also provided investors with misleading signals resulting in large, unexpected losses. Furthermore, mathematical economists who have favoured the use of dynamic disequilibrium modelling have argued that there was never any reason to assume that an economy should function on a linear basis, particularly as economic theory provides virtually no support for such an assumption.[12]

The pervasive view of equilibrium analysis however did not stop the handful of financial market practitioners from analysing streams of data that at times appeared linear and random but can suddenly change, demonstrating non-linear and deterministic patterns. These investors tended to snap up anyone with a PhD in non-linear dynamics in order to extract useful information from the market. These investors have also accepted that market behaviour cannot be forecast, and that the general trend shifts through time as an economy changes, thus requiring the portfolio to be adjusted to new conditions.

In terms of data analysis there are two general approaches that investors can use which help indicate the position of an economy in relation to the business cycle on an ex-ante basis. Firstly, is an analysis of the streams of credit- and economic-related data that indicate future shifts in the Wicksellian Differential as the ex-ante Wicksellian Differential is an unobservable measure. The second is an analysis of the extent of long-term memory in the asset class indicators themselves.

Asset prices rise when the expectations of future earnings rise. The streams of credit-related data represent the expectations of economic units. When expectations are positive, leverage increases expanding the volume of money which may be put to use to increase the return on capital or to invest in financial assets to generate returns. However, at some stage this increase in leverage becomes so large that the market's expectation of the ability for debtors to repay their loans as the rate of profit slows begins to change thus excess leverage which initially fuelled an increase in the rate of profit growth amplifies its fall as the economy deleverages. In essence, leverage has a dual and contradictory impact on the economy which is driven by changing expectations as the economy evolves. Further insight into the general trajectory of a portfolio can thus be gleaned by analysing streams of data on the growth in leverage of key economic agents through time. This includes the rate of growth in leverage of consumers, non-financial corporations, financial institutions and governments. The rate at which economic agents leverage up has an impact on the Wicksellian Differential due to the ability of increasing leverage to raise profits. However, the relationship of each of these factors to the Wicksellian Differential changes through time as the underlying structure of the economy shifts, with the potential for the variables to move contrary to each other as well.

The consumer leverage ratio generally has the greatest impact on the Wicksellian Differential given it heavily influences aggregate demand for products and is the largest contributor to GDP in most advanced economies. Corporations increasing leverage to invest also have an impact on raising the Wicksellian Differential. Indeed, the potential for corporations to dramatically increase their investment through leverage is closest to Hayek's theory of capital where overinvestment takes place. The ability of banks to leverage up to provide financing for both consumers and corporations also remains a key factor. In all of these instances rising leverage would lead to an increase in the Wicksellian Differential by sustaining profit growth until leverage becomes unsustainable as the rate of profit growth slows. This in turn would then lead to falling leverage and a falling Wicksellian Differential. Finally, one needs to take into account a change in government leverage. Governments that are not heavily leveraged and decide to increase debt to pay for productive investment which is then spent efficiently will have a positive impact on the Wicksellian Differential. An example might be a government that uses debt to increase spending on a road or airport building programme to reduce the costs of travelling for consumers and corporations, thus generating a productivity increase for the economy. It may well be that the time horizons of the private sector related to the investment are insufficient, thus requiring the government to step in to ensure that the investment is made. However, there are clearly more instances where governments use debt for unproductive purposes, and as such increasing leverage would be perceived negatively. This is particularly problematic when a government is already highly leveraged causing expectations to fall. However, it does explain why some governments are able to leverage up significantly more than others. For instance, Japan's debt to GDP ratio is substantially higher than Greece's, with incredibly low bond yields. At some stage however perception by Japanese savers of the ever-increasing amount of debt will lead to changing expectations causing yields to jump. As Minsky argued, it cannot continue forever.

Although credit expansion is critical to fuelling an increase in the Wicksellian Differential, other factors also play a role. The nominal rate of interest clearly has an impact on the Wicksellian Differential. Furthermore, the increase in the availability of credit requires that companies deploy credit in a productive way. This means that credit is used to generate productivity increases by investing in people and/or new tools. Thus we need to add a measure of the growth in human capital or output per worker.

Finally, given the importance of high levels of inflation impacting profitability, the general price level also needs to be taken into account. This is because there is now a great deal of evidence that economies with higher levels of inflation do impact investment and therefore reduce the return on capital.[13] From a micro level this comes about when input costs are rising faster than consumers are willing to pay for final consumption goods, thus reducing the margins of firms. Clearly other factors such as inventories and tax rates could be added in; however, the objective is to focus on the major dynamic factors that influence the expectations of future profits.

As the streams of data are published, an analysis of the relationships between the factors pertaining to the Wicksellian Differential is undertaken to ascertain the likelihood of a change in expectations shifting due to the delay in being able to calculate the ex-post data. Figure 5.1 is an example of the dynamic and non-linear nature of the way in which credit impacts the economy. It shows the relationship through time of the US consumer leverage ratio versus the Wicksellian Differential. The chart demonstrates there are periods when the consumer leverage ratio is rising

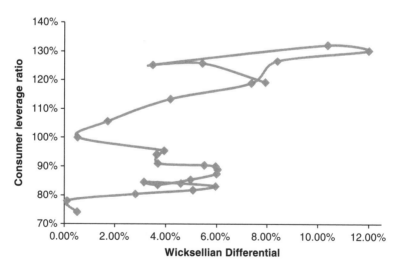

Figure 5.1   US consumer leverage ratio vs Wicksellian Differential
Source: Thomson Reuters Datastream, Credit Capital Advisory.

along with the Wicksellian Differential. At other times it shows an asymmetric deleveraging process and a falling Wicksellian Differential. The relationship is also punctuated by data anomalies which are related to the dynamic nature of the issue where other factors are impacting profits/losses more than consumer debt, highlighting the complexity of the problem. Indeed, for each potential value of the Wicksellian Differential there are multiple solutions through time. Moreover, consumers do not deleverage from the same level through time. Thus, using historical averages is not particularly helpful, given that the underlying structure of the economy at a point in time will impact individuals' appetite for debt. Thus any attempt to forecast when consumers might stop deleveraging is not going to generate anything useful, although an analysis of the data as it comes in can provide insight to changing patterns.

Besides analysing the underlying credit factors related to leverage that represent expectations of economic units through time, it is also possible to model asset prices themselves in order to estimate the extent of long-term memory present in a series. The presence of long-term memory provides another stream of data to analyse with regard to asset bubbles. There has however been a great deal of debate about whether long-term memory exists in financial markets at all. Samuelson's position that markets are micro-efficient but not macro-efficient suggests that EMH will hold at the stock level but not at the index level. This was further backed up by evidence from Shiller and Jung. Although EMH does not appear to hold at the macro level, the ability to demonstrate long-term memory is still a matter of debate. This debate is largely a technical one between the financial economists and the econophysicists, a movement that was started in the 1990s based on statistical physics and was highly influenced by Mandelbrot's breakthrough in the 1960s. A number of financial economists who have looked at this in depth have suggested that long-term memory may well manifest itself, however it will not be easy to detect using current statistical techniques.[14] Hence the econophysicists remain focussed on the challenge of developing appropriate techniques to show long-term memory detection.[15] One tool that has become prevalent within the econophysics movement to detect long-term memory is the Hurst exponent, which was introduced to finance by Mandelbrot and has also been used by financial market practitioners.[16]

The origins of this measurement tool are linked to the world of hydrology and the arrival of Harold Hurst in Cairo in 1906.[17] Hurst was a hydrologist who spent most of his career in Egypt measuring the annual flood of the river Nile in order to understand how much it might flood from one year to the next. The discharge of the Nile could vary almost three-fold, which was clearly problematic for a hydrologist trying to control flood waters that appeared to have no predictable pattern. After several years of measuring water flows up and down the river, Hurst dismissed normal distributions as a way of predicting the size of floods. The data clearly showed that the highs were higher and the lows were lower. Hurst eventually discovered that what mattered was the sequence of events rather than the size of each individual flood. This meant that statistically a flood was more likely to be followed by another flood rather than to revert to any mean. The observations were therefore not independent of each other.

Mandelbrot applied these ideas to finance and soon discovered that the Hurst exponent, which is a number between 0 and 1, did not maintain a figure of 0.5 which would imply a normal distribution of Brownian motion, or a random walk. Mandelbrot found that over periods of time H increased above 0.5, thus indicating the effect of stored memory with yesterday's price being more important to today's price. This is Mandelbrot's Joseph effect. However, this stored memory process is finite and at some stage becomes unsustainable, resulting in a fall below 0.5 where assets display characteristics with sudden discontinuous changes. This is akin to Mandelbrot's Noah effect.

It is also worth bearing in mind that at times assets do have an exponent of 0.5, thus giving the impression of randomness. This is important because such random behaviour mimics the stochastic behaviour of a linear function which generates a time series of data that appears to follow a random walk. This is why many studies do indeed demonstrate that over periods of time, prices do follow a random walk; however, these movements do not hold in the medium term at the macro level. A calculation of H thus provides the markets' view of expected returns which can help investors manage downside risk on their portfolios. Thus if $H = 0.5$, then it is entirely appropriate to use a normal distribution of expected returns; however, this is unlikely to remain constant given the dynamic nature of credit. As H increases above 0.5 the probability of fatter tails will increase until the Noah effect takes place. Given the discontinuous nature of the Noah effect, distributions of severe events in these periods are of course far more common. Thus the Generalised Hurst Exponent[18] can be used as a secondary measurement tool allowing investors to see turning points in the market's reaction to the business cycle based on the fundamental drivers of credit expansion and contraction. Such a calculation is best carried out on index tick-by-tick data due to the need for hundreds of thousands of observations to detect long-term memory. Moreover, a significantly larger number of observations increases the confidence levels of the results, which can be problematic.

Finally, from an ex-ante modelling perspective, one cannot assume that all asset bubbles are grounded in the release of credit into the economy. Thus the measurement of the Wicksellian Differential will not detect asset bubbles that have no link to increased credit. Indeed it is quite feasible for the Wicksellian Differential to be in decline with individual asset prices rising due to an investment frenzy, with tulips being a good example. Although tulip mania in 17th-century Netherlands took place against the backdrop of a robust economy that displayed signs of increased credit due to falling interest rates and increasing international trade, the prices that tulips reached in 1637 had little in common with any incremental release of credit. Charles Mackay in his book *Memoirs of Extraordinary Popular Delusions and the Madness of Crowds* noted the value of one rare tulip called the *Viceroy*, as recorded by a contemporary author (Table 5.1).[19]

Table 5.1 Value of a Viceroy tulip at the height of Tulip Mania

Goods exchanged for one Viceroy tulip	Value in florins
Two lasts of wheat	448
Four lasts of rye	558
Four fat oxen	480
Eight fat swine	240
Twelve fat sheep	120
Two hogsheads of wine	70
Four tuns of beer	32
Two tons of butter	192
One thousand lbs. of cheese	120
A complete bed	100
A suit of clothes	80
A silver drinking cup	60
TOTAL	2,500

Source: C. Mackay (1852) *Memoirs of Extraordinary Popular Delusions and the Madness of Crowds*

Turbulence in economics

Understanding an economy based on the analysis of streams of data is a much more effective way in making sense of the dynamics of such a complex system. Just as the physicists abandoned the pipe dream of being to model the real world, economists need to do the same. The challenge with attempting to analyse an economy according to one economist is that 'although economies are permeated with nonlinearities and discontinuities, there are still many times and places where simple linear and continuous models of a Marshallian or Walrasian sort will be quite adequate'.[20] This is what makes modelling so ineffective yet so enticing to work on. However, given that we know credit largely drives the evolution of the complex system in which we live, a neo-Wicksellian analytical approach that can generate streams of data provides a great deal of insight into the general trajectory of the system. Despite the fact that outcomes of a complex system are unpredictable, it does not mean that we are unable to influence the economy through policy, only that our ability to see beyond the present is limited. Hence, all economic forecasts ought to be treated with a significant degree of scepticism. So when the Fed announced it was publishing its long-term forecasts, Charles Goodhart rightly responded in the FT that this was largely an irrelevance.[21]

Before we go into detail as to how one might be able to use this system as part of an investment process and what the system has to say about how policy can impact capital values, it is imperative to return to our ex-post analysis and demonstrate the validity of Wicksell's framework. Wicksell's framework permits the calculation of the ex-post Wicksellian Differential, which in turn highlights the extent of ex-post cumulative imbalances within an economy. Indeed, unless the empirical analysis on credit bubbles using this framework is compelling, the idea of creating investment products on this framework remains firmly in the world of dreams.

Chapter 6

Testing Wicksellianism

Well when events change, I change my mind. What do you do?

Paul Samuelson[1]

In 2011 the IMF published a study looking at the drivers behind the asset allocation decisions of long-term investors in an attempt to ascertain the risks that sudden changes in asset allocation have on global financial stability. The analysis concluded that investor decisions were largely driven by positive growth prospects as indicated by real GDP growth forecasts.[2] This implies that when forecasts suddenly reverse, as they did during the financial crisis, it can lead to dramatic capital flows out of bond and equity funds into cash or liquid credit-worthy government bonds such as US Treasuries. Such rapid movements can of course exacerbate the stability of the economy and increase the volatility of asset prices. The challenge in the lead up to the financial crisis was that most investors' real GDP forecasts were wrong. The reality is that any attempt to forecast the future is fraught with complexity and more than likely to be misleading.

However, even if they had been right, the link between higher rates of GDP growth leading to higher earnings growth and therefore higher returns appears to be indirect at best. Indeed, several studies have concluded that the correlation between real GDP growth and equity returns is in fact negative.[3] In recent years, a number of arguments have been developed that support that perspective. In the 1990s, the Nobel Laureate Paul Krugman and Alwyn Young argued that much of the real economic growth in emerging markets came from high savings rates and the more efficient utilisation of labour, neither of which necessarily translates into higher profits.[4] This partially explains the stellar performance of Chinese GDP growth figures and the relatively poor performance of its stock market. Thus the aggregation approach of measuring output has no necessary correlation with the rate of profit. It is therefore possible to have countries with high levels of output and low profit rates and vice versa. However, one would expect there to be some kind of relationship between equity returns and GDP growth during significant drops in output which would most likely impact short-term profitability. In essence the relationship between output and profits is indirect. Investors need an aggregation measure that focuses on the nature of profits, which in turn is linked to the growth in credit. Hence one would expect the Wicksellian Differential to be a far better indicator of rising profits than GDP growth.

The Wicksellian Differential permits an investor to understand just how far an economy has deviated from its equilibrium level due to a growth in credit. Moreover, this measurement process provides insight into how long an economy has deviated from its equilibrium level. This is critical because Wicksell's process is cumulative, which means that the longer an economy has operated above its equilibrium level due to a sustained increase in leverage, the greater the bubble in credit and therefore the greater the peaks and troughs of the business cycle. Hence any increase in the rate of excess profit growth or the Wicksellian Differential should filter through more quickly to higher expectations of future profits and hence equity returns.

Using the defined measurement process, the aim is now to test the relationship between the Wicksellian Differential against real equity returns and real GDP growth. Given that the Wicksellian Differential is a measure of excess profit growth which in turn is fuelled by credit expansion, theoretically we should expect to see that a rising Wicksellian Differential generates increased equity returns. Conversely we would expect to see falling returns as the Wicksellian Differential decreases. In periods where the Wicksellian Differential is negative, markets remain focussed on future expected profits, and if the future is too uncertain then markets would remain muted. In essence, the relationship between the Wicksellian Differential and equity returns ought to be strong.

There is of course one big caveat in that sometimes the market mis-prices assets. Equity prices contain forward-looking information representing the markets' expectations of the future. However, as we have seen, investors can be fooled for a considerable period of time, thus in the medium term markets do tend to correct themselves after such periods of mispricing and expectations adjust. Hence, there may be instances when equity returns, due to capital gains, rise in conjunction with falling profits or indeed fall with rising profits. Moreover, trends in equity returns ought to be punctuated by sudden falls due to changing expectations related to the unsustainability of leverage as the rate of profit slows. At its core, the Wicksellian Differential should be able to indicate the nature of the business cycle which oscillates between higher and lower rates of profit growth based on the availability and expansion of credit. So is the theory borne out by the empirical data?

A very brief credit history of the United States

Over the last 30 years, the US economy in terms of real GDP has experienced four slowdowns in output, starting from the early 1980s recession to the early 1990s, followed by the dot-com crash and finally the recent financial crisis which started in the summer of 2007. Figure 6.1 shows the various trends in relation to real GDP growth, equity returns and the Wicksellian Differential. Although the charts start from 1980, the first observation for the Wicksellian Differential is in 1985. This is because the time series for US bond yields does not start until 1980, and due to the five-year moving average calculation the first derived data set starts in 1985.

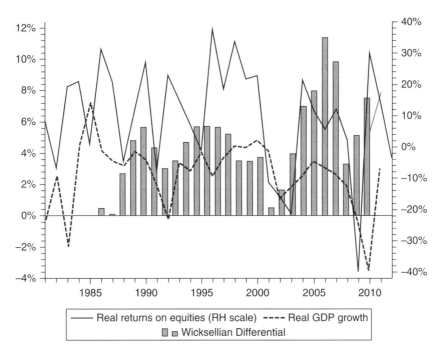

Figure 6.1 US Wicksellian Differential, real GDP growth and equity returns

Source: Thomson Reuters Datastream, Credit Capital Advisory.

The 1980 and 1982 downturns were both accompanied by rising equity returns with the positive rebound in growth in 1981 coinciding with substantial negative equity returns, highlighting an inverse correlation between GDP growth and equity returns. An analysis of 1970s interest rate data from February of each year shows that the Wicksellian Differential fell in 1981 but improved in 1982 along with equity returns.[5] The levels themselves, if the February data is representative of each year, were close to zero, highlighting that the economy was close to its 'equilibrium' position as it was in 1986. Price indices between January 1980 and August 1982 remained flat during this period; however, there were significant changes that can also be explained by credit. The dramatic fall in interest rates by almost 5 per cent in May 1980 as credit controls were relaxed was largely responsible for the positive equity market performance in 1980. However, rising inflation meant that Paul Volcker at the Fed then increased rates by over 5 per cent at the end of 1980, thus increasing the cost of capital for 1981 which the estimated Wicksellian Differential calculations pick up. Paul Volcker's actions of course did tame inflation, but at a cost. In January 1983, President Reagan's popularity reached record lows at 35 per cent due to the slowdown. Thus it would appear that the simple test of looking at the rate of acceleration or deceleration on an ex-post basis highlights that the Wicksellian Differential provides more insight into equity returns than real GDP growth.

From 1986 the Wicksellian Differential continues on an upward rate of growth until 1990 which roughly corresponds to equity returns. The growth in excess profits was fuelled by an increase in the return on capital in combination with falling interest rates. The financial deregulation of the first Reagan Administration also explains some of the growth in credit driving up the Wicksellian Differential. As a result equity prices remained on a solid upward trajectory, reflecting an increase in future expected profits. The exception of course was the fall in 1987 due to the stock market crash. Clearly such dramatic gyrations in asset prices are not going to be picked up by any fundamental analysis. With the exception of 1988, the rate of real GDP growth was broadly in decline over the period despite a strong equity market. The Wicksellian Differential maintained its growth along with the equity market until the end of 1989. Between 1990 and 1991 the Wicksellian Differential declined in conjunction with the economy, resulting in a recession for both years; however, somewhat surprisingly the equity market picked up in 1991. The main reason behind this increase was most likely due to the sustained fall in inflation from 6 per cent to 3 per cent during 1991. Such a fall in inflation would not immediately get picked up in the ex-post figures as it would take time to filter through to actual increased profits. However, the ex-ante model described in Chapter 5 takes this into account, thus providing a positive signal for increased profits.

The next noteworthy section in the chart shows the Wicksellian Differential starting to decelerate in 1996 due to a fall in the return on capital or natural rate of interest. However, this was taking place just as equity markets exploded on an exponential growth curve with the rise of ridiculous dot-com valuations. According to the theory espoused in previous chapters, equity markets should have begun to fall and not rise with a falling rate of profit. This therefore provides clear evidence of an asset class becoming decoupled from fundamentals, given that the outlook for future profits was falling and not rising. Indeed, this is exactly the kind of behaviour associated with Tulip mania. The preceding 12-year cumulative process of excess profit growth had set off an unsustainable growth in credit creation looking for returns. In this instance excess credit was being invested in financial instruments which drove asset prices upwards, as investors believed that technology companies would generate untold riches. During the late 1990s as the Wicksellian Differential fell, real GDP growth remained strong in combination with low inflation. These indicators were critical in duping investor expectations into believing that the rise in equity valuations was not in fact a bubble but rooted in improving fundamentals. Given that the value of an equity is predicated on future profits which were falling, the subsequent crash in equities was only to be expected once investors had realised their folly and changed their expectations.

The final section of note in the chart highlights a substantial increase in the Wicksellian Differential from 2003. The growth in profits was real this time, unlike in the late 1990s, and was fuelled by an increase in the return on capital and the maintenance of low interest rates. Some of this excess credit went into increased consumption and to a lesser extent investment; hence, real GDP growth during the period showed little sign of running out of control. Indeed between 2004 and 2007, real GDP growth was in decline. This highlights one of the problems with Hayek's assumptions where he expected that excess credit would be automatically invested. The reality is that companies can continue to increase profits without having to invest if demand continues to grow and corporations can maintain reasonable productivity growth. Once credit has been created, the increased volume of money goes to where it can generate the best returns, and in this instance it was largely going into housing.

What came to be known as the sub-prime crisis is without doubt one of the best examples of a cumulative but clearly unsustainable credit creation process that fed back on itself due to the reflexive nature of credit. A system of highly leveraged financing was set up whereby banks, mortgage companies and rating agencies all profited from the creation of – in the most part – low-quality financial assets that were priced and rated at similar levels to high-quality assets. The underlying premise of the cumulative process was that individuals with limited income could afford to buy reasonably expensive houses. Hence, the growth in excess profits was in fact real, but of course could not be sustained, thus differentiating this period to the late 1990s where excess profits were declining. Between 2004 and 2006 there is again a divergence between real GDP growth and equity prices, with equity prices increasing as the rate of GDP growth declined. Hence, it would appear that the link between real GDP growth and equity returns is indirect at best, although during downturns the link is more direct. From a fundamental economic perspective the Wicksellian Differential is a more direct driver of equity prices which in turn is impacted by either a fall in the money rate of interest or a rise in the natural rate of interest or a combination of the two.

Figure 6.1 provides us with an ex-post perspective of the relationship between the Wicksellian Differential, GDP growth and equity returns. However, as ex-post data sets are mostly unhelpful for investors due to the time delay in calculation, the monitoring of signals that explain ex-ante expectations will provide investors with information allowing them to invest through the business cycle. Wicksell was very clear that economic imbalances are caused by an expansion of credit. Hence, ex-ante profit expectations can be monitored regularly and these include leverage ratios of consumers, corporations and governments as a percentage of income, investment and expenditure. Bank leverage ratios have not been used in the analysis due to the lack of a long-time series, and due to the fact that increased bank leverage is broadly captured by the corporations and consumers they are providing credit to. Figure 6.2 shows the relationship between the Wicksellian Differential and the leverage ratios for consumers, corporations and the government. When leverage is sustainable it provides impetus for growth. However,

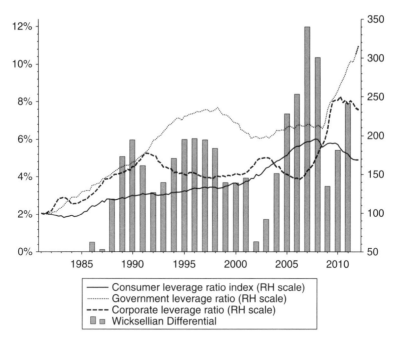

Figure 6.2 US leverage ratios and Wicksellian Differential
Source: Thomson Reuters Datastream, Credit Capital Advisory.

when leverage is over-extended in conjunction with a slowing rate of profit, it helps send the economy backwards. This process is dynamic through time and is the result of a non-linear, deterministic process.

The left of the chart shows increasing leverage across all sectors explaining the rise in the Wicksellian Differential to a peak at the end of 1989. The slowdown in the growth of rising consumer leverage between 1990 and 1992 explains the reversal in the Wicksellian Differential despite a continuous rise in corporate and government leverage until 1991. Corporate leverage then began to reverse due to the 1991 recession reducing aggregate demand. Indeed corporate leverage remained subdued throughout the 1990s. Steadily rising consumer leverage supported by continued government expansion explained the rise in the Wicksellian Differential through to 1996 when it began to fall with faltering consumer leverage and a very high level of government leverage.

Consumer leverage starts to increase from 2002, explaining the rise in the Wicksellian Differential up to record levels. The net result of this increase in consumer leverage was the creation of a significant amount of excess liquidity. It was therefore unsurprising that *The Economist*, on 3 February 2005, wrote an article subtitled 'The global economy is awash with liquidity, being pumped by America'. However, this extension of leverage was not sustainable as it relied on the presence of ever-rising house prices. The turning point came of course in 2007 when it became clear that many subprime assets were indeed worthless, and by 2008 consumers had started to retrench.

Although the Wicksellian Differential dropped substantially between 2007 and 2008 due to the consumer retrenching, during 2009 consumer leverage increased once more, thus explaining a rising Wicksellian Differential. Moreover, companies pursued aggressive cost-cutting policies to reduce aggregate supply which in turn led to a substantial increase in productivity or output per worker. This rise in productivity ensured the Wicksellian Differential continued its increase through 2010 despite falling consumer and corporate leverage. By 2011, the once-off shift in productivity growth had run its course, thus leading to poor ex-ante expectations of a growth in future profits and falling equity prices. Hence the ex-post Wicksellian Differential for 2011 is likely to have fallen once all full-year results have been announced and the data assembled.

Finally, one crucial observation relevant to investors is that since 1987 the US economy has been operating significantly above its equilibrium level with the exception of the 2001 fall towards zero. In essence, the performance of financial assets through the period can partially be explained by non-inflationary excess credit growth which went largely undetected. This should raise alarm bells for any investors who remain wedded to the assumption that the market will still be able to generate 8 per cent returns in the future just because it did so during the Great Moderation.

The 1970s and stagflation

The relationship between leverage and the Wicksellian Differential mostly explains equity returns and the relative movement in equity prices over the last 30 years. Increasing leverage has the capacity of boosting the Wicksellian Differential due to excess credit releasing a larger amount of money into the economy, thus driving asset prices up due to improving expectations of higher future profits. However, increased levels of leverage are unsustainable as the rate of profit slows, leading to a period of de-leveraging which negatively impacts equity returns. This analysis is predicated on the fact that inflation and productivity are reasonably stable. As the previous analysis showed, this is not necessarily the case as inflation expectations can shift as they did in 1992 and productivity tends to be boosted after severe cost cutting by companies. Thus inflation expectations do matter, which is why testing the theory out on the 1970s is critical. There is no necessary correlation between an increase in the volume of money and output as any increase in volume needs to be invested. Investment is only going to take place if there is an increase in the expectations of future profits. Inflation of course impacts ex-ante expectations of future profits for a variety of reasons.

Firstly, ex-ante nominal returns on capital may shift due to increasing uncertainty of future price movements. For instance, rising input costs may not be able to be passed on to consumers which may result in lower productivity, thus curtailing investment. This could be from either rising commodity costs or from increased wages without a proportional increase in productivity, as was the case in the 1970s. Secondly, falling purchasing power of consumers may result in a lower volume of goods being consumed, affecting production runs. Thirdly, the cost of funding is much more volatile due to frequent changes in short-term interest rates set by central banks in their attempt to control inflation. Unfortunately the lack of data prevents us from testing this theory in detail over the 1970s. However, equity returns performed poorly between 1977 and 1981 with the bounce in 1980 due to credit regulations being relaxed, reducing interest rates by 5 per cent. Figure 6.3 demonstrates that inflation and equity prices are broadly inversely correlated, implying that inflation is bad for the return on invested capital.

We now have a broad-based business cycle theory that appears to explain the reasons behind the cyclicality of the last 40 years. However, for any theory of business cycles to have any credibility it needs to explain the 1920s and 1930s. This has to remain a litmus test for the relevance of any business cycle theory.

The roaring 20s

According to Friedman there was no bubble in the 1920s. Friedman's argument was based on the fact that prices remained stable throughout the 1920s and that there was no significant rate of acceleration in the money supply. The Great Depression according to him was purely caused by the Fed's incompetence in the way

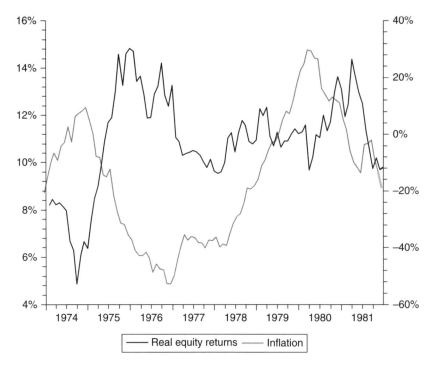

Figure 6.3   US inflation vs real equity returns
Source: Thomson Reuters Datastream.

it conducted monetary policy between 1929 and 1933, particularly when the Fed raised the discount rate. As the Great Depression panned out, Friedman and Schwarz's data set suggested that money was deliberately being taken out of the economy by the Fed at a time when prices, income and industrial production were falling. Banks were also deleveraging too. Friedman's ex-post recommended solution was therefore clear. All that ought to have been done to have resolved the crisis was for the Fed to have pumped money back into the system. This would have reflated the economy, leading to rising prices and therefore a stabilisation of the system.

Friedman's theory although backed up by over a century of data and the Quantity Theory of Money was of course flawed. Friedman was right to argue that the Fed's decision to tighten monetary policy by raising the discount rate did take money out of the economy which clearly exacerbated the situation. Worse still was the fact that over 7,000 banks defaulted during the Depression, which reduced the amount of money circulating in the economy substantially. Friedman's solution to pump money back into the economy had already been largely dismissed in the 1930s as being devoid from the reality of how an economy functions. 'Cheap money does not of itself give any great immediate impetus to business,'[6] wrote one of the leading monetary economists at the time. Moreover, Keynes' liquidity trap due to negative expectations was also a significant breakthrough in the economics tree of knowledge whereby a poor economic outlook curtailed investment with economic agents keeping their money in cash (or today's cash equivalents). Perhaps more interesting was Friedman's assertion that there was no bubble in the 1920s because there was no inflation. Friedman's assertion is almost identical to the theorists behind the Great Moderation, who believed that the business cycle had been conquered because inflation had been tamed. The economics profession is now coming to terms with the fact that these policies generated one of the largest ever credit bubbles in the history of financial markets.

Friedman's assertion that there was no bubble in the 1920s is however at odds with the data. The label 'roaring' clearly stuck for good reasons, many of which are present in Fitzgerald's novel *The Great Gatsby*, particularly the rise in wealth of the period. Indeed, during the 1920s the US economy went through a dramatic change due to the age of mass production and improved communication through the automobile and the radio. In order to determine whether the US economy passed through a classic Wicksellian cumulative process, we would expect to identify the following key characteristics. Firstly, the rate of profit growth would need to have remained strong across the period. Secondly, the money rate of interest ought to have remained low relative to profits across the period, thus stimulating the cumulative process further. Thirdly, there needs to be signs of increasing leverage. Finally, an explanation will be required as to why inflation did not accelerate. Unfortunately, most of this data is not readily available in a raw time series, so we will need to search for proxies to use.

The economic indicators between 1924 and 1929 highlight a period of robust expansion accompanied by strong productivity growth in tandem with falling commodity prices, and a marginal increase in wages. During the period, consumer goods and durable goods production expanded in tandem with each other, highlighting another of the flaws in Hayek's theory.[7] Steel production increased by 49 per cent and pig iron by 36 per cent.[8] Data between 1923 and 1929 demonstrates that manufacturing output grew by 18 per cent, with wages increasing by only 6 per cent. This boom led to share prices more than trebling in the period. However, this was not a dot-com bubble as it was based on a high rate of profit growth. According to stats from the New York Fed, the total profits of 99 industrial companies grew from $416 million in 1924 to $1.065 billion in 1929.[9] This amounts to roughly a 20 per cent compound annual growth rate of profit between 1924 and 1929, which is really rather astonishing. According to Hawtrey, this accounted for a large part of the trebling of share prices, but not all. Highly levered investment trusts which saw a huge growth in assets during the period also had an impact on boosting the stock market.[10]

Of interest in relation to the nature of Capital Theory are Hawtrey's views that the 'increase in profits was the fruit of the improved processes and improved organisation'.[11] Clearly there was a jump in capital outlay as companies invested in new semi-automated production systems. However, for Hawtrey, profit growth derives from the interaction of people with equipment. Thus the separation of labour and capital is not a particularly helpful approach when it comes to trying to understand the drivers of productivity growth. The evidence would appear to be unequivocal that the roaring twenties were a decade with robust productivity growth, highlighting that the natural rate of interest would have been on an upward trend throughout the period.

So what happened to interest rates in the 1920s? Data compiled by Homer and Sylla highlights that long-term bond yields fell during the 1920s from 5.32 per cent in 1920 to 3.33 per cent in 1928 – a substantial decline in the cost of funding.[12] Interest rates however did rise in 1929, driven by the Fed raising its rediscount rate which increased both short- and long-term yields. In summary between 1924 and 1928 we have a natural rate of interest growing at 20 per cent per annum with the money rate of interest falling by 18 per cent over the period. These conditions are clearly characteristic of a Wicksellian cumulative process. As Hawtrey argued, 'from 1925 the Fed pursued a policy of credit expansion at a time when record profits were being produced'.[13] This leaves us with the need to understand the nature of leverage in the system. And indeed, it was considerable.

Firstly, the total loans and investments of the member banks of the Federal Reserve system increased significantly from $26.5 billion in 1923 to $35.7 billion in 1929, which was a 35 per cent increase.[14] Moreover, during this period banks induced their depositors to transfer their funds from checking accounts to saving accounts, in order to take advantage of lower reserves and obtain a larger basis for credit expansion.[15] This credit expansion saw an increase of over

100 per cent for loans on urban real estate and on securities. Thus we have the classic reflexivity of credit as described by Soros. The rise in loans in order to acquire these assets was justified because of the rising value of the assets themselves. Finally, bond issuance saw a growth of nearly 90 per cent during the period.[16] Phillips et al. summarise the leveraging of the 1920s in the following way:

> Banks during this period were tying up an increasing share of their resources in assets not readily liquidated; they were extending to business men and to industry, or through their banking operations they were enabling business men and industry to acquire, long-term or capital credit, with fixed assets of one character or another pledged as security.[17]

One final point needs to be explained as to why inflation remained subdued in the 1920s. The subdued nature of inflation provided investors who believed that rising inflation was a sign of an overheating economy with false signals. Firstly, there clearly was a structural shift in manufacturing processes whereby equipment required less labour participation to produce an exponentially larger quantity of goods. Thus the demand for labour was weaker despite the significant increase in output. Indeed, data from Hawtrey highlights that the number of wage earners employed between 1923 and 1929 increased by less than 1 per cent. Besides the jump in productivity, the 1920s saw much lower levels of immigration due to tighter immigration laws and a static male workforce between 25 and 44. Female participation in the workforce however did increase in the 1920's by around 18 per cent. Although the female workforce remained about a quarter the size of the male workforce[18] the growth in this pool of labour was of course cheaper than the existing male pool of labour due to clear discrimination policies. The net result of these factors was a very small increase in the overall wage bill, which rose at only 6 per cent over the period.[19] Clearly in a period of falling commodity prices there is less pressure for wage increases as it is the fall in prices that increases real wages.

By the summer of 1929, the cumulative Wicksellian credit expansion driving higher rates of growth in excess profits was becoming unsustainable. Most economic agents at the time did not understand the consequences of this, as commodity prices had been subdued in conjunction with soaring equity and house prices. Increasing credit expansion it seems was being progressively spent on financial investments. However, from June 1929, the manufacturing index began to decrease, in particular due to falls in the output from the steel, motor car and building industries.[20] The rise in asset prices throughout the 1920s was based on the notion that the rate of growth of future profits could be maintained. This rise was fuelled by a credit boom which in turn relied upon rising collateral values. However, the slowdown during the summer of 1929 began to change expectations, which in turn caused stock market growth to level off and then crash in October 1929. Once the bubble burst it was clear that a period of deleveraging had to follow. Without doubt Friedman's view that the Fed did exacerbate the situation by increasing the money rate most likely above the natural rate was accurate. Moreover, the lack of support for the 7,000 defaulted banks which in turn substantially reduced the amount of money in circulation also worsened the situation to a significant degree.

This is not to say that the only consequence of a credit expansion is in fact misery, with falling incomes and rising unemployment. According to Phillips et al. there was no reason to believe that a depression need necessarily ensue from an expansion. Indeed, had the increase in productivity been accompanied by a proportionate fall in prices:

> The fall in prices would in itself serve to constitute an effective check upon *inordinate* capital development because it would bring about a decline in the rate of return going to capital; as the rate of return to capital declined consequently upon the fall in prices the rate of accumulation of capital goods would tend to diminish. Under such conditions the system is automatically self-corrective. It is just this self-corrective process which is essential to the smooth functioning of the economic machinery. And it is in this way that the system would work were it not for the disturbing factor of credit. The injections of new credit not only permit an increase in the rate of capital accumulation, but also tend to disrupt progressively the normal equilibrium relationships between costs and prices over many sectors of the pricing front.[21]

The United Kingdom's credit history

The recent credit history of the United Kingdom is very similar to that of the United States with its economy operating substantially above equilibrium for most of the period. Both countries

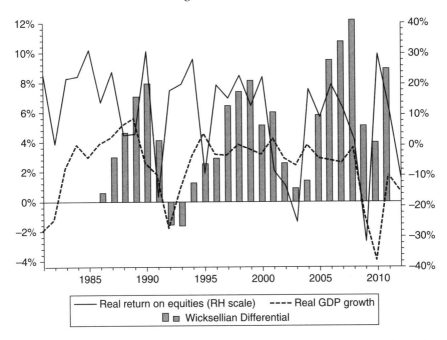

Figure 6.4 UK Wicksellian Differential, real GDP growth and equity returns
Source: Thomson Reuters Datastream, Credit Capital Advisory.

entered into the 1980s in a recession from a period of stagflation and poor equity returns in the late 1970s. UK interest rates were however somewhat higher than in the United States.[22] As shown in Figure 6.4, throughout the 1980s, the Wicksellian Differential rose due to both an increase in the return on capital as well as a fall in the cost of credit. This was partially driven by the financial dereg-ulation of the Thatcher Administration, leading to an injection of credit driving up equity and house prices. Real GDP growth in gen-eral increased with the Wicksellian Differential and equity returns until 1988 when it began to fall. Thus using changes in the real GDP growth rates as a simple trigger would have missed the high returns of 1989 of 31 per cent.[23] However, it did provide an early warning of the early 1990s recession.

The Wicksellian Differential then grew robustly from 1992 right through to 1998 when it started falling, signalling a decline in the rate of profit growth despite soaring equity valuations, low inflation and rising real GDP which misled investors and central bankers. The inevitable readjustment of the equity market occurred two years later when the dot-com boom crashed. Finally, the years lead-ing up to the recent crisis almost completely mimic the United

States. The Wicksellian Differential grew substantially between 2003 and 2007 to record levels of excess profit, creating a world awash with liquidity. Indeed, the 11 per cent level reached was far higher than the 7.5 per cent peaks of 1989 and 1998. This record growth in excess profit generating a significant credit bubble was accompanied by a gradual decline in real GDP growth over the period, with the excess liquidity being directed towards financial investments rather than physical investment. As such the gradual decline in real GDP growth in conjunction with low inflation gave investors further comfort that the economy, if anything, was performing at below capacity rather than above it. Moreover, it highlights further issues in trying to use real GDP growth as a proxy for stock market performance. However, as expected during downturns, real GDP growth, the Wicksellian Differential and equity returns all fell together in 2008 with the economy before rebounding in 2010.

One further advantage of using the Wicksellian Differential as an investment trigger is that it allows investors to compare levels across countries. Figure 6.5 shows the early 1990s recession in more detail and explains why the US stock market outperformed that of the United Kingdom. The fact that the United Kingdom had

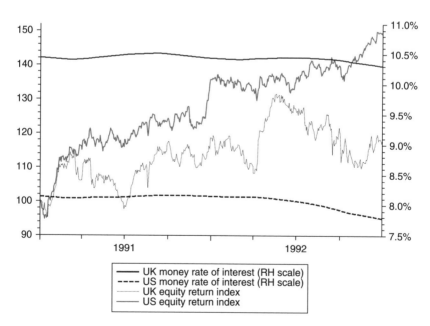

Figure 6.5   UK vs US in the 1990s recession
Source: Thomson Reuters Datastream, Credit Capital Advisory.

a negative Wicksellian Differential of –1.4 per cent compared to 3 per cent in the United States was the main difference between the two economies. This was due to both a lower return on capital and significantly higher funding costs which are shown in the chart. Given that the United Kingdom had a negative Wicksellian Differential which implies capital destruction, equity prices ought to have fallen to an extent. One key issue when it comes to anticipating stock market performance is to understand the nature of the correlation of global stock markets. Given the US stock market accounts for around a third of global market capitalisation, when it moves up and down it tends to influence the behaviour of other markets. This can be observed over and over again in multiple markets.

In terms of looking at the ex-ante expectations of the United Kingdom's Wicksellian Differential, the leverage ratios in Figure 6.6 highlight rising consumer debt in the 1980s explaining an increase in the Wicksellian Differential. This proved unsustainable in relation to the rate of profit, leading to a decline in consumer leverage and a dramatic fall in the Wicksellian Differential. As the economy

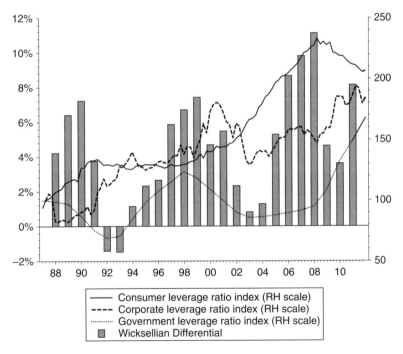

Figure 6.6 UK leverage ratios vs Wicksellian Differential
Source: Thomson Reuters Datastream, Credit Capital Advisory.

came out of the recession, the Wicksellian Differential began to grow again, this time with significant increases in corporate and government leverage accompanied by a steadily rising level of consumer leverage. The 1990s came to an end with record corporate leverage increasing the Wicksellian Differential partly driven by the telecommunication companies investing in new infrastructure. This example in many respects is close to Hayek's description of 'overinvestment' driving the cycle. As corporate leverage collapsed in the early 2000s, the consumer took on the responsibility of fuelling the rise in the Wicksellian Differential until the market peaked in 2007. Since the onset of the recent financial crisis consumer leverage has fallen, with the corporate and government sectors taking up the slack once more.

One final aspect of the United Kingdom's credit history that needs to be understood in relation to this theory is the so-called Great Depression of the 1880s. Indeed, it was this very problem that got Wicksell interested in monetary economics. However, as was stated previously, his argument to explain this period was flawed because output in fact rose over the period whereas he assumed it was in decline as prices were falling.

The Great Depression? 1873–1896

Between 1873 and 1896, the British wholesale price index fell by nearly a third. This depression in prices or deflation was considered to have caused economic conditions to deteriorate over the period. Indeed, the contemporary view that conditions were bad led to the appointment of a Royal Commission in 1885 on the Depression of Trade and Industry. The aim of the Commission was 'to inquire and report upon the extent, nature, and probable causes of the depression now or recently prevailing in various branches of trade and industry, and whether it can be alleviated by legislative or other measures'. The profits of British industry it seems were eroding, and such was the influence of the industrialists that the government was persuaded to look into the issue for them. However, as summarised by a number of economists, although profits did erode, real wages rose as did production, with unemployment rates only marginally higher than in previous epochs.[24] Moreover, not all contemporaries were convinced that there was a problem. According to the great Alfred Marshall, 'a depression of prices, a depression of interest, and a depression of profits; there is that undoubtedly. I cannot see any reason for believing that there is any considerable depression in any other respect.'[25] Indeed, the evidence that has been accumulated since the 'depression' is counter to the notion that there was a depression at all. Selgin's excellent summary of the 'Great Depression' closes referring back to the Cambridge economist Arthur Pigou who argued that 'if there ever was a protracted depression at the end of the 19th century, it occurred not during the oft-maligned era of falling prices, but immediately afterwards when output prices began to rise'.[26]

So how can this be explained in Wicksellian terms given that Wicksell's analysis on the 'Great Depression' was rather muddled? It is clear from the fact that a Royal Commission was set up in the first place that the natural rate of interest (return on capital) was unlikely to have been growing. Hence it is also unlikely that there was a significant surge in leverage given the lower future profit expectations. This would have provided a backdrop most likely for poor equity returns, although the lack of data makes this difficult to test. However, the bond market in the second half of the 19th century went through a roaring bull market, thus reducing the cost of funding. Yields fell on 3 per cent Consols, which can be used as a proxy for long-term interest rates from 3.24 per cent in 1873 to 2.28 per cent in 1896, with prices rising from 92 5/8 to 110 7/8.[27]

Given that output increased during the period, it appears unlikely that the Wicksellian Differential was negative for any if not all of this period. Thus we have a situation where for a significant period of time there was most likely a positive, albeit small but stable Wicksellian Differential. This would have been bad for equity valuations of course, but good for bond investors. Interestingly, from a monetary policy perspective it would appear that this period mimicked Myrdal's ideal approach to monetary policy. Prices according to the model described in Chapter 5 ought to move in relation to productivity growth. The increased level of competition with the industrialisation of the United States, Germany and France had a considerable pressure on pushing prices down. This means that the rate of excess profit was not substantial enough to maintain constant prices but significant enough to maintain a positive growth in output. From the investor perspective this is clearly less than ideal, as it implies that asset values are unlikely to grow. However, knowing this information provides investors with a simple asset allocation decision, allowing assets to be moved into growth markets based on the trajectory of the Wicksellian Differential, or into bonds which performed well throughout the period. In the 20th century, a country where such an asset allocation strategy would also have worked well would have been Japan.

Japan's great leap forward and the lost decade

The Japanese economy has remained an enigma for many economists and investors, particularly those who use a current monetary policy framework for investment signals. This has led to many false hopes and in many cases substantial losses. However, when analysed using a neo-Wicksellian framework, the situation in Japan is reasonably straightforward to understand. Starting with the first oil shock in 1973, Figure 6.7 shows equity returns fell in both the United States and Japan as inflation rose. However, Japan's dependency on OPEC oil supplies had a much bigger impact on short-term inflation with rates rising to 25 per cent in 1974. By the end of 1975 Japan's inflation was under control and converging with the rate in the United States in the 7–8 per cent range, before dipping below the US rate in late 1977 where it has remained ever

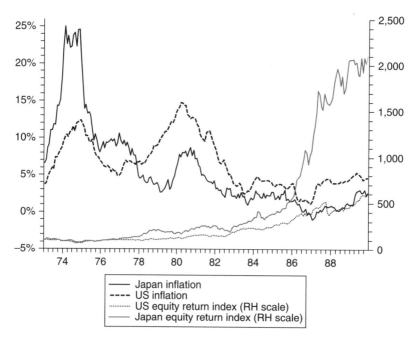

Figure 6.7   US and Japan inflation vs equity returns
Source: Thomson Reuters Datastream.

since. From 1976 the Japanese equity market began to outperform the US market, which it consequently did for the next 14 years until the market crashed.

The divergence of Japan and the United States in the latter half of the 1970s meant that the Japanese economy entered the 1980s on a very different trajectory than the United States. Japan was able to maintain an increase in expected profit growth due to substantially lower and falling interest rates in conjunction with lower inflation. The United States was impacted by the early 1980s recession disrupting Wicksell's cumulative process of credit creation. This cumulative process of credit creation in Japan set the scene for one of the most impressive equity bull runs of any market that naturally resulted in a crash once leverage ratios became unsustainable in relation to the rate of profit growth. Indeed, from 1985 this cumulative process of credit creation, which had been in train since 1976, triggered an exponential growth in equity prices as shown in Figure 6.7, as well as a substantial bubble in property prices.

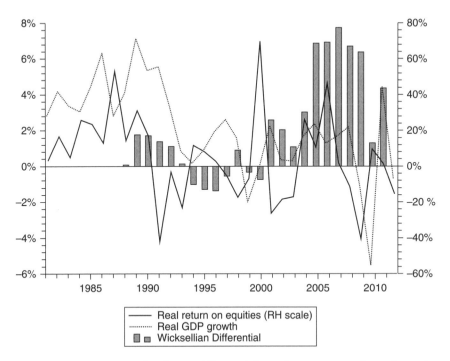

Figure 6.8 Japan Wicksellian Differential, real GDP growth and equity returns
Source: Thomson Reuters Datastream, Credit Capital Advisory.

Returning to the relationship between the Wicksellian Differential, equity returns and real GDP growth, the first calculated figure we have for Japan's Wicksellian Differential is for 1987, which is just above equilibrium. Using interest rate estimates, the Wicksellian Differential for 1986 was most likely around the 2 per cent mark. Although the performance of equities was still positive in 1987, it did fall dramatically from the 1986 highs of over 50 per cent. One striking aspect of the analysis is that Wicksellian Differentials were much lower in the 1980s than in recent periods. Hence one has to take into account the span of an uninterrupted cumulative process, and whether the Differential is on an upward or downward rate of acceleration from an ex-ante signalling perspective. One other factor that also has a bearing on asset values is the correlation effect of global equity markets. Without doubt, the rate of growth of Japanese equity prices from 1986 was supported by the recovery of the US market. However, from 1989 the Wicksellian Differential began to decline, signalling falling profits and equity values becoming negative in 1993 causing capital destruction. This fall was exacerbated by the subsequent policy of the Bank of Japan which in many respects was similar to that of the Fed in the 1930s with interest rates being pushed up instead of down. Finally, after a decade of false starts including the dot-com boom and bust, the Japanese economy in 2003 embarked upon a sustained upward cumulative process which saw a substantial increase in equity returns. Unfortunately for Japan, the driver behind this revival was related to a higher level of global aggregate demand, driven by increasing leverage in the United States and elsewhere. Thus from 2008, equity prices began to fall as global aggregate demand shrunk in conjunction with real GDP growth and the Wicksellian Differential. The Wicksellian Differential did increase in 2010 with equity returns barely generating a positive return. Thus the ex-post increase in 2010 profits does not tally with the ex-ante perception of no change in expected profits. The main reason behind this was the general price level. The general price level fell between 2009 and 2010, which can be bad for future profits and therefore capital values as the ex-ante expectations of profits were based on known production costs and higher-prices at the point of sale.

Returning to the explanation of Japan's lost decade, the left-hand side of Figure 6.9 shows the rate of interest, as influenced by the Bank of Japan, increasing in 1990. This put the cost of funding, on a spot basis, above the aggregated return on capital. As a result it precipitated a much deeper fall in the Wicksellian Differential with

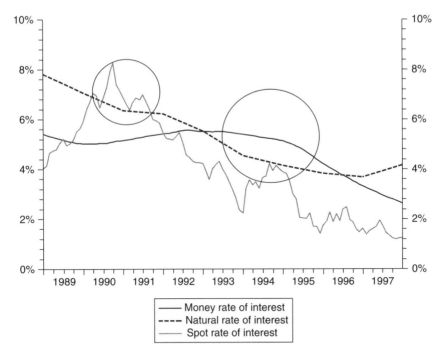

Figure 6.9   Japan natural rate of interest vs money rate of interest
Source: Thomson Reuters Datastream, Credit Capital Advisory.

higher rates of funding feeding through to future years, leading to a fall in the Wicksellian Differential and the destruction of capital, as shown on the right-hand side of the chart, between 1993 and 1996. Wicksell's cumulative process works in both ways, with three years of excess losses making it more difficult for Japan to emerge from its predicament.

   This economic backdrop is also mostly responsible for explaining the disastrous performance of Japanese equities, with the Wicksellian Differential unable to sustain a ratio of 2 per cent or more for two years until 2003. Indeed, the absolute level of its Wicksellian Differential which in 2010 was around 4 per cent compared to 8 per cent in the United States can explain a great deal of the difference in equity market performance. The difference in absolute returns highlights that Japanese companies are, on average, roughly 50 per cent less productive in the way they deploy capital than their US counterparts. One of the major reasons behind the lower productivity of capital is the fact that there remains over supply in Japan. In general, companies do not shed large numbers of workers, and companies do not tend to go bankrupt, which is why Japan's credit default swap market has traditionally traded at spreads of up to a third lower than the United States. In essence, Japanese companies have been unable to adjust effectively to a world of lower aggregate demand.[28]

In terms of explaining the different trends of the Wicksellian Differential in Japan, a brief analysis of Japan's leverage ratios provides further insight. In Figure 6.10, we can see the massive build-up in leverage in the mid-1980s, fuelling the rise in the Wicksellian Differential. During the 1990s we see corporate and consumer leverage drifting, explaining the largely static Wicksellian Differential which briefly spiked in 1998 before falling again, despite a dramatic increase in government leverage. Consumer leverage has drifted for much of the last decade too and at levels akin to the United Kingdom and the United States. The lack of any meaningful consumer deleveraging in Japan means that the outlook for consumption growth remains subdued. Moreover, the deflationary

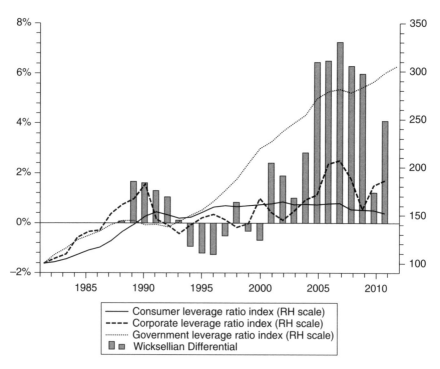

Figure 6.10   Japan leverage ratios vs Wicksellian Differential
Source: Thomson Reuters Datastream, Credit Capital Advisory.

trend over the last decade or so has exacerbated the level of consumer debts, as a fall in the general price level increases the value of that debt.

From 2004, corporate leverage did increase considerably, boosting the Wicksellian Differential as exports rose along with equity prices. However, this was soon curtailed by the recent financial crisis. Corporate leverage has started to rise again, which explains the recent jump in the Wicksellian Differential. However, with the consumer now on a downward trajectory in combination with massive government debts, the ex-ante outlook for rising profits in Japan remains clouded at best.

One striking aspect of the analysis of all the above three countries has been the fact that the relationship between real GDP growth and equity market performance has not been consistent. Indeed, there is clearly a much closer relationship between the Wicksellian Differential and equity returns, using simple acceleration or deceleration triggers. This should not be surprising given the Wicksellian Differential is a measure of the growth in the rate of profit. This highlights why those investors who decide to allocate their portfolios to countries with strong GDP growth may not see the returns they expect. As argued by Ritter, the owners of capital do not necessarily benefit from economic growth, as a country can grow rapidly by applying more capital and labour without seeing an increase in the marginal productivity of capital.[29] During the 1880s 'Great Depression' in Britain, output was also growing but profits were not due to falling prices.

China's recent growth story is also a partial good example of this. China's rate of investment has been unsurpassed at over 40 per cent of GDP, which has been the major factor why it has had the highest growth in output of all the BRIC economies by a significant margin. The ability of China to tap into a huge pool of labour and to direct savings into production does not necessarily require there to be increases in the productivity of the deployment of capital and labour. However, a paper in 2006 by three Chinese economists found that the return on capital between 1998 and 2004 was 20 per cent per annum.[30] This means that there was a productive deployment of capital and labour, although the inability of this rate to increase suggests that there is something to the Krugman–Young argument, although it is much more nuanced than originally stated. The authors do put a caveat on their conclusions which are hampered by the quality of data available, which is generally an issue of many emerging markets.

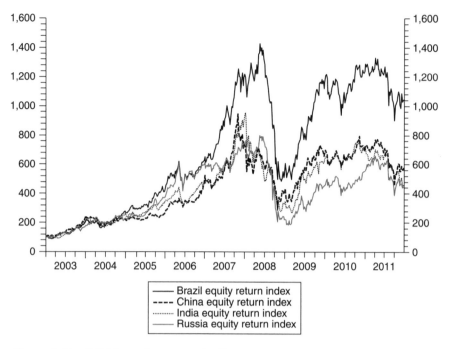

Figure 6.11   BRIC equity return indices
Source: Thomson Reuters Datastream.

Figure 6.11 shows that despite the high investment rates, China's equity market relative to the other BRIC economies has not performed any better. Indeed, Brazil with a lower rate of real GDP growth has outperformed China over the last 10 years by a significant margin. It is important to note however that all BRIC economies have outperformed developed market economies over the last decade, highlighting that there is an indirect link between GDP growth and increased profit growth.

Besides the Krugman–Young thesis explaining why returns may not correlate with GDP growth which most likely explains the difference between Brazil and China, Ritter also highlighted some other explanations that are worth noting, including the fact that equity prices in high-growth economies can be over-valued, thus reducing returns and that it is often new companies that spur economic growth rather than existing ones. Also of note is the fact that multinational companies' profitability is dependent on the health of the global economy rather than the local economy.[31] Hence using real GDP growth signals as a barometer for equity market performance ought to be treated with greater scepticism by investors, particularly the assumption that non-inflationary increases in output should generate higher-than-expected profits, and hence higher equity prices. During the period of the Great Moderation this non-inflationary growth took place at the expense of increasing leverage and hence was not sustainable, leading to a crash in equity prices and investors losing money. Although there are many instances of equity prices following real GDP growth, there are also instances where it does not happen. For example, between 2004 and 2007, the rate of US real GDP growth declined but equity markets increased.

One further test of the extent to which real GDP growth provides misleading market signals to investors in developed markets is to compare the performance of a country that did not go into recession during the recent financial crisis with those that did. The following analysis uses Australia, which maintained a robust rate of growth over the last five years compared to Canada, which in terms of GDP growth pretty much mimicked the US economy following it in and out of the recession.

Australia and Canada: growth and profits

Australia escaped the worst of the crisis without any period of negative real GDP growth. As a result one might have expected equity markets in Australia to have substantially outperformed its peers, signalling higher expected future profits. However, the data once again reveals that the relationship between real GDP growth and equity returns, which capture expectations of future profits, is not consistent. Figure 6.12 shows that over the last five years, Australia's real GDP growth rate on a cumulative basis has substantially outperformed Canada and the United States. Both Canada and the United States had half the level of growth rates pre-crisis and both suffered from deep recessions compared to Australia. Thus the results on the bottom pane are surprising on two fronts. Firstly, one needs to ask the question as to why Canada outperformed the United States by such a significant margin despite having such a similar real GDP growth trajectory. Secondly, the question as to why Australia was unable to outperform Canada arises.

Stock markets do respond negatively to sharp falls in real GDP growth as was the case in 2008 with all markets indicating lower future profits. The fall in 2008 also demonstrates the importance of the correlation of global stock markets with the profits

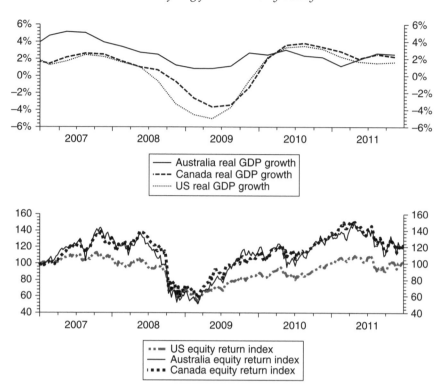

Figure 6.12 Real GDP growth and equity market performance – Canada, Australia and the US
Source: Thomson Reuters Datastream.

of many companies generated internationally rather than domestically. However, the recovery in real GDP growth in 2011 was accompanied by falling rather than rising stock markets. Such signals if they had been followed would have resulted in investors losing money in 2011. In order to explain the behaviour of each stock market we need to return Wicksell and the rate of profit growth. Figure 6.12 demonstrates that profits and economic growth are not synonymous with each other although there are clearly periods when both can and do move together. However, it also highlights that countries can have high growth rates and lower expected future profits as well as lower growth rates and higher expected future profits.

Figure 6.13 demonstrates the closeness of the relationship between the Wicksellian Differential and equity market returns in Australia and Canada. The left of the chart shows a negative Wicksellian Differential and muted stock market performance in both countries between 1992 and 1994, which is to be expected.

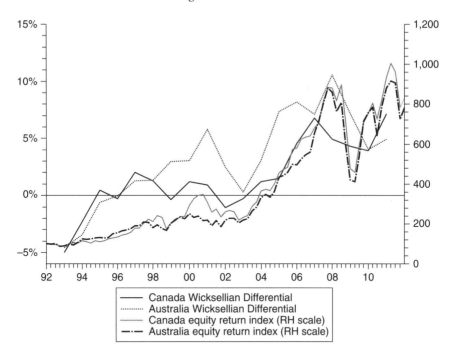

Figure 6.13 Canada and Australia Wicksellian Differential vs equity market performance
Source: Thomson Reuters Datastream, Credit Capital Advisory.

As the Wicksellian Differential maintained a positive outlook, equity markets began to rise with the expectations of higher profits through to 1996. The year 1997 saw an easing in the rate of growth of the Wicksellian Differential in both countries and a corresponding fall in equity returns.

By the end of 2000 however the two economies were moving in different directions. Canada's Wicksellian Differential declined in 2000 although equity prices maintained their ridiculously high trajectories due to the interdependency of the Canadian economy on the United States. Equity prices had clearly become decoupled from underlying fundamentals where higher valuations were not justified by higher future expected profits – hence the crash at the end of 2000 through 2001. Australia's Wicksellian Differential, unlike the other Western economies, showed an increasing rate of its Wicksellian Differential, thus justifying higher valuations. It is important to note that as a result of the dot-com crash, Australia's equity market was the least impacted of developed markets, experiencing substantially lower falls. Indeed, the Australian market actually declined in 2000, although this was most likely due to a spike in inflation in conjunction with its perception as an 'old economy' market – the kind that actually generates profits. Investors with access to this information could have improved their asset allocation decisions, thus improving the returns on investment.

The right hand section of the chart shows the rise of Canada's Wicksellian Differential from 2001 until 2006 when it declined until 2009. Australia's Wicksellian Differential was rather more volatile, falling in 2006 and then rising in 2007 before falling again. Both economies by 2010 were seeing a rise in their Wicksellian Differentials once more.

One issue that stands out is the fact that both equity markets saw substantial rises in 2009 when the Wicksellian Differentials for both countries fell, thus providing a false signal for investors. The reason behind this is related to a weakness in the methodology itself for smaller economies, due to the need for large amounts of data. Specifically this relates to the number of constituents in each index to ensure that the industry aggregates are not impacted significantly by changes in the return on capital invested by individual companies. Indeed, it is important for there to be a sufficient number in each sector to ensure that specific economic factors do not impact sub-sectors which are disproportionately represented in the indices, thus creating distortions in the estimate of the aggregated return calculations. This is of course the very issue that Myrdal raised in his analysis. Both Japan and the United States have 1,000 constituents in the Datastream indices with the United Kingdom over 550. However, Canada has 250 and Australia only 150, thus the volatility of Australia's Wicksellian Differential ought not to be entirely unexpected.

Indeed, the returns by the Australian financial services sector dropped from 10.51 per cent in 2008 to −5.09 per cent in 2009. This fall in the returns to financial services companies thus skewed the 2009 Wicksellian Differential calculations, causing it to fall from 12.7 per cent to 9.7 per cent. The reason behind this fall was that 14 of the companies in the financial services sector were property companies, with all 14 companies having to write down the value of their assets by around $20 billion in total, due to falling property prices. The impact of falling property prices did not affect the broader performance of the economy and thus needs to be taken into account when running a neo-Wicksellian analysis using listed companies with a small number of constituents. Furthermore, the listed Australian construction sector only has nine constituents, highlighting that individual company returns which may be idiosyncratic in nature can move the industry aggregate disproportionately, particularly if the sector is reasonably large from a gross value added perspective. Construction accounts for 17 per cent of GVA in Australia.

Canada is no different in that its Wicksellian Differential can be impacted by macro shifts. In 2009 this was because the price of oil fell fourfold in the latter half of 2008 to around $35 per barrel of Brent crude. Canada has 27 listed oil exploration and production companies within the overall industry and energy sector of around 140 constituents. Thus wild swings in oil prices drive significant changes to the return on capital of these companies, which in turn impacts the industry aggregates and hence the country Wicksellian Differential. The return on invested capital for the industry and energy sector fell in 2009 to 4.34 per cent down from 6.45 per cent in 2008. If these 27 companies are excluded from the analysis the returns for the sector actually grew from 3.55 per cent to 4.14 per cent. Just to stress the point, the aggregated returns of the 27 companies fell from 17 per cent in 2008 to 5 per cent in 2009.

These data issues are critical to recognise, particularly if one is attempting to run tactical asset allocation strategies within smaller economies such as Canada and Australia. Moreover, the ability to generate sufficiently robust calculations is even more challenging in emerging markets due to shorter time series, a smaller number of constituents as well as the corporate governance issues. The number of constituents in the larger economies is however broadly sufficient to provide strong indicators of shifts in the valuation of capital. The difference in the number of constituents between smaller and larger economies also has an impact on the general correlation of global equity prices. In essence, an attempt to run asset allocation strategies on smaller economies will require an analysis to be done on the larger economies, as they will also influence the general movement of global asset values.

In returning to the question as to why Canada was able to outperform both the United States and Australia over the last five years, the ex-post analysis provides limited insight. However, the ex-ante perspective provides a great deal more information which is clearly critical given the limitations of an ex-post analysis for investment triggers. The ex-ante model is of course based on the neo-Wicksellian theory of credit, where excess credit creation fuels the growth in profits. Thus we look first at the growth in consumer leverage as driving incremental demand for goods, as it has the largest impact on increasing the rate of return – assuming that the production of an incremental unit of output requires less than an equivalent input. Hence, consumer behaviour plays a significant role in driving excess profits. In 2011 consumption in Canada accounted for 57 per cent of GDP, whereas the figure in Australia was slightly lower at 54 per cent. However, for consumption to maintain its level of growth, savings need to decrease and/or consumers need to leverage up. Increasing consumer leverage requires the banking sector to provide consumers with access to credit, which in turn raises leverage in the banking sector. Although this leverage can kick start an increase in profits, it can also turn in on itself if the market perceives the level of leverage to be unsustainable in relation to the rate of profit growth.

Figure 6.14 demonstrates the importance of the relationship between consumer leverage and equity market performance. Over the last five years the Canadian consumer has been on a constant upward trajectory in terms of leverage, whereas the Australian consumer has been deleveraging except for a short period between late

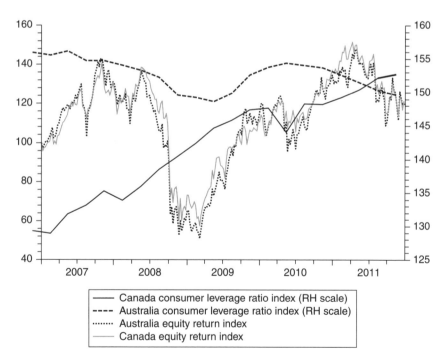

Figure 6.14   Canada and Australia consumer leverage vs equity market performance

Source: Thomson Reuters Datastream.

Table 6.1   Australia and Canada average banking sector leverage ratios (common equity/total assets)

Year	Canada (%)	Australia (%)	Difference in leverage (%)
2006	4.43	4.97	12
2007	4.68	5.59	19
2008	4.19	5.56	33
2009	5.34	6.83	28
2010	5.38	7.32	36

Source: Fitch Solutions.

2009 and early 2010. Despite the fact that Australia had a larger Wicksellian Differential until 2010, from 2008 the Canadian stock market was already outperforming its Australian counterpart driven by ex-ante expectations of consumer behaviour which were negative for Australia and positive for Canada. The US market performed worst of the three because of more aggressive consumer deleveraging reducing expected future profits. The fall in global stock market values in 2011 highlights the fact that Canadian companies were unable to escape from falling markets elsewhere (in particular the United States) due to the high levels of correlation. Despite such falls, the performance of the Canadian stock market remains stronger relative to its peers.

For consumers to be able to leverage up it requires the banking system to provide those consumers with easy access to credit. A comparison of the leverage ratios of the Australian and Canadian banking systems in Table 6.1 shows that in 2010 Canadian banks were roughly a third less leveraged than their Australian counterparts, highlighting that Canadian consumers are more likely to be able to access credit. Leverage of course is good when it is sustainable and helps drive growth in capital values, but it causes a fall in capital values when it becomes unsustainable. As a result, over the last five years the fact that consumers are becoming more leveraged and have access to credit is clearly a driver of improved equity market performance.

Canada it seems wins hands down when it comes to consumer and bank leverage in terms of ex-ante expectations of future profits when compared to Australia. Indeed, the fact that the Canadian banking system was not impacted by the subprime mortgage crisis meant that it was able to maintain its provision of credit to Canadian consumers, allowing them to leverage up. Hence Canada outperformed Australia and the United States despite higher real GDP growth in Australia and similar levels in the United States. When it comes to investment the picture is marginally favourable to Canada despite investment in Canada accounting for 19 per cent of GDP whereas in Australia it was a much larger 27 per cent. The fact that investment is over 40 per cent higher in Australia as a percentage of GDP partially explains the higher growth in output. However, investors are interested in increasing the rate of profit rather than absolute levels of output and Canada's Wicksellian Differential has been more resilient than Australia's since the onset of the crisis. Finally, Canada's government sector is also more leveraged than Australia's with both countries on an upward trend. It is however difficult to make generalised assumptions about government expenditure as what counts is the ex-ante expectations of the impact government spending might have. The views of most neo-Hayekian capital theorists tend to be rather absolutist, arguing that any government expenditure by definition has to be negative as it increases the cost of funding and requires the transfer of real resources from the private sector. Moreover, given that future government deficits have to be paid for by taxation, the savings rate increases reducing consumption, thus worsening the downturn.[32]

Hayek himself was not so absolutist about this from a policy perspective. Indeed, he alluded to the fact that there might be reasons to support capital-intensive industries with credit to prevent too much capital destruction, although he did doubt the practicality of the policy.[33] Capital losses of course will reduce future output to such an extent that it would take years just to return to previous levels of output. Neo-Hayekian economists like Garrison describe deficit financing as a form of taxation. From a logical model perspective this may indeed be the case, and Garrison's argument that the deficit financing of the Vietnam War is a good case in point as it did lead to a crowding out effect and higher interest rates. However, to assume that all government financing would lead to negative ex-ante expectations does not fit the facts.

For example, a comparison of government bond rates between Canada and Portugal suggests that sometimes the level of government debt can be seen as negative, and sometimes positive. In May 2010, the five-year benchmarks for Canada and Portugal were on par with each other at just under 3 per cent. By January 2012, Canada's five-year benchmark had fallen to under 1.5 per cent with Portugal's rising to over 15 per cent. The bond market clearly had much more faith in Canada being able to spend its money more wisely than Portugal.

From the theoretical perspective it is possible that government-financed projects can generate a positive return on capital invested without raising interest rates, which Keynes argued was a prerequisite for deficit financing. Unfortunately due to poor public sector management this does not always happen, hence Garrison's arguments in some respects are well made although not necessarily for the right reasons. Poor public sector management has been cited as one of the major obstacles to productivity growth by management theorists for decades.[34] This lack of efficiency in the public sector does not mean that all public sector managers by definition are unable to deploy capital effectively. For example, if a particular department of education has demonstrated it can spend money wisely thus increasing the skill of the labour force leading to rising productivity, then surely they would be a good bet for further investment, even if it did mean increasing the deficit in the short run. Moreover, it is feasible that the rate of return on certain infrastructure projects may not attract sufficient private capital due to the amount required and the time horizons of the return. Furthermore, it is plausible that such an investment could indeed have a multiplier effect, providing jobs and increased productivity for local companies with cheaper transportation costs. The problem of course is that many neo-Keynesian economists fail to make these distinctions, tending to make quite ridiculous sweeping statements that all such projects are beneficial, when in fact many of them, as Garrison argues, are just an extra tax. For example, the debate over the 2009 US stimulus package had two quite different perspectives with Christina Romer predicting a multiplier of 1.5, whereas John Taylor et al. had it substantially lower at 0.5.[35] No doubt the debate about fiscal stimulus will roll on as it has done since the New Deal. In reality the debate about government expenditure is less about economics and more about management theory, something which economists unfortunately seem loathe to accept. Moreover, neo-Keynesians seem to conveniently forget that Keynes was clear that *every* government investment had to have a positive return on capital.

From a practical perspective, using the long-term government bond yield can provide a good indication as to whether there is a crowding out effect from increased government spending. If long-term yields do indeed fall, this would suggest that at least some of the expenditure has been useful and potentially may be aiding capital values in a positive way. Although demand for 'safe' assets pushes yields down, the reason why they are perceived as safe is because they are considered fiscally sound with low inflation expectations. This means that countries can quite easily lose their safe haven status should poor public spending decisions be taken and inflation rise. When Canada and Australia are compared on these benchmarks, Canada wins on this too with its five-year rate yielding 1.296 per cent on 2 January 2012 compared to Australia's 3.27 per cent This suggests that despite both a higher level of government leverage and increase of that leverage over much of the last five years, the market believes that there has been no crowding out effect given long-term interest rates have fallen almost 3 per cent from June 2007.

An empirical analysis using an ex-post Wicksellian Differential explains the growth in capital values, whereas real GDP growth provides mixed signals which in some cases have generated significant losses for investors. The ex-ante explanations of the neo-Wicksellian model provide further insight into the relationship between the Wicksellian Differential and capital values, allowing investors to make the appropriate asset allocation decisions. Thus, it is reasonably straightforward to understand why Canada's stock market has significantly outperformed Australia and the United States.

The above analysis highlights the rather limited relationship between capital values and real GDP growth. It would appear that there is a relationship between the two when a severe downturn hits, otherwise output and capital values can move quite independently of each other. This clearly has ramifications for asset allocation strategies that use real GDP forecasts as a factor, particularly those strategies which assume that over time growth rates of economies converge resulting in converging stock market performance. For example, when the euro was set up, a series of eurozone indices were offered by the asset management industry to provide investors with exposure to the main companies across the eurozone block. The rationale being that as the economies in the eurozone converged, there was little excess return to be extracted from eurozone country effects. Research in 2005 concluded that in the late 1990s and early 2000s an industry-based approach outperformed a country-based approach.[36] This seemed to mark a permanent shift from the early 1990s when the country effect was more profitable.

This research was also substantiated by a significant body of macroeconomic research with regard to the benefits of creating a single currency leading to economic convergence. Eurozone members would benefit from increased trade in goods and services with each other, higher levels of cross-border investment and falling transaction costs, as well as reduced foreign exchange volatility.[37] The implication is that this would enhance economic performance and accelerate economic convergence for the eurozone economies. There were of course a series of pre-requisite criteria that each country had to meet in order to join the club as laid out in the Maastricht Treaty. These included the convergence of inflation and long-term interest rates, as well as anchoring the currency within the exchange rate mechanism. Finally, the criteria stated that the ratio of gross government debt to GDP could not exceed 60 per cent and the deficit to GDP ratio no larger than 3 per cent. It is worth pointing out that given inflation can be exogenously determined, China probably did more for many peripheral European countries' inflation rates, interest rates and currency stability than their respective central banks did as part of meeting the criteria. The challenge in joining a common currency is of course whether the benefits outweigh the loss of the ability to control the rate of interest, combined with a floating exchange rate during times of economic stress.

Unfortunately, for investors the theory did not seem to work in practice. The eurozone debt crisis has shown that a two-speed Europe has developed. An analysis using a neo-Wicksellian model however would have exposed the lack of convergence in the Wicksellian Differentials across specific economies within the eurozone. Moreover, the single rate of interest for all eurozone countries meant that countries with higher Wicksellian Differentials would see a significant boost to their cumulative credit creation process, generating excess profits and liquidity. Knowing this would have allowed investors to have over-weighted countries experiencing asset bubbles and then moving into less risky government bonds as they fell, thus generating significantly higher returns than a broad eurozone index.

The trials and tribulations of the eurozone

In order to ascertain the growth in the Wicksellian Differentials over time in the eurozone, four countries were analysed, including two core and two peripheral countries: France, Germany, Spain and Ireland. Greece was not selected due to 'statistical errors' with regard to its budget deficit. From an analytical perspective it is of more interest to run the analysis against those economies that did legitimately pass the tests but have since fared less well. The period

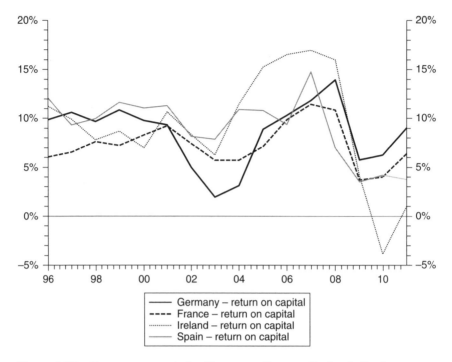

Figure 6.15   Return on capital – Germany, France, Ireland, Spain
Source: Thomson Reuters Datastream, Credit Capital Advisory.

analysed from 1995 included the pre-euro period which factors in individual central banks' interest rate policy in relation to exchange rate convergence.

Figure 6.15 shows the return on capital for all four countries remained reasonably high from 1995 until 2001 when Germany fell back considerably leaving Spain and Ireland as the best performers. Ireland then led the pack by a considerable margin between 2004 and 2008 with returns on capital significantly higher than the other three countries. However, the onset of the credit crisis has seen the return on capital in Ireland severely curtailed, with Irish companies on a weighted basis now showing a negative return on capital, largely driven by the troubled construction and banking sectors. The post-crisis data shows Germany as the strongest country followed by France, with Spain seeing a decline in 2010.

Figure 6.16 plots the Wicksellian Differential for each country which subtracts the average cost of capital over the previous five-year period from the return on capital. Because of the deflationary effect from China, interest rates remained lower than they ought to

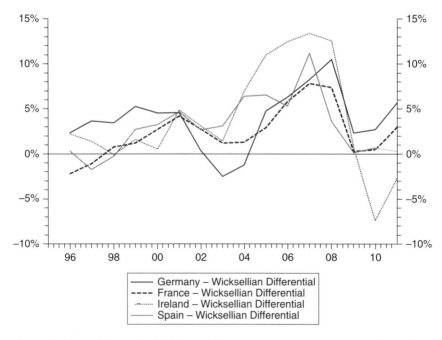

Figure 6.16 Wicksellian Differential – Germany, France, Ireland, Spain
Source: Thomson Reuters Datastream, Credit Capital Advisory.

have been in the 1990s, as they were in the United States and the United Kingdom. This drove a classic cumulative credit process in Germany in the 1990s with increasing leverage generating excess profits and liquidity due to the reunification process. By the early 2000s the return on capital was falling for all countries, although in particular for Germany which turned negative in 2002, resulting in capital destruction. Ireland and Spain saw only a marginal fall in their Wicksellian Differentials which both remained positive, thus continuing the cumulative credit creation process started in 1998. By 2005 all economies were generating significant excess liquidity due to large and growing Wicksellian Differentials, although Ireland's rate of growth of excess profits was clearly on a different trajectory to the rest of the eurozone. The reason behind this is that the interest rate for Ireland is largely determined by the ECB which sets the level appropriate for the core of the eurozone economy in relation to price stability. These rates were clearly too low for Ireland which set off an aggressive, sustained credit bubble leading to an almighty crash in 2009 as its banking system came close to defaulting. It was only the crash in Ireland which resulted in a divergence between long term interest rates and the short term ECB rate. Indeed, in the run up to the credit crisis, the credit compression of long-term sovereign bond yields highlighted the impact that short-term ECB rates had on the long-term yields of all countries, including Greece.

The post-crisis data shows that the core countries of France and Germany remain strong and on an upward trend in comparison to Spain's declining levels and Ireland's negative levels, highlighting capital destruction. For a country to generate positive returns on capital, a structural shift needs to take place to increase the outlook for profits, thus encouraging investment. This generally requires a reduction in aggregate supply in conjunction with increasing unemployment, unless there is a significant demand for exports. For Spain and Ireland much of the excess liquidity went into a construction boom, and given that construction activity has fallen dramatically, which was a reasonable chunk of prior output in conjunction with an oversupply of houses and flats, this is unlikely to pick up significantly any time soon.

Returning to asset allocation decisions within the eurozone, it is clear from the Wicksellian Differentials in Figure 6.16 that up until 2007 Ireland and Spain should have been overweighted given the cumulative credit creation process was larger and sustained for longer. Figure 6.17 shows that this would have generated excess returns although France performed reasonably well. Germany however performed poorly and lagged the other markets by a considerable margin. The main reason for this was that it had a negative Wicksellian Differential in the middle of the period leading to capital destruction and the cumulative process having to start again. Figure 6.17 also shows the inexorable rise of house prices in Ireland which outperformed Spain by a considerable margin. This can be explained as Spain had a consistently lower Wicksellian Differential over the latter half of the period, generating less excess liquidity than Ireland. Excess liquidity is invested wherever the best returns can be extracted. If the future returns from physical investment look less than exciting, financial assets may well provide investors with what they need – at least for a while. In this instance many investors considered housing a more attractive bet and for those who managed to get out at the right time, it was indeed a great investment.

As the financial crisis unfolded, Figure 6.18 shows the German Wicksellian Differential beginning to forge ahead and accelerating in 2009, far ahead of the other economies, although France did follow Germany but at lower levels. This difference is reflected in

Figure 6.17   Germany, France, Ireland, Spain equity market performance and Ireland and Spain house prices (1996–2007)
Source: Thomson Reuters Datastream.

equity values, with German equities on a relative basis being the star performers and Ireland falling away by a considerable margin. The fall in property prices can also be seen in Spain and Ireland, with Ireland suffering worst because it had a larger credit bubble. Thus it would appear that the analysis by Estrada et al. was indeed a temporary phenomenon. Wicksell's theory of credit which drives capital values is a far better explanatory variable than any GDP factor.

The lessons of Wicksell's theory are clear. The relationship between the Wicksellian Differential and equity returns is much stronger than between real GDP growth and equity returns. This relationship should not be surprising given the Wicksellian Differential measures the excess rate of profit growth. Economies that have increasing but sustainable leverage ratios in combination with a rising Wicksellian Differential look like good investment opportunities. However, economies that have unsustainable or falling leverage ratios in combination with a falling Wicksellian Differential conversely look like bad investments. Moreover, the ex-ante indicators of leverage highlight how an investor can use this approach as a way

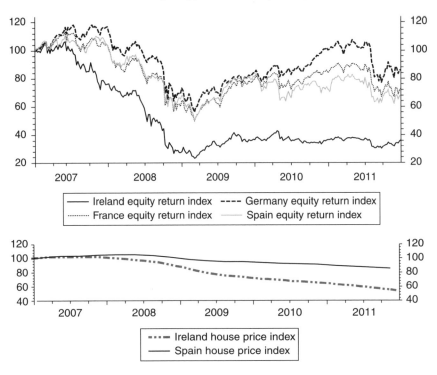

Figure 6.18   Germany, France, Ireland, Spain equity market performance and Ireland and Spain house prices (2007–2011)
Source: Thomson Reuters Datastream.

of improving investment returns and avoid owning assets which are about to crash in value.

When analysing the process of the creation and destruction of capital, the way in which governmental institutions operate can have an inordinate effect on the outcome of capital values. Inflation targeting during the Great Moderation masked one of the greatest credit bubbles in the history of financial markets that led to a crash in asset values. Moreover, the continuation of monetary policy experiments since the onset of the crisis continues to generate uncertainty in equity markets. Regulatory policy of the banking sector can also have a substantial effect on constraining growth, as well as stimulating too much growth. Finally, it is the government that is responsible for creating the underlying economic framework that can have long-term implications for capital values. This includes the way in which its citizens are educated, infrastructure provision, energy distribution, land use and the way in which the public finances are managed. This requires governments to actively pursue these policies, hence it is not more government or less government that is needed, but effective government. This is a point that has largely been ignored since the onset of the crisis with the focus on a largely irrelevant debate of austerity versus stimulus. These are issues that with the help of streams of data allow investors to park their capital in those countries that do take capital preservation seriously. This will become increasingly important to ensure that sufficient returns are generated for pension schemes.

Chapter 7

The creation and destruction of capital

A capitalist economy is not and cannot be stationary. Nor is it merely expanding in a steady manner . . . . Economic progress in a capitalist society means turmoil.

Joseph Schumpeter[1]

The investment management community faces a daunting challenge to provide the pensions sector with the desired rate of return, given that the recent financial crisis resulted in such an extensive destruction of capital. The current outlook for profits remains uncertain due to the massive amount of debt outstanding in developed markets. Moreover, the outlook for bond returns is also clouded due to the impact of interest rates having to rise at some stage, which will result in falling bond prices. Although the sector cannot beat the market overall, it can change the way it thinks about the benchmarking of returns through time by reducing the volatility of returns and investing through the business cycle. This can be achieved by analysing the Wicksellian Differential of an economy which as Chapter 6 demonstrated is closely linked to the rate of profit and therefore the performance of equities. Hence such an approach could be used in an investment process to trigger asset allocation decisions between equities and bonds providing pension funds with more stable returns through time to help match their liabilities. Given that monetary policy was unable to identify one of the largest credit bubbles in the history of financial markets, there is no reason why the signals emanating from central banks today are likely to be of much use in preventing capital destruction in the future. The neo-Wicksellian framework can therefore be exploited to develop simple and cost effective investment strategies such as an annualised switching approach between equities and bonds based on the rate of growth of excess profit. This allows investors to benefit from credit expansion in the way it drives equity valuations and from returns on government bonds when the rate of growth of excess profit falls. Crucially, such a strategy generates long run equity-like returns but with bond-like volatility, thus providing pensions schemes with a better risk return payoff. Equally as important is that investors can use this framework to invest in countries that are more disposed towards capital preservation policies. However, capital preservation policies are not just purely related to the way in which central banks move the nominal rate of interest impacting credit growth. They include all aspects of economic and social policy as Myrdal stated. Monetary policy is thus a broad term to encompass the superstructure upon which an economy sits.

Central banks, despite their central role in setting the nominal rate of interest, do not own centre stage with their crude tools of economic management. However, it has been convenient for professional politicians to allude to the fact that central bankers are in control as a way of deflecting any criticism of their own track record of economic policy making. In reality of course, it is governments that have more tools at their disposal to alter the superstructure. However, the economic returns from changing the structure may not yield results for many years, therefore making them less interesting for politicians to pursue. Investors when making their asset allocation decisions can therefore also profit from other types of monetary policy by investing in those countries which improve their superstructure in the interests of capital preservation and by pulling money out of those countries that do not.

From an investor perspective, there are at least three kinds of changes that might impact the superstructure, thus influencing the creation or destruction of capital. These include the framework that governs the objectives of monetary policy to be pursued by central banks. The regulation of the banking sector is also critical given that banks remain the main providers of credit to an economy. Finally, developments related to changes in the underlying productivity of the private and public sector also impact capital values. This is particularly relevant in understanding the sustainability of rising government debt and why bond yields can jump when some economies attempt to spend their way out of a recession but fall when even more indebted countries do the same thing.

Business as usual for central bankers

This study has argued that the theoretical framework that governs monetary policy generated false signals for investors, resulting in large and unexpected losses. It proposes a new approach to assessing capital values by understanding the difference between the return on capital and the cost of capital at the macroeconomic level, defined as the Wicksellian Differential. As the Differential increases due to rising profits fuelled by excess leverage, capital values will increase, however, an eventual decline in the rate of profit leads to deleveraging, hence capital values will fall. Such a framework allows investors to monitor the business cycle and ensure that their investment process is constructed around preserving capital through time.

One concern for investors might be why could not such a framework be used as a basis for monetary policy itself, thus eliminating excess credit growth and increasing equity values? Indeed, the so called "productivity norm" that has been championed by the economist, George Selgin, attempts to do just that. This would require the introduction of a policy that moves general prices inversely proportional to changes in productivity or the nominal interest rate in line with the natural rate. From an equity bond switching strategy this would most likely result in fewer buy signals for equities. If this were to happen, the switching strategy between equity and bonds would still provide equity-like returns with lower volatility; although, the returns on equity would most likely be lower than they have been historically.

However, if central bankers did pursue such a policy it is not clear what the other consequences might be; the history of monetary policy is not filled with many success stories. The indebted French government's support for John Law in the 18th century was a disaster. The laissez-faire political ideology of central bankers in the 1930s meant that many were generally loathe to intervene as they felt that a prolonged downturn was necessary to purge the economy of the excesses of the 1920s. The post-war Keynesian relationship between inflation and employment proved little better, as Friedman demonstrated with his attack on the Phillips Curve leading central bankers to conclude that Friedman had all the answers through his resurrection of Fisher's quantity theory of money equation which also did not work. During the Great Moderation, the new neoclassical synthesis argued that interest rates ought to remain low because there was little inflationary activity. Thus it missed one of the largest ever credit booms in financial history due to the exogenous shock to prices from China and India entering into the global supply chain. The onset of the financial crisis has in turn led to another set of experiments with the lowering of short-term rates to effectively zero, which to date has had limited effect on stimulating demand. As a consequence, central bankers have maintained their track record by using more untested measures to stimulate the economy, such as quantitative easing whereby the central bank injects money into the economy by the purchase of financial assets. This in many respects is a replay of monetarism based on the theory that an increase in the quantity of money increases the general price level with the belief that this will stimulate the economy. These latest sets of experiments started back in March 2001 when the Bank of Japan increased its target for current account balances of commercial banks in excess of their required reserve levels. The idea behind the policy was to lower the cost of capital, thus leading to increased investment and growth. In turn this growth would be inflationary, thus dislocating Japan from its deflationary spiral in conjunction with its high debt levels. The Bank of Japan also set up a programme to buy Japanese government bonds to maintain lower long-term interest rates and reduce the cost of financing of Japan's ever-increasing levels of government debt. The policy did have the effect of lowering long-term interest rates; however, as Chapter 6 demonstrated, the key to growth is in fact an increase in future demand. Given that corporate Japan did not substantially reduce its capacity to meet the lower level of demand, the policy of lowering long-term interest rates had a limited impact on this objective. The policy was abandoned in March 2006 as the Japanese economy began to reflate due to rising exports driven by the global credit boom. According to the San Francisco Federal Reserve, although long-term interest rates did indeed come down, 'in strengthening the performance of the weakest Japanese banks. [the policy] may have had the undesired impact of delaying structural reform'.[2]

Since the onset of the financial crisis in 2007, these monetary experiments have continued with central bankers in the United States, the United Kingdom and the Eurozone embarking on a similar series of policies. In November 2008, the Federal Reserve embarked on a programme of buying $500 billion of mortgage-backed securities and a $100 billion of government-sponsored enterprise (GSE) debt. In March 2009 the purchases of US Treasuries, GSE debt and mortgage-backed securities were extended by a further $1.15 trillion. In November 2010 the Fed announced a second round of quantitative easing by buying a further $600 billion of US Treasuries. Finally in September 2011, the Fed embarked upon a third stage by buying $400 billion of longer-dated securities whilst selling a similar amount of shorter-dated securities. All of these policies were an attempt to reduce the cost of capital and therefore hopefully stimulate demand, thus kick starting the economy. The United Kingdom pursued a similar policy in March 2009, of purchasing £200 billion of mostly government bonds, which was extended in October 2011 by £75 billion and February 2012 by £50 billion. The ECB pursued a slightly different approach by auctioning low-interest loans to banks and accepting lower-quality assets as collateral to reduce the cost of capital.

As was the case in Japan, the cost of capital did fall as a result of these measures,[3] which has also reduced the cost of government borrowing. Although reducing the cost of capital has benefits, the aspirations of quantitative easing (QE) beyond this remain unproven and controversial as the BIS has argued.[4] Indeed, the idea that increasing the money supply has an impact on inflation is about as close to Friedman's monetarism as one can get. Friedman did not believe in liquidity traps as described by Keynes, thus his theory ignored them. However as Keynes argued, an increase in the supply of money can, on occasion, lead to a fall in output if consumers' expectations about the future have deteriorated. This of course is a possible reason why investment remains sluggish although central banks in their 'analysis' of their QE programmes appear not to have even contemplated such an effect. Indeed, some of the claims from central banks of the benefits of QE seem to conveniently ignore aspects of what has been happening in the real economy such as the productivity jump after the cost cutting of 2008 and 2009 being the main driver of equity price rises in 2009 and 2010 rather than due to the success of QE. Investment is predicated on a rise in future profits, and given that consumers in most countries are deleveraging, future demand has not increased and productivity growth has not been able to maintain its stellar rise into 2011 and beyond. Thus, it should not be surprising that corporations in 2011 were hoarding cash rather than investing it. If a central bank really wanted to stimulate investment, the most effective policy would of course be to pay off every consumer's mortgage, although this would certainly lead to high inflation due to a sudden jump in demand, given consumers would have money to spend again.

The anti-QE camp has unfortunately also been duped by Friedman arguing that any increase in the money supply will increase inflation.[5] This again highlights the lack of understanding of money in relation to the economy. This issue is the same one Cantillon pointed out centuries ago, in that it all depends on where the money goes into the economy. QE may well impact relative prices of certain goods depending on the transmission of the wealth effect through the economy; however, it is quite possible that it could lead to a fall in the general level of prices, no change in prices or an increase. Moreover, exogenous factors may remain more important drivers of the general price level and thus it is quite possible for inflation to pick up without the economy expanding at all.

Investors have of course been able to profit from these actions by buying the same high grade bonds the government has been buying which has sent bond prices soaring. There have been other knock on effects too which have given rise to opportunities in particular the impact on international capital flows. As the US government has been buying US Treasuries and depressing yields, many investors have moved their money elsewhere to find higher-yielding assets. This in turn has led to large financial flows into emerging markets and an excess supply of credit to these growing economies, thus stimulating other credit bubbles. A comparison of the five-year credit default swap rates for the United States, Brazil and China, as shown in Figure 7.1, highlights the credit compression that has taken place in emerging markets as a result of QE in March 2009, which is similar to the compression that took place in developed markets pre-crisis.

It would appear that central banking experiments with monetary policy are here to stay, although it is not clear whether

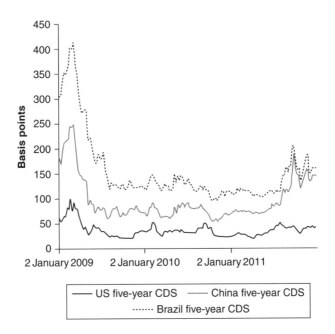

Figure 7.1   Five-year CDS spread – US, China and Brazil
Source: Fitch Solutions.

any experimentation ought to be welcome given the confusion it can have on investor expectations. Hence, if a productivity norm approach were to be used for monetary policy, whereby the absolute level of prices moved inversely proportional to productivity by ensuring that the money rate of interest was close to the natural rate, then several decades of research ought to take place first on the impact of these ideas. In particular, it is not clear at what level central bankers should minimise inflation or deflation jumps and at what level expectations might impact prices. Thus, for instance, a leap in productivity growth might take place leading to a growth in excess profits. As the money rate of interest increases, prices should start to fall. However, it is possible that if prices fall too far, corporations might decide to cut back their supply too aggressively, leading to higher unemployment. The challenge is to build up the tree of knowledge rather than to base decisions on a half dying, scrawny shrub. However, this line of research may indeed prove fruitful given that it has a strong intellectual heritage to act as a foundation. The stage has now been set for a move away from the new neoclassical framework as argued by Buiter, Borio, Goodhart, Stiglitz and Kay, amongst others. Whatever the outcome of this new strand of research in monetary policy, investors can still generate improved returns by rejecting the current framework now. Even if a new monetary framework is eventually established, it is highly unlikely that credit cycles will be eliminated; thus, the opportunities for investors to switch between equities and bonds based on rising leverage will still generate equity-like returns with reduced volatility.

There are of course other factors besides monetary policy that impact the release of credit into an economy, the most important being the banking sector. Indeed, the banking sector is now poised to go through its biggest ever change in the way it is regulated due to the banking sectors' role in the recent crisis. Hence, investors need to be aware of the impact this regulation is likely to have on capital values.

Banks are dead, long live the banks!

The failure of politicians and central bankers to support the banking system during the 1930s undoubtedly worsened the Great Depression. Banking failures led to a further loss in confidence, impacting the supply of working capital to businesses, and of course limiting the supply of new credit for those few businesses who were attempting to expand. During the Great Depression over 7,000 banks alone in the United States failed. The recapitalisation of the global banking sector using tax payers' money was therefore an important step taken by the world's politicians in 2008. However, the use of large amounts of tax payers' money has quite rightly led to the banking system becoming a key focus of regulation. One particular issue worth highlighting is that over the last century capital ratios have been falling in tandem with an increase in leverage. As a result banks were using a smaller and smaller capital base whilst lending out a higher multiple of customer deposits. This is one of the main reasons why the return on equity of banks has increased so significantly in the decades leading up to the crisis.[6] The reality of course is that this was an unsustainable rise in leverage which generated large short-term profits for bankers. When the system came crashing down, the lower rates of capital held by the banks were unable to absorb the shock of the financial crisis, thus requiring the government to intervene.

Since 2010 the world's regulators have begun to crank out the new structure of how banks will be regulated. Of particular note are the new Basel III regulations, announced in 2010 by the Basel Committee on Banking Supervision aimed at strengthening the capital base of the banking system. One of the most important changes brought about by Basel III has been the tightening of the definition of what counts as capital to ensure that banks are resilient enough to survive during periods of financial stress. The Basel II definition of capital comprised multiple elements with a complex set of minimums and maximums, including Tier one capital, innovative Tier one, upper and lower Tier two and Tier three capital. Each element had its own limits and was sometimes a function of other capital elements. The complexity in the definition of capital thus made it difficult to determine what capital would be available should losses arise during a period of stress.[7] This combination of weaknesses permitted tangible common equity capital, the best form of capital, to be largely omitted from a bank's capital base. Indeed, the actual level of the most robust form of capital (tangible common equity) in the period leading up to the financial crisis was between 1 per cent and 3 per cent, or a risk-weighted leverage of between 33:1 and 100:1.

The new Basel III rules increase the amount of tangible common equity or core tier one capital that banks must hold in relation to their risk-weighted assets. As a result, core tier one capital will increase from an average of 2 per cent to around 10.5 per cent in many jurisdictions. On top of this core tier one capital, further non-core tier one capital charges will be added if a bank poses a systemic risk to the financial system of up to a further 2.5 per cent.

According to a recent report, core tier one capital in Switzerland and the United Kingdom will be as high as 12 per cent with additional tier one capital charges rising to 20 per cent and 15 per cent respectively.[8]

Furthermore, banks will also be forced to increase capital charges levied in relation to counterparty credit risk exposures. During a systemic downturn, the risk exposures to other counterparties increase considerably, impacting the sustainability of the banking system itself. Indeed, two-thirds of counterparty losses during the crisis were related to deteriorating systemic conditions increasing Credit Valuation Adjustment charges to cover increasing unexpected counterparty losses. This was the reason why implied default rates derived from CDS indices in May 2010 were at 45 per cent for the global banking sector.[9]

Besides the incremental capital charges, banks will also be forced to manage their businesses within a certain leverage ratio, which is a bank's tier one capital as a percentage of its total assets, including off balance sheet exposures and derivatives. The idea being that many assets under the risk-weighting scheme, such as senior subprime CDO tranches that had a AAA rating, were in reality far riskier. Finally, banks will also be subject to minimum liquidity and funding ratios. These two ratios are to ensure that if banks experience a period of financial instability, they have enough liquid assets to cover net outflows and that they are not dependent on short-term financing given the challenges of trying to raise finance during unstable periods.

The reality of all these new regulations is that the banking sector will now need to substantially increase the amount of core tier one capital in relation to their risk-weighted assets. This will cause a fall in the profitability of the banking sector with returns on equity most likely falling back to where they were in the 1970s. From a regulatory perspective there are clearly benefits from doing this in order to prevent the banking system from becoming as leveraged as it was in the run up to the financial crisis. Risk-weighted leverage ratios based on core tier one capital will thus fall from around 50:1 in the pre-crisis period to below 10:1, which is a substantial decrease in leverage. Moreover, the credit that will be made available will be more expensive. However, it would appear that much of this leverage was not put to productive use as it had little impact on the rate of growth of output.[10] This is further evidence that excess liquidity does not necessarily boost production with much of this excess liquidity flowing into financial assets, driving asset prices up in the short run due to higher demand. Some of this leverage did get used productively, thus a fall in leverage will impact output to an extent.[11]

However, the timing of these reforms could not have been worse. As Stiglitz and Greenwald highlighted, forcing banks to recapitalise during the depths of an economic crisis will not facilitate the provision of credit to the corporate sector to invest and generate jobs, which will be crucial in changing expectations. Moreover, the non-financial corporate sector is not particularly leveraged at the moment and therefore has the capacity to increase debt to expand should firms spot an opportunity. As a result investors can expect little let up in negative expectations in the short term. However, in the medium term, companies involved in finance, which may or may not be banks, will find a way of channelling credit to those who most need it. Such is the nature of the sector as Minsky pointed out. Thus investors looking to understand when the trajectory of equity values might change due to an injection of credit would do well to observe developments in the non-banking sector, particularly in the bond market. The reason why the bond market will become more important now the cost of borrowing from banks will increase is that there has been a fundamental structural shift in the source of savings that can be channelled into capital investment over the last few decades.

The pension fund system in the United Kingdom alone now has $2.4 trillion in assets compared to $1.9 trillion of retail deposits. The US pension fund sector manages over $16 trillion with $10 trillion in retail deposits.[12] Clearly from a reserve banking operation, deposits can be leveraged up, thus dwarfing the amount that can be invested back into the economy. However, the new banking rules are likely to accelerate the source of financing for many businesses away from banks to the bond market.

In the United States the bond market has long been an important source of capital, and since the advent of the euro there has been a shift within Europe too, with many larger companies who traditionally used bank loans now raising capital via the bond market instead. Indeed, the high yield or leveraged finance market is seeing significant growth despite the on-going challenges facing the global economy.[13] A large bulk of these bond investors are indeed pension funds, with the insurance sector also acquiring a large amount of investment grade assets. Although this growth in capital market funding is to be welcome, it unfortunately does not help the most important sector of the economy with respect to employment and output, the small- and medium-size enterprises (SMEs). In the United States, SMEs account for around half of GDP and employment with exports at around 30 per cent.[14] In Europe it is estimated that SMEs' contribution is around 67 per cent in private sector employment but account for 85 per cent of new jobs created.[15]

SMEs are unlikely to be able to tap into the capital market directly due to the small size of loans required and the fact that there are too many of them for bond investors to analyse default risk effectively. However, an economy with listed companies is only able to do well if it has an expanding supplier base to support these companies. Hence the availability of financing for SMEs from the banking sector is important to equity investors. The challenge though is that the cost of funding for SMEs is going up because the new capital charges for banks will be passed on to the market in the form of higher-priced loans, thus potentially reducing the amount of funding available at acceptable levels.

This is where the banking sector might be able to reinvent itself using securitisation in order to support the provision of credit to SMEs despite the new banking regulations. Securitisation has been much maligned since the onset of the financial crisis. According to Joseph Stiglitz, 'securitization was based on the premise that a fool was born every minute.... Globalization meant that there was a global landscape on which they could search for those fools – and they found them everywhere'.[16] More than $27 trillion of securitised securities were sold from 2001, leading up the crisis which bundled mainly mortgages (often very poor quality ones) into securities with supposedly different risk profiles. The industry has been particularly attacked, because by onwardly selling the risks, banks had no reason to maintain high underwriting standards to ensure that original loans were of sufficient quality. Indeed, the number of mortgages issued to consumers who clearly had no means to repay the loans was rife across the industry. Lending money to a person who has limited income to buy a house with no deposit is clearly a very foolish act. This foolish act was then rubber stamped by the banks securitising these loans, and the rating agencies who rated tranches of subprime CDOs AAA.

However, if the quality of loans being securitised is good and the securitisation structures are transparent and simple, then it can be an extremely effective method of providing financing for SMEs. Recent research from the BIS has highlighted that securitization can indeed work effectively.[17] So how might securitisation be effectively applied to provide financing to SMEs? Banks are without doubt in the best position to provide loans to SMEs because they have the accumulated knowledge and infrastructure as well as having a local presence which is critical to understanding the nature of the SMEs business and environment. New securitisation rules based on the Capital Requirements Directive (CRD) announced by the European Union effectively permit up to almost 50 per cent of a bank's SME balance sheet to be securitised as long as assets remain on the balance sheet in an amount exceeding 5 per cent of the securitisation exposures, assuming the asset selection process is transparent and public.[18] These loans could then be packed up into a collateralised loan obligation (CLO) and sold to pension funds. In essence this allows the banks to increase leverage in order to increase the provision of credit to the SME sector.

But why should pension funds buy such complex instruments given what happened with subprime CDOs? Indeed, the search for yield most likely will still lead investors to make foolish decisions. In 2001 a fund manager asked the company I was working for at the time to price a CDO for them. We requested more information on what were the underlying assets of the pool, only to receive the response from the client that they did not know. They had just bought the bond for a bit more yield. This approach to investment was in fact largely the case right up until the credit crisis with very little loan-level analysis of these structures being undertaken. An investor should be able to see the performance of every loan inside the pool in order to make an effective analysis of the concentration risks of the security. At present, the amount of SME CLOs in the market is limited, mainly because there is not sufficient transparency yet to provide investors with the confidence in the instrument at the yields offered. However, this is clearly one avenue that might be developed by the banking sector to increase the availability of credit.

The new banking regulations will increase the cost of capital and reduce the availability of credit, thus impacting equity values in the short term. However, in the medium term this will not necessarily impact the returns to equities as the non-banking sector looks to find a way round the regulatory framework to provide the corporate world with the credit they need for investment, and therefore a growth in asset values as expectations shift. The bond market in combination with a banking sector focussed on SME funding using the securitisation route may well be sufficient to meet future demand. Without doubt, the sector will come up with a whole series of other ideas too, not all of which though are likely to be good.

An understanding of the cost and availability of credit is critical for equity investors to assess the trajectory of future capital values. However, investors ought to also be focused on how well companies and governments utilise the credit they receive. Indeed, a comparison of the Wicksellian Differentials between US and Japanese companies shows that in aggregate US companies are twice more productive in their use of capital than their Japanese counterparts at 8 per cent and 4 per cent respectively. Thus productivity remains critical to the future growth in equity values. Furthermore, given that the next decade is unlikely to see such high growth rates in consumer credit, productivity may become far more important to investors with respect to future returns.

The productivity conundrum

I started my career as an analyst for a company that specialised in turning around failing businesses. Companies on the brink of bankruptcy that are losing millions of dollars every month are generally very unproductive. Pretty much, the only way for companies to come back from the brink is to dramatically shrink the number of employees and focus on the part of the business that is actually profitable or close to being profitable. If this is not done, then in general the company will go bankrupt with the loss of all jobs. The end results were generally similar in that after the turnaround the business was back up to its prior revenue, generating a profit but with roughly 50 per cent of the workforce. This is purely about productivity or how you can generate a higher output with the same input or the same output with a lower input. There are a number of factors that are critical to driving this productivity. Firstly is the quality of the workforce which is highly correlated to educational attainment. Secondly is the quality of the management who run the company on behalf of the shareholders. In essence, human capital is the most important aspect of capital formation in developed economies. Other factors include core input costs into the production function, such as energy and property which every productive enterprise is forced to buy. These can often be impacted by government rules and regulations distorting market forces. This is by no means an exhaustive list but rather an attempt to focus on a few universal issues related to driving productivity growth that impacts the private sector. Clearly each industry will have its own drivers that impact both productivity growth and capital values, such as the impact of anti-trust legislation for the cement sector or patent protection for pharmaceuticals or regulatory changes for utilities on carbon emissions.

In a recent essay the economist Tyler Cowen highlighted that there were now no easy wins to boost productivity. Given the main driver for capital growth is the way in which people interact with tools, education is one of his key focuses. Despite the fact that many countries are spending more on education services, the returns to education appear to be in decline. Between the early 1970s and 2009, spending on education in the United States more than doubled per pupil with no change in the average scores for literacy and numeracy.[19] This is backed up by OECD evidence showing that 89 per cent of 55- to 64-year-olds completed an upper secondary education compared to 88 per cent of 25- to 34-year-olds. More importantly, whilst the baby boom generation were far more educated than every other country, defined in terms of per cent completion of an upper secondary education, this advantage has vanished with the 25- to 34-year-olds now ranked 12th in secondary school completion rates.[20] For tertiary education, the United States has also seen little improvement with the rate marginally improving over the two generations from 41 per cent to 42 per cent. South Korea has the highest per cent of tertiary education completion at over 60 per cent, up from below 15 per cent for the 55- to 64-year-olds which is a very impressive generational shift. Finally, in international comparisons on literacy and numeracy, the United States fares poorly, coming 17th in the OECD table for reading and 26th for mathematics and 23rd for science.[21]

So why does this matter so much? Educational achievement is strongly linked to average earnings with graduates of tertiary education on average earning over 50 per cent more than those completing an upper secondary education.[22] Moreover, average unemployment rates are far lower for graduates of tertiary education. Thus the higher productivity growth driven by educational attainment should be a factor in boosting capital values over time. Higher levels of education are of particular importance during a downturn when unemployment increases. Given wages are sticky and do not fall dramatically in a recession, the lower levels of productivity growth that are generated with unskilled labour are less effective in supporting a recovery. Highly skilled workforces with strong management can drive an increase in productivity growth, thus reducing prices and increasing consumers' purchasing power, which if highly leveraged becomes critical in maintaining output. It is interesting to note that the Korean stock market has substantially outperformed the US stock market in the last decade and it would not be surprising to find that education is one of the most important contributory factors to the growth in capital values. Thus investors assessing the expected growth in capital values for long-term asset allocation bets would do well to take note of such international differences.

However, a highly educated workforce will not on its own drive capital values up. Firms need to have quality management teams in place in order to exploit the available human capital in conjunction with tools to generate returns to shareholders. For instance, although Japan has a highly educated workforce, its firms have not on average generated significant returns on capital compared to the United States. This is of particular interest given Japan's investment rate has been substantially higher than the United States. Hence it is not how much money that is invested that matters, but rather the productivity of that investment. For private sector companies this is reasonably straightforward to measure using the annualised returns on capital by country or the natural rate of interest. Thus it would appear that the management of US companies is superior when it comes to generating stronger returns on capital than those in Japan. It is worth pointing out however that Japan's educational attainment is gained at a much lower cost than the United States, suggesting that the education establishment which includes the bureaucracy, head teachers as well as government support for educational policies is far more productive in Japan than in the United States. Investors may therefore want to decide on which countries to run the equity bond switching scheme to take advantage of a strong management approach and a highly educated workforce, generating higher returns.

One concern for equity investors is that given the current state of highly indebted consumers in the United States and other countries, what potential is there for strong growth in capital values. The evidence from Chapter 6 is clear that the growth in consumer credit during the period of the Great Moderation played a substantial role in driving capital values due to increasing demand. One approach to the asset allocation process is to set up a switching strategy in a country like South Korea, where consumers are less in debt than in say the United Kingdom or the United States but where other factors such as education are strong. Another might be to focus on countries that currently have the most productive management teams as measured by the natural rate of interest. If consumer demand is unlikely to rise in a country of more productive managers, the set of firms will be forced to innovate and drive productivity growth, and hence capital values. Indeed, it is striking that when Hawtrey was writing about the 1920s, he put down the success of the increase in output down to management and not technical progress, which is what the neoclassical growth model tells us. Leverage of course was also growing too, so this may have been over-stated somewhat. However, the data is reasonably clear that productivity growth jumps substantially in recessions as firms reduce labour whilst maintaining marginally reduced levels of output. This suggests that during the good times firms tend to become fat and less well managed.

Indeed, it would appear that management teams have not been sufficiently tested as to their potential, given that during the Great Moderation the more important task was to ensure that rising demand was met. The reality is that when the rate of profit growth is already growing, management teams will focus on the easiest way of making money which is related to increasing costs at a slightly lower rate than demand. It is a much harder task to manage a business when demand is stable, and the objective is to deploy resources internally more effectively to generate similar output using substantially lower inputs. Indeed, there is no reason to believe that with a bit more shareholder activism the rate of productivity growth can not increase significantly. My own experience of executive committees across multiple industries suggests that the room for improvement is substantial. Moreover, without such an increase in productivity growth it is hard to see how equity values can generate the kinds of returns they generated in the past given the general deleveraging trend.

Besides nurturing and exploiting the relationship between people and their tools, managers need to take other input costs into account. Clearly in times of rising energy costs there is not much that can be done, particularly for energy-intensive sectors. However, in the medium term governments more open to exploiting cheaper energy sources may well see productivity gains resulting in rising profits. The 'fracking' revolution in the United States is a good example of this. Another input cost that can be reduced through regulation is the cost of land or rent. Indeed, it is striking that Cowen in his essay highlighted free land as one of the reasons for the rise in productivity in the 19th century. Hence it is odd that today there are few arguing for the logic of capitalism to be applied to the property market which would reduce input costs, boost productivity and drive equity values – except for those businesses that generate profits from fleecing the productive sector of the economy by charging high rents in both senses of the word. Of course it could be argued that given the ability of land owners to extract economic rent from the productive sector of society, they ought to be good places to invest money in. Indeed, the Hong Kong stock market is heavily weighted in such companies whose profits are generated from rising demand for office and residential space on assets they monopolise. Unfortunately for investors such a bet can be highly volatile as when demand starts to fall, the inflated asset prices which were extracting large amount of economic rent can fall dramatically.

The Canadian economist Galbraith once wrote that 'the inadequate provision of housing at modest cost in contrast with that of say automobiles or cosmetics, can be considered the single greatest default of modern capitalism'.[23] Given every productive enterprise has to pay for land somehow, as it is required to have a registered office somewhere in the world, investors during the asset allocation process may want to assess which countries are willing to support capital and introduce market forces to the property sector. This may count against economies like the United Kingdom in the medium term that remain wedded to their support for landlords who continue to extract significant amounts of economic rent from the productive sector of society at the expense of lower profits and lower wages. Tenants in the United Kingdom are still subject to upward-only rent reviews. During the recent financial crisis, the rate of bankruptcies has accelerated in the United Kingdom largely due to landlords refusing to reduce rent in line with market rates, leading to capital destruction and rising unemployment, and therefore lower aggregate demand.[24]

The fact that governments may decide not to support the preservation of capital in the way they decide to regulate an economy in many respects should not be surprising. Since the end of the Second World War, governments all around the world have got bigger and generally more ineffective. Cowen's data on education is a case in point. However, the role of government in the economy is critical. Markets fail. If there were no government to intervene in the event of a banking collapse, society would break down. As such what really matters is public sector productivity. The bond market provides some general information about this, given that some countries are able to raise debt and spend it in such a way that it generates a positive return on capital. As a consequence they have lower funding costs. However, many governments do not have the ability to spend tax payers' money productively. There is a reason why Sweden, Denmark and Switzerland can raise debt cheaply. The bond markets believe that the money raised is used effectively due to higher levels of public sector productivity. This partially explains why Sweden and Denmark have higher levels of public expenditure because their level of public sector productivity can support it. However, bond market expectations can change quickly. The fact that interest rates are currently low does not mean they will stay that way. Indeed, one possible explanation why the United Kingdom has been able to continue to raise debt cheaply is that it has gone for austerity. The United Kingdom is well below average in the international comparisons on public sector productivity.[25] If the UK government suddenly decided to raise another £50 billion to spend, what would happen to interest rates?

The recent debate between Paul Krugman and Kenneth Rogoff highlights this point implicitly.[26] Rogoff's repost to Krugman's stimulus programme ideas is that interest rates can rise very quickly if the market becomes concerned about how the money is being spent, thus making the debt overhang even worse. However, there is a consensus that where projects are seen to generate a positive return on capital which might include infrastructure investment, there is some value in proceeding. The challenge is of course predicting up front which ones are worth betting on. The most effective way of managing this process would be to run a predictive market and ask bond investors their views on how much each project ought to yield back to investors. This is a much more effective way of assessing the risk than some abstract economic model that has no bearing on the real world. A predictive market provides a continuous stream of data for officials to analyse and would be an extremely effective method for governments to help support capital.[27]

For example, if a specific project was put forward to mimic Keynes' famous quip about paying unemployed workers to dig holes, how would the market price its funding costs? Without doubt the employment of unemployed workers to dig up disused coal mines and extract bottles filled with banknotes is clearly sustainable. It is how mining works. However, Keynes does not make it clear how much it would cost the Treasury officials to fill the bottles with notes, deposit them in the old mines, cover them up with town rubbish and provide sufficient security to ensure the site is not robbed until the bidding process for the rights to extract the bottles is complete. I doubt that investors would think this would be a sensible use of scarce resources and the cost of funding would most likely be high. Thus Keynes' digging holes experiment would most likely worsen the debt overhang.

Furthermore, the way in which money is spent is just as critical in assessing the cost of funding as the nature of the project. Indeed a series of poorly implemented projects would no doubt cloud the judgement of investors to invest in other projects proposed by the same government. Unfortunately, this leads us back to the issue of poor public sector productivity that Peter Drucker highlighted two decades ago. However, that is not to say it can not work. Indeed, there are a handful of examples where increased public expenditure has turned around floundering economies. One of the best examples that highlights this issue is how the US economy emerged from the Great Depression in the Second World War. Investors were willing to finance the government war effort because the country felt this was the right thing to do to protect the democratic values of America. However, what was more important was the way in which the money, roughly $3 trillion in today's money, was spent. As Arthur Herman describes in his recent book, Bill Knudsen of General Motors persuaded FDR that federal dollars *had* to follow the trail of productivity and innovation, and if FDR could wait 18 months, he would ensure that American industry was prepared to move towards a war economy.[28] The results are frankly astonishing. By the end of 1943, the US economy was producing more military equipment than Germany, United Kingdom and the Soviet Union combined.

The current austerity versus stimulus debate therefore misses the point. What matters is the productivity of the private and public sector to spend the money they currently have, as well as any new money that might be raised. This means that the focus needs to be shifted towards who is spending the money, for what purpose and what experience those individuals or groups have to convince investors and tax payers that they can spend money wisely, thus generating a positive return on capital. Unfortunately, this debate does not lead to attention-grabbing headlines, but it is the daily grind of how capital is created. As Herman emphasised, one of the most important aspects of the US success story during the Second World War was the fact that FDR decided to give the money to those with expertise, which was contrary to his own political ideology. This was a rare case of the triumph of the practical experience of managers over the abstract ideas of economists. The creation of capital is not easy to accomplish: To invest successfully, and to create jobs is much harder to achieve than theorising about capital and creating an abstract model which more often than not leads to capital destruction. The sooner investors realise this, the better.

Junk the models and look at the data

The dynamism and turbulence of the modern economy is totally at odds with the foundations upon which the economy is analysed by governments, economists and many investors today. The economy does not oscillate around an equilibrium level. The central bank does not have the ability to fine tune an optimum level of output through the movement of the nominal rate of interest. Stable prices do not equate to a stable economy. The trajectory of an economy is not a linear one accompanied by random movements. Real GDP forecasts are unable to forecast the destruction of capital, which has led to a shortfall in pension fund returns.

If the investment industry is going to be able to generate the kinds of returns the pensions industry requires, it will need to ignore signals emanating from the current macroeconomic framework of price stability and general equilibrium. The preservation of capital through the business cycle necessitates the analysis of streams of data from a credit-based framework. This includes an understanding of the growth in profits driven by increasing leverage and whether the central bank is stimulating credit growth or causing capital destruction by its actions. It will also require an understanding of whether the financial sector can allocate sufficient credit to those who demand it, which is linked to the extent of financial regulation and the areas of finance that are unregulated. Finally, an understanding of more structural issues related to productivity can also provide an insight into those jurisdictions that are most favourably disposed towards the protection of capital. Ultimately investors will need to accept that although the general trend of asset values can be monitored, attempts to model and forecast are pointless. It is only by analysing streams of actual data can one determine the turning points of the cycle, allowing investors to switch asset classes and preserve capital, thus generating the required returns for pension funds.

Chapter 8

Where are the customer's yachts?

Sailing into the harbour at Newport, William R. Travers saw many beautiful yachts at anchor on the sunny water.
'Whose boat is that?' he asked.
'It belongs to So-and-So, the great Wall Street broker.'
'Whose yacht is that big one over there?'
'It belongs to So-and-So, another great Wall Street broker.'
'And whose is that big steam yacht almost as large as an ocean liner?'
'It belongs to the greatest of all the Wall Street brokers and bankers, So-and-So.'
Travers looked at the different yachts, asked about them, and got always the same answer. At last with his usual stutter, he asked: 'Where are the customers's yachts?'
There were no customers's yachts to be seen.

William R. Travers[1]

Between 2001 and 2010 the average OECD pension plan returned 0.1 per cent per annum. Savers who started putting money aside for their pension ten years ago are discovering that the value of their savings has only managed to increase marginally above the rate of inflation. Inflation has been low over the last decade, which means the performance of their investment has been shocking. The main reason behind this poor performance is that capital values have fallen dramatically because capital preservation has been largely ignored by the investment community. Roughly 25 per cent of all investment funds are passive funds benchmarked against an index. A large chunk of the remaining assets are active funds benchmarked against the same set of indices. Hence the main issue that fund managers care about is whether they have beaten their benchmark index or not, rather than whether they have increased the value of a savers' pension pot. To the saver who is paying someone to increase the value of their assets, the idea that someone gets paid for not generating positive returns can be difficult to comprehend. Moreover, those fund managers that try and beat the market using asset allocation strategies tend to use the current macroeconomic framework for investment signals, in particular real GDP forecasts. However, these signals have proven to have been unreliable as the dot-com crash and the recent Financial Crisis have shown. Although some fund managers are focussed on absolute returns, they are few and far between.

The reality is that most of the investment management industry was duped by the financial and economic theory behind the Great Moderation which turned out to be a Great Myth. The theory argued that as long as inflation remained stable, the economy was oscillating around equilibrium, and therefore future returns would be similar to historical returns. Investors' expectations would maintain the economy oscillating around equilibrium as long as monetary policy responded to these changed expectations. Thus, all that had to be done was to buy and hold assets and the returns would roll in. Active investors using real GDP forecasts for asset allocation assumed that the relationship between output and inflation would hold, thus allowing them to generate excess returns above the market. However, as the Financial Crisis has amply demonstrated, inflation targeting does not stabilise an economy. Employment and output have both fallen without much change in the general price level. As such it calls into question whether the economy has been operating around equilibrium. Hence there is no reason why future returns will have any relationship to historical returns. Indeed, the data described in Chapter 6 demonstrates that the US and European economies were in fact operating at levels substantially above equilibrium for the last 20 years or so. Thus it should not be surprising that there is a great deal of evidence that markets at the macro level are not efficient. Investors have behaved rationally only to the extent that they believed in the Great Myth, a Myth that prioritised an analysis of inflation and largely ignored credit.

However, ignoring credit turned out to be a rather large flaw as the last decade coincided with one of the largest credit bubbles in the history of financial markets. Excess credit expansion led to an unsustainable rise in capital values, which in turn resulted in capital destruction and investors losing trillions. Credit is inherently unstable, and given it is the driving force of the modern capitalist economy, an economy will not naturally tend towards equilibrium. As the crisis has worsened, the criticism of current macroeconomic theory from many parts of the industry has grown. However, as of yet nothing has taken its place. That leaves investors in a quandary as to how best to allocate their assets to generate returns when they know the existing framework they have been using no longer works. Moreover, it also calls into question the utility of standard index benchmarks, given that future returns remain uncertain without any necessary connection to the past.

However, alternative macroeconomic theories based on credit do exist, upon which a new investment paradigm can be constructed. During the first half of the 20th century a body of economic thought based on the nature of credit originating from the ideas of Knut Wicksell was developed and systematised. Wicksell's model, which was the first credit-based economic theory, described the nature of equilibrium for a credit economy, whereby the cost of capital equalled the return on capital. As the logic of this argument was taken forward by Hayek and then Myrdal, the view that the economy was in a natural state of dynamic disequilibrium became clear, meaning that there are no equilibrating tendencies. However, an equilibrium based on Wicksell's two rates of interests can be measured, providing investors with the general trend of the business cycle.

With a credit-based foundation in place, investors can now reject current monetary policy with its ideas that inflation targeting leads to macroeconomic stability, thus maintaining the economy oscillating around equilibrium. The fact that future returns have no necessary connection with historical returns has therefore substantial implications for the way in which pension assets are managed. One approach to the problem of pension deficits would be to develop business cycle investment products which have capital preservation as central to their strategy. The ability to measure and monitor the business cycle thus allows an investment product to be constructed that can provide equity-like returns with a substantially lower volatility. This is predicated on a simple annualised switching strategy between equities and bonds based on the rate of growth of excess profits which is linked to the growth in credit.

What this approach cannot do is to predict when the cycle will turn. An economy is a complex dynamic system and can shift dramatically even with very small changes. As such the turning points are identified in analysing streams of macro and credit-related indicators. This is similar to the approach that the natural sciences took in the 1970s when scientists gave up trying to model complex dynamical systems moving towards the analysis of patterns in data instead. Thus streams of macro and credit-related data need to be fed into the asset allocation process to signal to investors when to move out of equities into bonds and vice versa.

The implication of this approach is that what matters is capital. The ultimate owners of capital today are of course mostly savers through their pension holdings, which are attempting to generate future income streams to provide a decent standard of living when they are unable to work. The preservation of capital is thus crucial for pensioners and tax payers, which a simple switching strategy between equities and bonds based on a number of factors including credit growth can facilitate. The framework also provides signals identifying which countries are actively pursuing policies of capital destruction and which ones are in favour of capital creation. Country asset allocation strategies can therefore be established to prioritise investment in those countries that are focussed on capital preservation rather than relying on real GDP forecasts which have not been of much help.

As the demand grows from pension schemes to improve returns with lower volatility, the investment management sector will need to fundamentally change its approach to investment. This will require the industry to reject the current monetary framework based on price stability and general equilibrium, and embrace a credit-based dynamic disequilibrium framework instead. Hopefully in the next few years the fund management sector will begin to introduce low-cost business cycle tracker funds: index funds based on a foundation of credit disequilibrium rather than the myth of price stability and general equilibrium.

Chapter 9

Post-script – Constructing business cycle tracking funds

The analysis in this book demonstrates that increasing leverage is the driving force of an economy fuelling the growth in profits. In essence it is debt that drives equity values as increasing leverage filters through to higher profits and rising capital values. However, increasing levels of debt are unsustainable as the rate of profit will eventually slow down, thus when economic agents begin to deleverage it impacts equity values. Although this trend can be observed, the turning point of a cycle when agents begin to deleverage and the profit expectations have shifted cannot be predicted. An analysis of multiple streams of macro and credit-related data does however highlight shifting expectations. The challenge of course is how can fund managers take advantage of this analytical framework in order to generate less volatile returns for the pension sector by preserving capital through the business cycle?

One key conclusion in the analysis was the distinction between the efficiency of markets at the micro level versus the macro level. There remains compelling evidence that EMH does still hold at the micro level. Indeed, this formed the basis of the passive management revolution of index funds founded by John Bogle of Vanguard Asset Management. Bogle argued that the prevailing structure within asset management gave rise to a potential conflict between fund shareholders and the operating fund management company seeking to grow profits by providing portfolio management services. As such the products offered by the fund management industry seemed far from ideal in being able to provide individuals with quality savings products for their retirement. Critically he believed that the ability of a fund to consistently outperform the market was remote. This claim went back to his student days at Princeton, where he wrote a thesis which concluded that mutual funds should 'make no claim for superiority over the market averages'.[1] Bogle's view was based on the notion that given all investors as a group are the market, they cannot as a group outpace the market. These ideas were shared by Professor Samuelson at MIT and Charles Ellis of Greenwich Associates who argued in 1975 that in the previous decade 85 per cent of institutional investors had underperformed the return of the S&P 500 index.

Since Bogle set his index funds up, a great debate has developed between the merits of active investment, where a fund management company uses its skill to select stocks and time the market to beat the index, versus passive management. Passive management requires no stock selection process or skill, and provides the returns of the index which is a proxy for the market. The challenge for an active manager is that to consistently beat the market over a significant time period is difficult. Indeed, the vast bulk of academic studies have found that most actively managed mutual funds should be avoided.[2] As a leading investment professional once quipped, 'Who still believes markets don't work? Apparently it is only the North Koreans, the Cubans and active fund managers.'[3] However, there is evidence that it is possible to consistently outperform the market, the problem being that given this is such a rarity, it is hard for savers to know who that star performer is going to be.[4] It is not that fund managers are not able to pick good companies, they are. The problem is that it is quite difficult to avoid picking bad companies and it is the bad companies that can often bring down the returns. This is why many academics and index providers have argued that in the long run investors are better off investing in index funds. There are of course numerous trading strategies besides under-weighting/overweighting companies in an equity or bond index that can beat the market. However, in general these strategies do not scale sufficiently to take on a large amount of assets.

Although EMH seems to hold at the micro level, there is a great deal of compelling evidence that EMH does not hold at the macro level. Thus the opportunity to invest through the business cycle needs to be driven at the macro level through asset allocation. Indeed, the successful hedge fund managers who have been able to invest through the cycle are the global macro funds who place bets on under-valued asset classes by going long, whilst shorting over-valued asset classes. Indeed, empirical evidence backs up this approach as being central to generating excess returns.

It's all in the allocation

A study published in 1986 highlighted that getting the asset allocation right accounted for more than 93 per cent of return variance with stock selection and market timing the other contributors.[5] Although this number is still debated somewhat, asset allocation is without doubt the core of generating excess returns. One of the best examples of a successful asset allocation investment strategy is Jim Rogers' commodities fund that he set up in 1998. Rogers argued that commodities were due for a booming super-cycle because of increasing demand from emerging market countries. The nature of the super-cycle is related to the fact that it takes so long to increase supply in the sector. If $100 had been invested in commodities, UK equities and UK government bonds in 1998, by 2010 equities would have returned $118, government bonds (gilts) $128 with Jim Rogers' commodities fund well over $400.[6] Brinson et al's argument is thus well made. The decision to overweight commodities would have generated most of the return than any effort focussed on improving individual stock or bond selection. The challenge of course is deciding when to invest and in which asset classes.

Although investors who decided to put money in equities in 1998 would have lost out, historically equities have outperformed other asset classes, including government bonds. Indeed, over the last 50 years, an investment in equities would have generated an annual real rate of return of 5.8 per cent in the United States compared to US government bonds at 2.9 per cent. Over the period this would have generated a difference in money returns around four times higher. The problem with equity markets is that they are extremely volatile. The peaks of the dot-com boom in 2000 led to a falling market until 2003. The market then rose until 2007 falling again in 2009 before getting back on an upward trajectory. Such volatility is bad for two main reasons. Firstly, it highlights why the return on equities over the last decade has been poor. Secondly those retirees who need to cash in their portfolio might see dramatic changes in the value of their retirement fund – and usually for the worst. For example, anyone who had the luck of retiring in 1999 based on an equity portfolio started in 1960 would have generated returns of 7.7 per cent per annum, over 50 per cent more per annum than the person who retired in 2008, which generated returns of only 5.1 per cent per annum.[7]

Significant drops in retirement income can cause pensioner poverty, broader social issues as well as feeding back negatively into the economy. Although investors in equity index tracker funds would on the whole have seen better returns than actively managed equity funds over the last decade, the returns would still have been way below expectations. Indeed, those opting for a government bond index tracker would have done better and those who invested in Jim Rogers' commodity index fund would have earned a substantially larger amount. Although index funds are revolutionising the industry by taking costs out and handing those returns back to investors, getting asset allocation right is by far the most important aspect of investing.

So what can be done about the risk return paradigm to ensure that low-cost products can be offered that generate equity-like returns, but are less volatile through avoiding the peaks and troughs of the business cycle? Let's assume we now have a crystal ball and know in which year equities will outperform and in which year bonds will outperform. If we decide to move money between the two asset classes based on the strongest performance for that particular year, the average annual real return for the United States is 15.3 per cent from 1986. This is substantially higher than the equities figure of 6.8 per cent and 5.1 per cent for government bonds.[8] The idea of tactical asset allocation – or switching between asset classes to outperform standard benchmarks – has been around for several decades, but in general has fallen short of its promise. There are a handful of successful funds in the space but they tend to charge high fees and do not appear to be able to scale effectively. For those investors switching between equities and government bonds, one of the biggest challenges is related to how one values the equity market, as it is this valuation that in effect triggers the buy/sell order for the fund.

Theories of equity valuations are numerous and have led to a large equity research market developing. One of the investment strategies that has been in operation at the stock level for many years is a micro version of Wicksell's theory. This is where fund managers go long on companies whose cost of capital is much lower than their return on capital and short on those whose cost of capital is higher than their return on capital. The challenge with stock selection of course is that good companies can become bad companies sometimes quite quickly; thus, getting the asset allocation right remains a potentially more profitable approach.

The empirical analysis conducted in Chapter 6 demonstrated the close relationship between the Wicksellian Differential and the equity market, indicating that the Wicksellian Differential can be used as an ex-post benchmark for tactical asset allocation. To see how well the Wicksellian Differential functions as an investment indicator, it was used as a trigger to buy either equities or bonds based on whether the Differential itself was in growth mode or in decline. The time series from 1986 shows that the Wicksellian Differential generated an annualised real return of 8.2 per cent, which is substantially higher than the 6.8 per cent for equities as published by Barclays. It is worth noting that the returns of the switching strategy are slightly over stated given the costs of switching between index funds, although between 1986 and 2010 this only happened nine times. Of more interest, however, was the volatility of the returns. The standard deviation over the mean (relative standard deviation) generated a figure of 1.73 which is in fact significantly lower than the standard deviation of the real returns to US government bonds which was 2.10. The volatility of equities was much higher at 2.72.

The returns based on the movement of the Wicksellian Differential of 8.2 per cent not only outperformed equities but they did so by investing in bonds between 1996 and 1999, when the US stock market almost tripled. This was because the rate of profit growth was falling, thus indicating an investment in government bonds. The fact that equity prices maintained their rise for four years as profits were declining is a clear indication of irrational exuberance where asset prices become decoupled from fundamentals. In 1996 Alan Greenspan in a now famous speech posed the question, 'How do we know when irrational exuberance has unduly escalated asset values which then become subject to unexpected and prolonged contractions?'[9] The answer is pretty straightforward using a neo-Wicksellian analysis. However, such an asset bubble clearly provides issues for those investors who believed that equities were going through a classic bubble. Throughout the dot-com boom, those investors who believed that it was a bubble and stayed in bonds were heavily criticised by other market participants as 'not getting' the new economy, an economy in which the rate of profit was falling. Indeed, many savers decided to pull their money out of bearish funds and allocate them to tech funds instead. The result of this was that these savers wiped out a very large portion of their initial capital. Pension funds need to ensure that they can maintain consistent positive returns in the long run, and it is hard to see how that can be achieved without a sufficient focus on the preservation of capital.

One such strategy is to switch between bonds and equities driven by the Wicksellian Differential, which is based on 40 years of research by numerous economists at the turn of the 20th century. This neo-Wicksellian macroeconomic framework provides a universal explanation of the business cycle, something that new neoclassical theory has failed to do as it assumed an economy was oscillating around its equilibrium. Furthermore, the empirical data is also compelling. Thus it is possible to construct a low-cost investment product that invests through the business cycle providing equity-like returns with significantly less volatility.

Although the ex-post Wicksellian Differential indicator looks promising as an investment trigger for an equity-like return and bond-like volatility product, it is of course the ex-ante signals that matter due to the time delay in calculating the ex-post data. Chapter 6 looked in some detail at the various factors that help explain the ex-ante expectations of the Wicksellian Differential, including leverage ratios. The challenge now is to therefore use the ex-ante framework to show that expectations of profit growth have shifted from positive to negative or vice versa to act as the actual trigger to switch between equities and bonds.

Ex-ante signalling

The rise or fall of the Wicksellian Differential is due to the change in the rate of growth of profits, which influences economic agents' expectations of future profits and an agents' appetite for leverage over time. However, there is no reason to assume that an economic agents' expectations of appetite for leverage will have any bearing on previous levels, given economic conditions are constantly changing. For example after the early 1980s recession consumers started to leverage up from a debt to income ratio of 62 per cent, after the early 1990's recession from 82 per cent and in 2000 it was 90 per cent. Moreover, we know that these factors display highly non-linear relationships through time with the Wicksellian Differential itself. Hence, the main challenge is to aggregate the various streams of data on changing expectations of leverage in conjunction with the macro indicators as described in Chapter 5. So how does this work in practice?

An investor wants to make a decision in January whether to invest in equities or government bonds for that year. In order to make the decision on whether to buy equities or bonds, the latest actual leverage data is compiled with the macroeconomic indicators. In general it is preferable to use monthly data whose publication is lagged only by a month, limiting the time by which data inputs lag the real world. Actual data is required as the idea that these factors can be forecasted or one can find a leading indicator using econometric analysis is flawed, as was discussed in Chapter 2. Critically the factors need to be given a relative weighting as the leveraging of different agents has a different impact on the rate of profit growth. This weighting is dynamic as the relationship of each factor to the rate of profit changes through time. This is particularly important for the macroeconomic factors which, when stable, have limited impact on the rate of growth. It is only when the general price level or output per worker changes significantly that it impacts the profit rate in any meaningful way. Once the weightings have been compiled we need to aggregate all the individual changes into a single indicator providing the binary investment signal. One way of monitoring the output is to use an abstract mathematical system known as a phase space. This was the approach that Robert Shaw used to plot the nature of the dripping tap.

A phase space is a way of representing the relationship between a series of dynamic variables and the last known value. The advantage of the phase space is that it generates on a real-time basis an aggregated market signal from all independent variables in relation to the last known signal. In this instance, the latest indicators reflecting the most recent views on future expected profits can now be plotted against the previous year's ex-post Wicksellian Differential, providing the investor with the binary trigger, whether it is rising or falling. This information would also reflect the previous year's ex-post actuals as well. For instance, once it becomes known that last year's profits were falling across the board and a company's expectation of consumption has fallen, the company might decide to cut back, which would lead to lower leverage levels due to falling expectations. Indeed, that was largely the picture during the dot-com boom. The excess liquidity generated by the Wicksellian cumulative process was being poured into tech stocks instead. The ex-ante forecast and the ex-post actual are highly unlikely ever to equal each other once the ex-post figure is calculated, however, the investment process is only interested in the trend itself rather than attempting to forecast next year's Wicksellian Differential to any degree of certainty.

The phase space analysis can then be validated by a number of other approaches. Firstly, a calculation can be made of the extent of long-term memory using the last known equilibrium position as a reference point as it is the extent of a cumulative process that generates long-term memory. The output of the Hurst Exponent calculation based on tick data can provide a useful validation indicator. The main challenge with these kinds of calculations is the confidence levels of the output, which is largely a function of the number of observations. Finally, it remains important to monitor the slow, changing nature of factors that can increase or reduce productivity and availability of credit that would therefore impact future profit rates.

Although this system has been developed to provide low-cost index funds, it can also generate market signals for active investors too. Clearly each active investor will have a different approach as to which trade might be the most appropriate. For example, the divergence between the growth in the rate of profit and equity markets in the 1990s was a clear signal of an asset bubble, or capital values diverging from underlying fundamentals. There are many cases of active investors recognising bubbles as such, and riding the wave successfully. The key is to ensure that one gets out in time as Cantillon did during the South Sea bubble. There is nothing irrational about investing in a bubble. The challenge is to ensure that the assets can be liquidated before the turning point, thus allowing the assets to be shorted as well.

Capital preserving asset allocation strategies based on the current monetary framework are almost impossible to achieve, because the underlying economic theory states that rational expectations and general equilibrium will eliminate any such deviations reasonably quickly. However, the EMH data at the macro level is not at all compelling. Investors like Soros have assumed that the world is more akin to a dynamic disequilibrium system which provides a better framework for profitable asset allocations strategies. Wicksell's credit-based framework permits the extent of disequilibrium to be measured, thus allowing investment strategies to preserve capital through the business cycle. Such strategies can provide pension schemes with the returns they need, eliminating the massive volatility that has so plagued pension fund returns in recent years.

Notes

Introduction

1. R. Novy-Marx and J. Rauh (2010) 'Public Pension Promises: How Big Are They And What Are They Worth', p. 5.
2. www.usgovernmentspending.com
3. OECD Pensions Outlook (2012), p. 20.
4. M. Lewis (2010) *The Big Short* (Penguin Books).
5. OCED Pensions Outlook, p. 20.
6. IMF Global Financial Stability Report (2011), See Chapter 2.
7. 'Minutes of the Federal Open Market Committee' (27–28 June 2007), http://www.federalreserve.gov/
8. 'Introductory Statement' (6 June 2007), http://www.ecb.int
9. Datastream Total Market Indices.
10. 'More of a Low Rumble', (22 August 2007) www.economist.com
11. Fitch Solutions CDS Indices www.fitchsolutions.com, Markit iTraxx & CDX Indices, www.markit.com
12. 'Fund Industry Overpaid by $1,300 bn' (3 April 2011), www.ft.com
13. H. Minsky (2008) *Stabilising an Unstable Economy* (McGraw Hill); J. Stiglitz & B Greenwald (2003) *Towards a New Paradigm in Monetary Economics* (Cambridge University Press).
14. W. White (2006) 'Is Price Stability Enough?', www.bis.org
15. W. Buiter (2009) 'The Unfortunate Uselessness of Most State of the Art Academic Monetary Economics', www.ft.com
16. J. Kay (2011) 'Economics: Rituals of Rigour', www.ft.com

1 The Great Moderation and the unravelling of a Great Myth

1. K. Popper (1974) *Objective Knowledge: An Evolutionary Approach* (Oxford University Press), p. 266.
2. M. Friedman (1968) 'The Role of Monetary Policy', *The American Economic Review*, Vol. 58, No. 1, pp. 1–17, p. 12.
3. J-C. Trichet, 'Remarks at the Farewell Event' (19 October 2011) www.ecb.int
4. C. Reinhart and K. Rogoff (2009) *This Time Is Different* (Princeton University Press), p. 181.
5. The Federal Reserve System: Purposes and Functions (2005) www.federalreserve.gov, p. 15.
6. J. Locke (1691) 'Some Considerations of the Consequences of the Lowering of Interest and the Raising the Value of Money', http://www.economics.mcmaster.ca/
7. J. Law (1705) 'Money and Trade Considered with a Proposal for Supplying the Nation with Money', Chapter 2, http://www.economics.mcmaster.ca/
8. R. Cantillon (1755) *An Essay on the Nature of Trade in General*, Book II, Chapter VI, http://www.economics.mcmaster.ca/

9. Cantillon, *Essay*, Book II, Chapter VII.
10. D. Ricardo (1951) *The Works and Correspondence of David Ricardo*, Ed. P. Sraffa, Vol. 10, 'As Loan Contractor', http://oll.libertyfund.org./
11. D. Ricardo (1995) *On the Principles of Political Economy and Taxation* (Cambridge University Press), p. 88.
12. Ricardo, *Principles*, pp. 164–165.
13. L. Walras (2010) *Elements of Pure Economics* (Routledge), p. 47.
14. Walras, *Elements*, p. 224.
15. Walras, *Elements*, p. 327.
16. I. Fisher (1971) *The Purchasing Power of Money* (Augustus M. Kelley), p. 156.
17. Fisher, *Purchasing*, p. 95.
18. Fisher, *Purchasing*, p. 155.
19. Fisher, *Purchasing*, p. 55.
20. J.M. Keynes (1993) *The General Theory of Employment, Interest and Money* (Macmillan and Cambridge University Press) p. 300.
21. Keynes, *General Theory*, p. 305.
22. Keynes, *General Theory*, p. 305.
23. Keynes *General Theory*, p. 299.
24. Keynes *General Theory*, p. 172.
25. A.W. Phillips (1958) 'The Relationship between Unemployment and the Rate of the Change of Money, Wage Rates in the United Kingdom 1861–1957', *Economica*, Vol. 25, No. 100, pp. 283–299, p. 291.
26. G. Selgin (1997) *Less Than Zero* (Institute of Economic Affairs), pp. 49–53.
27. J. Stiglitz (2008) 'The Failure of Inflation Targeting', www.Project syndicate.com
28. G. Mankiw (2006) 'The Macroeconomist as Scientist and Engineer', p. 16.
29. Mankiw, 'Macroeconomist', p. 21.
30. F. Canova and L. Gambetti (2008) 'Structural Changes in the US Economy: Is There a Role for Monetary Policy?'.
31. R. Solow (2010) 'Prepared Statement to House Committee on Science and Technology'.
32. M. Hume and A. Sentence (2009) 'The Global Credit Boom: Challenges for Macroeconomics and Policy', www.bankofengland.co.uk
33. C. Borio (2011) 'Central Banking Post Crisis, What Compass for Unchartered waters?', www.bis.org

2   From model failures to streams of data

1. J.M. Keynes (1993) *The General Theory of Employment, Interest and Money* (Macmillan Cambridge University Press), p. 33.
2. B. Bernanke (2005) 'The Global Saving Glut and the US Current Account Deficit', www.federalreserve.gov
3. Bernanke, Saving Glut.
4. B. Bernanke (2009) 'Financial Reform to Address Systemic Risk March', www.federalreserve.gov
5. C. Borio and P. Disyatat (2011) 'Global Imbalances and the Financial Crisis May', www.bis.org, Footnote 3.
6. Borio and Disyatat, 'Global Imbalances', p. 3.
7. J. Taylor (2007) 'Housing and Monetary Policy', www.kansascityfed.org

8. 'The Federal Reserve Purposes & Functions', www.federalreserve.org, p. 24.
9. Federal Reserve Purposes & Functions, p. 22.
10. A. Orphanides and S. Norden (1999) 'The Reliability of Output Gap Estimates in Real Time', www.federalreserve.gov
11. Monetary Bulletin (2005) 'Economic and Monetary Developments and Prospects', Appendix 2, www.cb.is
12. J. Twaddle (2005) 'Evaluating Starting Point Output Gap Estimate Errors', www.rbnz.gov.nz
13. R. Solow and J. Taylor (1999) *Inflation, Unemployment and Monetary Policy* (MIT Press), pp. 50–52.
14. M. Desai (1981) *Testing Monetarism* (Frances Pinter), p. 18.
15. E. Van Der Merwe (2004) 'Inflation Targeting in South Africa', www.resbank. co.za; J. Gregorio (2010) 'Recent Challenges of Inflation Targeting', www. bis.org
16. A. Galesi and M. Lombardi (2009) 'External Shocks and International Inflation Linkages', www.ecb.int; S. Snyder (2007) 'The Role of Inflation Targeting in Macroeconomic Effects of Oil Shocks: Evidence from Canada and Australia'.
17. C. Borio and A. Filardo (2007) 'Globalisation and Inflation: New Cross-country Evidence on the Global Determinants of Domestic Inflation', www.bis.org; 'How Has Globalization Affected Inflation' (2006) *World Economic Outlook 2006*, www.imf.org
18. S. Nickell (2005) 'Why Has Inflation Been So Low Since 1999?', www.nuffield. ox.ac.uk; Figure 3, CPI Goods Prices & 18a Imported goods.
19. R. Edge and R. Gurkaynak (2011) 'How Useful Are Estimated DSGE Model Forecasts', www.federalreserve.gov
20. M. Friedman and A. Schwartz (1993) *A Monetary History of the United States* (Princeton University Press). See Chart 62 particularly between 1870 and 1900 and the 1920s.
21. Friedman and Schwartz, *Monetary History*, p. 676.
22. P. Drucker (1994) *The Practice of Management* (Butterworth Heinemann), p. 45.
23. The Economist (6 August 2009) In Defence of the Dismal Science.
24. R. Thaler (1998) 'Giving Markets a Human Dimension', *Mastering Finance* (Financial Times), p. 193.
25. R. Shiller (2000) *Irrational Exuberance* (Princeton University Press), p. 44.
26. J. Campbell, A. Lo and C. Mackinlay (1997) *The Econometrics of Financial Markets* (Princeton University Press), p. 33.
27. P. Samuelson (1998) 'Summing up on Business Cycles: Opening Address', www.bostonfed.org
28. B. Mandelbrot and R. Hudson (2004) *The (Mis)behaviour of Markets* (Basic Books), pp. 200–202.
29. J. Jung and R. Shiller (2006) 'Samuelson's Dictum and the Stock Market', www. econ.yale.edu
30. J. Kay (2011) 'Economics: Rituals of Rigour', www.ft.com
31. W. Buiter (2009) 'The Unfortunate Uselessness of Most State of the Art Academic Monetary Economics', www.ft.com
32. J. Gleick (1988) *Chaos: Making a New Science* (Viking), p. 263.
33. Gleick, *Chaos*, p. 298, quoting Arnold Mandell.
34. Mandelbrot and Hudson, *(Mis)behaviour*, p. 28.

35. W. Barnett, R. Gallant, M. Hinich, M. Jensen and J. Jungeilges (1996) 'Comparisons of the Available Tests for Non-linearity and Chaos', in W. Barnett, G. Gandolfo and C. Hillinger (eds), *Dynamic Disequilibrium Modeling* (Cambridge University Press), p. 313.
36. C. Kyrtsou and C. Vorlow (2009) 'Modelling Non-Linear Co-movements between Time Series', *Journal of Macroeconomics*, Vol. 31, No. 1, pp. 200–211, p. 3.
37. C. Goodhart and B. Hofmann (2008) 'House Prices, Money, Credit and the Macroeconomy', www.ecb.int, p. 6.
38. C. Borio (2011) 'Central Banking Post Crisis: What Compass for Uncharted Waters?', www.bis.org, p. 10.
39. M. Friedman (1970) *The Optimum Quantity of Money* (Macmillan and Co), p. 189.
40. S. Homer and R. Sylla (2005) *A History of Interest Rates* (John Wiley & Sons), p. 17.

3 The problem of credit

1. C. Borio, N. Kennedy, S. Prowse (1994) 'Exploring Aggregate Asset Price Fluctuations Across Countries', www.bis.org, p. 67.
2. C. Borio and P. Lowe (2002) 'Asset Prices, Financial and Monetary Stability: Exploring the Nexus', www.bis.org; C. Borio, C. Furfine and P. Lowe (2001) 'Procyclicality of the Financial System and Financial Stability: Issues and Policy Options', www.bis.org; C. Goodhart (1995) 'Price Stability and Financial Fragility', in K. Sawamoto, Z. Nakajima and H. Taguchi (eds), *Financial Stability in a Changing Environment* (St. Martin's Press), pp. 439–510; B. Hofman (2001) 'The Determinants of Private Sector Credit in Industrialised Countries', www.bis.org; C. Goodhart, B. Hofman and M. Segoviano (2006) 'Default, Credit Growth and Asset Prices', www.imf.org; IMF World Economic Outlook (2000) www.imf.org; C. Goodhart and B. Hofman (2008) 'House Prices, Money, Credit and the Macroeconomy', www.ecb.int; T. Aubrey (2003) 'UK House Price Volatility'.
3. E. Mendoza and M Terrones (2008) 'An Anatomy of Credit Booms', www.federalreserve.org, p. 13.
4. Mendoza and Terrones, 'Anatomy', p. 21.
5. Goodhart and Hofman, 'House Prices'.
6. R. Merton (1974) 'On the Pricing of Corporate Debt: The Risk Structure of Interest Rates', *Journal of Finance*, Vol. 29, pp. 449–470.
7. R. Jarrow and S. Turnbull (1995) 'Pricing Derivatives on Securities Subject to Credit Risk', *Journal of Finance*, Vol. 1, No.1, pp. 53–85.
8. N. Taleb (2007) *The Black Swan: The Impact of the Highly Improbable* (Allen Lane).
9. G. Soros (1998) *The Crisis of Global Capitalism* (Little Brown & Company), pp. 41–42.
10. J. Stiglitz and B. Greenwald (2003) *Towards a New Paradigm in Monetary Economics* (Cambridge University Press).
11. Stiglitz and Greenwald, *Monetary Economics*, p. 104.
12. Stiglitz and Greenwald, *Monetary Economics*, p. 274.
13. C. Reinhart and K. Rogoff (2009) *This Time Is Different* (Princeton University Press), See Chapter 10.
14. Stiglitz and Greenwald, *Monetary Economics*, p. 207.

15. Stiglitz and Greenwald, *Monetary Economics*, p. 226.
16. Stiglitz and Greenwald, *Monetary Economics*, p. 37.
17. M. Miller and F. Modigliani (1958) 'The Cost of Capital, Corporation Finance and the Theory of Investment', *The American Economic Review*, Vol. 48, No. 3 (Jun., 1958), pp. 261–297.
18. Stiglitz and Greenwald, *Monetary Economics*, p. 134. Quoting Mayer who argued that about 70 per cent of investment comes from retained earnings, 20 per cent from debt and the rest equity/other.
19. Stiglitz and Greenwald, *Monetary Economics*, p. 176.
20. T. Aubrey (2010) *Inflation, Sluggish Growth, Disco and Flares: Will These Define the Next Decade?* (Thomson Reuters).
21. Stiglitz and Greenwald, *Monetary Economics*, p. 245.
22. Stiglitz and Greenwald, *Monetary Economics*, p. 201.
23. Stiglitz and Greenwald, *Monetary Economics*, p. 181.
24. Stiglitz and Greenwald, *Monetary Economics*, p. 294.
25. Stiglitz and Greenwald, *Monetary Economics*, p. 296.
26. Stiglitz and Greenwald, *Monetary Economics*, p. 239.
27. H. Minsky (2008) *Stabilising An Unstable Economy* (McGraw Hill), p. 11.
28. Minksy, *Unstable Economy*, pp. 112–113.
29. Minksy, *Unstable Economy*, p. 131.
30. Minksy, *Unstable Economy*, p. 338.
31. Minksy, *Unstable Economy*, p. 191.
32. Minksy, *Unstable Economy*, p. 237.
33. Minksy, *Unstable Economy*, p. 218.
34. Minksy, *Unstable Economy*, p. 253.
35. Minksy, *Unstable Economy*, p. 296.
36. Minksy, *Unstable Economy*, p. 250.
37. Minksy, *Unstable Economy*, p. 278.
38. Minksy, *Unstable Economy*, p. 272.
39. J.M. Keynes (1993) *The General Theory of Employment, Interest and Money* (Macmillan; Cambridge University Press), pp. 315–316.
40. Keynes, *General Theory*, p. 317.
41. Keynes, *General Theory*, p. 322.
42. Keynes, *General Theory*, p. 321.

4 The Vienna and Stockholm schools: A dynamic disequilibrium approach

1. F. Hayek (1966) *Monetary Theory and the Trade Cycle* (Augustus M. Kelley), p. 106.
2. C. Kindleberger and R. Aliber (2011) *Manias, Panics and Crashes* (Palgrave Macmillan); See Chapter 2.
3. E. Mendoza and M. Terrones (2008) 'An Anatomy of Credit Booms', www.federalreserve.org
4. M. Desai (1995) 'Kaldor between Hayek and Keynes, or Did Nicky Kill Capital Theory?' in M. Desai, *Macroeconomics and Monetary Theory: The Selected Essays of Meghnad Desai* (Elgar), p. 257.
5. C. Menger (2011) *Principles of Economics* (Terra Libertas), p. 16.
6. Menger, *Principles*, p. 51.
7. Menger, *Principles*, pp. 67–71.

8. Menger, *Principles*, pp. 257–285.
9. E. Bohm-Bawerk (1959) *Capital and Interest* (Libertarian Press); see Section XII in Book 1 on Exploitation Theory.
10. Bohm-Bawerk, *Capital*; See especially Book 1, Chapter 1 and Book II, Chapter 2.
11. Bohm-Bawerk, *Capital*, Book II, Chapters 2 and 4.
12. Bohm-Bawerk, *Capital*, Book II, p. 48.
13. Bohm-Bawerk, *Capital*, Book II, p. 114.
14. Bohm-Bawerk, *Capital*, Book II, pp. 290, 300.
15. K. Wicksell (1936) *Interest and Prices* (Macmillan & Co), p. 167.
16. Wicksell, *Interest*, p. 102.
17. Wicksell, *Interest*, p. 107.
18. Wicksell, *Interest*, pp. 116–117.
19. Wicksell, *Interest*, p. 96.
20. Wicksell, *Interest*, p. 189.
21. M. Woodford (2003) *Interest and Prices: Foundations of a Theory of Monetary Policy* (Princeton University Press).
22. Wicksell, *Interest*, p. 175.
23. G. Selgin (1995) 'The "Productivity Norm" versus Zero Inflation in the History of Economic Thought', *History of Political Economy*, Vol. 27, No. 4, p. 713, Table 1.
24. L. Von Mises (1981) *Theory of Money and Credit* (Liberty Fund), p. 164.
25. Mises, *Credit*, p. 378.
26. A. Tebble (2010) *Major Conservative and Libertarian Thinkers – Friedrich Hayek* (Continuum International Publishing), p. 6.
27. F. Hayek (1946) *Prices and Production* (George Routledge & Sons), p. 4.
28. Hayek, *Prices*, p. 11.
29. Hayek, *Prices*, p. 7.
30. F. Hayek (1966) *Monetary Theory and the Trade Cycle* (Augustus M. Kelley), p. 123.
31. Hayek, *Monetary*, p. 113.
32. Hayek, *Monetary*, p. 114.
33. Hayek, *Prices*, p. 28.
34. Hayek, *Prices*, p. 46.
35. Hayek, *Monetary*, p. 107.
36. Hayek, *Monetary*, p. 121.
37. Hayek, *Monetary*, p. 168.
38. Hayek, *Monetary*, p. 173.
39. Hayek, *Monetary*, pp. 201–202.
40. Hayek, *Monetary*, p. 189.
41. F. Hayek (1939) *Profits, Interest and Investment* (George Routledge & Sons), p. 84.
42. R. Garrison (2001) *Time and Money* (Routledge); M. Rothbard (2001) *Man, Economy and State* (Ludwig Von Mises Institute).
43. T. Cowen (1997) *Risk and Business Cycles* (Routledge), p. 29.
44. Hayek, *Profits*, p. 22.
45. Hayek, *Profits*, p. 35.
46. Cowen, *Risk*, p. 3. Quoting studies undertaken by Mayer and Sichel and Berna.
47. Hayek, *Profits*, p. 8.

48. H.M. Trautwein (1994) 'Hayek's Double Failure in Business Cycle Theory', in M. Colonna and H. Hagemann (eds) *Money and Business Cycles: The Economics of FA Hayek* (Elgar Publishing), pp. 79–80.
49. Cowen, *Risk*, p. 13.
50. M. Desai (1995) 'Task of Monetary Theory', in *Macroeconomics and Monetary Theory: The Selected Essays of Meghnad Desai* (Elgar), p. 163.
51. C. Ruhl (1994) 'The Transformation of Business Cycle Theory: Hayek, Lucas and a Change in the Notion of Equilibrium', p. 190 in Colonna and Hagemann (eds) *Money*.
52. Cowen, *Risk*, p. 101.
53. Cowen, *Risk*, p. 149.
54. G. Myrdal (1965) *Monetary Equilibrium* (Augustus M. Kelley), p. 16.
55. Myrdal, *Equilibrium*, p. 81.
56. Myrdal, *Equilibrium*, p. 36.
57. Myrdal, *Equilibrium*, p. 130; see footnote 7 on Davidson's theory.
58. Myrdal, *Equilibrium*, p. 192.
59. Myrdal, *Equilibrium*, p. 90.
60. Myrdal, *Equilibrium*, p. 40.
61. Myrdal, *Equilibrium*, p. 111.
62. Myrdal, *Equilibrium*, pp. 122–123.
63. Myrdal, *Equilibrium*, p. 74.
64. Myrdal *Equilibrium*, p. 159.
65. P. Sraffa (1932) 'Dr. Hayek on Money and Capital', *Economic Journal*, Vol. 42 (March), pp. 42–53.
66. Myrdal, *Equilibrium*, p. 199.
67. Myrdal, *Equilibrium*, p. 200.
68. Myrdal, *Equilibrium*, p. 184.
69. Myrdal, *Equilibrium*, p. 176.
70. 'Minutes of FOMC Meeting 31 January' (2006) Vice Chairman Geithner, p. 55, www.federalreserve.gov
71. Myrdal, *Equilibrium*, p. 195.
72. Myrdal, *Equilibrium*, p. 165.
73. Myrdal, *Equilibrium*, p. 153.
74. Myrdal, *Equilibrium*, p. 180.
75. D. Laidler (1991) 'The Austrians and the Stockholm School: Two Failures?', in L. Jonung (ed.) *The Stockholm School of Economics Revisited* (Cambridge University Press), p. 317.
76. G. Cederwall, 'Comment', in Jonung, *Stockholm*, p. 76.
77. B. Ohlin (1937) 'Some Notes on the Stockholm Theory of Savings and Investments II', *The Economic Journal*, Vol. 47, p. 233.
78. Ohlin, *Notes II*, p. 236.
79. Ohlin, *Notes II*, p. 237.
80. Ohlin, *Notes II*, p. 240.
81. E. Lindahl (1970) *Studies in the Theory of Money and Capital* (Augustus M. Kelley), p. 146.
82. B. Ohlin (1937) 'Some Notes on the Stockholm Theory of Savings and Investments I', *The Economic Journal*, Vol. 47, p. 56.
83. A. Leijonhufvud (1979) 'The Wicksell Connection', www.econ.ucla.edu, pp. 44–45.

84. Leijonhufvud, *Wicksell*, p. 25.
85. Leijonhufvud, *Wicksell*, p. 2.
86. A. Leijonhufvud, 'Comment' in Jonung, *Stockholm*, p. 463.

5 The neo-Wicksellian framework

1. A. Einstein (April 1934) *Philosophy of Science*, Vol. 1, No. 2, pp. 163–169. (Published by University of Chicago Press).
2. G. Mankiw, P. Romer and D. Weil (1992) 'A Contribution to the Empirics of Economic Growth', *The Quarterly Journal of Economics*, Vol. 107, No. 2, pp. 407–437.
3. P. Drucker (1993) *Post Capitalist Society* (Harper Business).
4. M. Desai (1981) *Testing Monetarism* (Frances Pinter).
5. Derived from Datastream indices which provide the largest constituent set over the longest time series in conjunction with the Worldscope database.
6. J. Stiglitz and B. Greenwald (2003) *Towards a New Paradigm in Monetary Economics* (Cambridge University Press), p. 134; Quoting Mayer.
7. A. Damodaran (2011) 'Equity Risk Premiums (ERP): Determinants, Estimation, and Implications', www.stern.nyu.edu; provides an excellent summary of the various methods and approaches.
8. Damodaran, *ERP*. p. 83.
9. Markit CDX & iTraxx indices www.markit.com, Fitch Solutions CDS indices www.fitchsolutions.com. (Prior to launching CDS indices Fitch Solutions analysed the average debt maturity profile of corporate entities rated by Fitch in EMEA which was 5.3 years.)
10. J. Barkley Rosser (1991) *From Catastrophe to Chaos: A General Theory of Economic Discontinuities* (Kluwer), p. 115, quoting Deneckere and Pelikan.
11. Rosser, *Chaos*, p. 322.
12. W. Barnett, R. Gallant, M. Hinich, M. Jensen and J. Jungeilges (1996) 'Comparisons of the Available Tests for Non-linearity and Chaos', in W. Barnett, G. Gandolfo and C. Hillinger (eds), *Dynamic Disequilibrium Modeling*, p. 313.
13. 'Real Effects of High Inflation' (2000), www.imf.org
14. A. Lo and C. Mackinlay (2007) *A Non-Random Walk Down Wall Street* (Princeton University Press), p. 180.
15. T. Di Matteo (2007) 'Multi-scaling in Finance', *Quantitative Finance*, Vol. 7, No. 1, pp. 21–36; Provides an overview of the various methodologies to detect long term memory.
16. E. Peters (1991) *Chaos and Order in the Capital Markets* (John Wiley & Sons).
17. B. Mandelbrot and R. Hudson (2004) *The (Mis)behaviour of Markets* (Basic Books), Chapter 9.
18. R. Morales, T. Di Matteo, R. Gramatica and T. Aste (2012) 'Dynamic Generalised Hurst Exponent as a Tool to Monitor Unstable Periods in Financial Time Series', *Physica A*, Vol. 391, 2012, pp. 3180–3189.
19. C. Mackay (1852) *Memoirs of Extraordinary Popular Delusions and the Madness of Crowds*, www.econlib.org
20. Rosser, *Chaos*, p. 324.
21. C. Goodhart (2 February 2012) 'Longer-term Forecasts Are a Step Backwards', www.ft.com

6 *Testing Wicksellianism*

1. As appeared in the transcript of the 'Interview with Professor Paul A. Samuelson, 1970 Nobel Laureate in Economics', on NBC Radio and Television Program "Meet The Press", 20 December 1970, Daily Report for Executives, 246 DER X-1 (21 December 1970). by The Bureau of National Affairs, Inc.
2. IMF Global Financial Stability Report September (2011) www.imf.org p. 66.
3. E. Dimson, P. Marsh and M. Staunton (2002) *Triumph of the Optimists: 101 Years of Global Investment Returns* (Princeton University Press); J. Ritter (2004) 'Economic growth and Equity Returns', www.ssrn.com; MSCI (2010) 'Is There a Link between GDP Growth and Equity Returns?', www.ssrn.com
4. Ritter *Equity Returns*. p. 4.
5. S. Homer and R. Sylla (2005) *A History of Interest Rates* (John Wiley & Sons), p. 399, Table 53b.
6. R Hawtrey (1932) *The Art of Central Banking* (Longmans) p. 400.
7. C. Phillips, T. MacManus, R. Nelson (1937) *Banking and the Business Cycle: A Study of the Great Depression in the United States*. (Macmillan) p. 127.
8. Phillips, MacManus, Nelson *Banking* p. 123.
9. Hawtrey, *Art*, p. 45.
10. Hawtrey, *Art*, p. 65.
11. Hawtrey, *Art*, p. 47.
12. Homer and Sylla, *Interest*, p. 351, Table 48.
13. Hawtrey, *Art*, p. 68.
14. Phillips, MacManus and Nelson, *Banking*, p. 105.
15. M. Friedman and A. Schwarz (1993) *A Monetary History of the United States 1867–1960* (Princeton University Press), p. 277.
16. Phillips, MacManus and Nelson, *Banking*, p. 136.
17. Phillips, MacManus and Nelson, *Banking*, p. 103.
18. C. Goldin (2006) 'The Quiet Revolution That Transformed Women's Employment, Education, and Family Table', www.nber.org
19. Hawtrey, *Art*, p. 46.
20. Hawtrey, *Art*. p. 77.
21. Phillips, MacManus and Nelson, *Banking*, p. 77.
22. Homer and Sylla, *Interest*, p. 448, Table 59.
23. Barclays Capital Equity & Gilt Study 2012.
24. Musson (1959) 'The Great Depression in Britain 1873–1896: A Reappraisal', *The Journal of Economic History*, Vol. 19, No. 2 (June), pp. 199–228; H. Beales (1934) 'The "Great Depression" in Industry and Trade', *The Economic History Review*, Vol. 5, No. 1 (October), pp. 65–75.
25. Musson, *Depression*, p. 200.
26. G. Selgin (1997) *Less Than Zero* (Institute of Economic Affairs), p. 53.
27. Homer and Sylla, *Interest*, p. 193, Table 19.
28. T. Aubrey (2010) 'Inflation, Sluggish Growth Disco and Flares: Will These Define the Next Decade?' (Thomson Reuters).
29. Ritter, *Equity Returns*, p. 12.
30. C. Bai, C. Hsieh and Y. Qian (2006) 'The Return to Capital in China', www.nber.org
31. Ritter, *Equity Returns*, p. 6.

32. R. Garrison (2001) *Time and Money* (Routledge), pp. 85–89.
33. F. Hayek (1946) *Prices and Production* (George Routledge & Sons), p. 97.
34. P. Drucker (1993) *Post Capitalist Society* (Harper Business), pp. 157–167.
35. http://johnbtaylorsblog.blogspot.com, 2 March 2012, Debating Stimulus and Harvard and Stanford.
36. J. Estrada, M. Kritzman, S. Myrgen and S. Page (2005) 'Countries Versus Industries in Europe: A Normative Portfolio Approach', *Journal of Asset Management*, Vol. 6, pp. 85–103.
37. R. Mundell (1961) 'A Theory of Optimum Currency Areas', *The American Economic Review*, Vol. 51, No. 4, pp. 657–665.

7 The creation and destruction of capital

1. J. Schumpeter (1994) *Capitalism, Socialism and Democracy* (Routledge), pp. 31–32.
2. M. Spiegel (2006) 'Did Quantitative Easing by the Bank of Japan "Work"?', www.frbsf.org
3. BIS Quarterly, p. 3 Review (December 2011) highlights the success of reducing long term bond yields.
4. F. Breedon, J. Chadha and A. Waters (2012) 'The Financial Market Impact of UK Quantitative Easing', www.bis.org
5. 'Open Letter to Ben Bernanke', 15 November 2010, www.wsj.com
6. A. Haldane, S. Brennan and V. Madouros (2010) 'The Contribution of the Financial Sector: Miracle or Mirage?', in *The future of Finance: The LSE Report* (London School of Economics), See charts 23, 24 & 26.
7. H. Hannoun (2010) 'The Basel III Capital Framework: A Decisive Breakthrough', www.bis.org
8. P. Härle, E. Lüders, T. Pepanides, S. Pfetsch, T. Poppensieker and U. Stegemann (2010) 'Basel III and European Banking' (McKinsey & Company).
9. T. Aubrey (2010) 'Inflation, Sluggish Growth, Disco and Flares' (Thomson Reuters).
10. D. Miles, J. Yang and G. Marcheggiano (2011) 'Optimal Bank Capital', www.bankofengland.co.uk
11. P. Slovik and B. Cournède (2011) 'Macroeconomic Impact of Basel III' www.oecd.org
12. Sources: Towers Watson Pension Survey @ www.towerswatson.com, www.bankofengland.co.uk, www.FDIC.gov
13. 'February HY volume hits record', 1 March 2012, www.Reuters.com
14. US International Trade Commission (2010) 'Small and Medium Sized Enterprises: Overview of Participation in US Exports', www.usitc.gov
15. 'Small Companies Create 85% of New Jobs' (16 January 2012) European Commission Press Release, www.ec.europa.eu
16. M. Pittman (27 October 2008) 'Evil Wall Street Exports Boomed with "Fools" Born to Buy Debt', www.bloomberg.com
17. A. Eramo and G. Salleo (2011) 'Securitization Is Not That Evil After All', www.bis.org
18. 'EU Capital Requirements Directive (CRD) Retention Rule and Incentives in Securitisation (2010)', www.FitchRatings.com

19. T. Cowen (2011) *The Great Stagnation* (Dutton), p. 39.
20. 'Education at a Glance: OECD Indicators' (2011), www.oecd.org, Figure 1.1.
21. Education OECD, pp. 87–89.
22. Education OECD, p. 38.
23. JK Galbraith (1987) *Economics in Perspective: A Critical History* (Houghton Mifflin), p. 290.
24. www.r3.org.uk, 'Rent Quarter Day Test for Struggling Businesses', 22 June 2012.
25. A. Afonso, L. Schuknecht and V. Tanzi (2003) 'Public Sector Efficiency: An International Comparison', www.ecb.int
26. 'The Decisive Issue for 2012: The Economy' (2012), www.cnn.com
27. F. Vibert and T. Aubrey (2007) *Prediction Markets: The End of the Regulatory State?* (European Policy Forum).
28. A. Herman (2012) *Freedom's Forge: How American Business Produced Victory in World War II* (Random House).

8   *Where are the customer's yachts?*

1. El Paso Herald, 26 March 1910.

9   *Post script – constructing business cycle tracking funds*

1. J. Bogle (1997) 'The first Index Mutual fund: A History of Vanguard Index Trust and the Vanguard Index Strategy', www.vanguard.com
2. K. Baks, A. Metrick and J. Wachter (2001) 'Should Investors Avoid All Actively Managed Mutual funds? A Study in Bayesian Performance Evaluation', www.finance.wharton.upenn.edu; See footnote 1.
3. Said by Rex Sinquefield at a conference in 1995.
4. Baks, Metrick and Wachter, 'Investors', footnote 2.
5. G. Brinson, L. Hood and G. Beebower (1986) 'Determinants of Portfolio Performance', *The Financial Analysts Journal*, Vol. 42, No. 4 (July/August), pp. 39–44.
6. Barclays Capital Equity Gilt Study 2012, Datastream.
7. Barclays Study.
8. Barclays Study.
9. A. Greenspan (1996) 'The Challenge of Central Banking in a Democratic Society', www.federalreserve.gov

Bibliography

A. Afonso, L. Schuknecht and V. Tanzi (2003) 'Public Sector Efficiency: An International Comparison', www.ecb.int

J. Aizenman, M. Hutchison and I. Noy (2008) 'Inflation Targeting and Real Exchange Rates in Emerging Markets', www.nber.org

E. Albertazzi and S. Gamabacorta (2011) 'Securitization Is Not That Evil After All', www.bis.org

A. Alvarez and V. Bignon (2010) 'L. Walras and C. Menger: Two Ways on the Oath of Modern Monetary Theory', http://economix.u-paris10.fr/

P. Arestis, M. Desai and S. Dow (eds) (2001) *Money, Macroeconomics and Keynes: Essays in Honour of Victoria Chick* (Routledge).

K. Arrow and G. Debreu (1954) 'Existence of an Equilibrium for a Competitive Economy', *Econometrica*, Vol. 22, No. 3 (July), pp. 265–290.

P. Asso, G. Kahn and R. Leeson (2007a) 'Monetary Policy Rules: From Adam Smith to John Taylor', www.dallasfed.org

P. Asso, G. Kahn and R. Leeson (2007b) 'The Taylor Rule and the Transformation of Monetary Policy', www.kc.frb.org

P. Asso, G. Kahn and R. Leeson (2010) 'The Taylor Rule and the Practice of Central Banking', www.kc.frb.org

T. Aubrey (2003) 'UK House Price Volatility'.

T. Aubrey (2010) *Inflation, Sluggish Growth, Disco and Flares* (ThomsonReuters).

T. Aubrey and D. Brigo (2010a) 'Corporate versus Sovereign Debt Risks – Reading CDS and Bond Market Signals', www.fitchratings.com

T. Aubrey and D. Brigo (2010b) 'Greek Bailout: Containment or Contagion? Reading CDS and Bond Market Signals Part 2', www.fitchratings.com

C. Bai, C. Hsieh and Y. Qian (2006) 'The Return to Capital in China', www.nber.org

K. Baks, A. Metrick and J. Wachter (2001) 'Should Investors Avoid All Actively Managed Mutual Funds? A Study in Bayesian Performance Evaluation', www.ssrn.com

L. Ball (1997) 'Efficient Rules for Monetary Policy', www.rbnz.gov.nz

Barclays Capital – Equity Gilt Study 2012 (Barclays Capital).

J. Barkley Rosser (1991) *From Catastrophe to Chaos: A General Theory of Economic Discontinuities* (Kluwer).

W. Barnett, G. Gandolfo and C. Hillinger (eds) (1996) *Dynamic Disequilibrium Modeling* (Cambridge University Press).

H. Beales (1934) 'The "Great Depression" in Industry and Trade', *The Economic History Review*, Vol. 5, No. 1 (October), pp. 65–75.

J. Benhabib, S. Schmitt Grohe and M. Uribe (2002) 'Chaotic Interest Rate Rules', www.nber.org

B. Bernanke (1999) 'Japanese Monetary Policy: A Case of Self-Induced Paralysis', www.princeton.edu

B. Bernanke (2005) 'The Global Saving Glut and the US Current Account Deficit', www.federalreserve.gov

B. Bernanke (2009) 'Financial Reform to Address Systemic Risk March', www.federalreserve.gov

B. Bernanke, M. Gertler and S. Gilchrist (1998) 'The Financial Accelerator in a Quantitative Business Cycle Framework Match', www.nber.org

BIS Quarterly Review, December 2011 www.bis.org

J. Bogle (1997) 'The First Index Mutual Fund: A History of Vanguard Index Trust and the Vanguard Index Strategy', www.vanguard.com

E. Bohm-Bawerk (1959) *Capital and Interest* (Libertarian Press).

M. Boianovksy, H.-M. Trautwein (2004) 'Wicksell after Woodford', www.columbia.edu

C. Borio (2011) 'Central Banking Post-Crisis: What Compass for Uncharted Waters', www.bis.org

C. Borio and P. Disyatat (2011) 'Global Imbalances and the Financial Crisis', www.bis.org

C. Borio and A. Filardo (2007) 'Globalisation and Inflation: New Cross-Country Evidence on the Global Determinants of Domestic Inflation', www.bis.org

C. Borio, C. Furfine and P. Lowe (2001) 'Procyclicality of the Financial System and Financial Stability: Issues and Policy Options', www.bis.org

C. Borio, N. Kennedy and S. Prowse (1994) 'Exploring Aggregate Asset Price Fluctuations across Countries', www.bis.org

C. Borio and P. Lowe (2002) 'Asset Prices, Financial and Monetary Stability: Exploring the Nexus', www.bis.org

F. Breedon, J. Chadha, A. Waters (2012) 'The Financial Market Impact of UK Quantitative Easing', www.bis.org

G. Brinson, L. Hood and G. Beebower (1986) 'Determinants of Portfolio Performance', *The Financial Analysts Journal*, Vol. 42, No. 4 (July/August), pp. 39–44.

G. Brinson, B. Singer and G. Beebower (1991) 'Determinants of Portfolio Performance II: An Update', *Financial Analysts Journal*, Vol. 47, No. 3 (May/June), pp. 40–48.

W. Buiter (1981) 'Macroeconometric Modelling for Policy Evaluation and Design', www.nber.org

W. Buiter (2009) 'The Unfortunate Uselessness of Most "State of the Art" Academic Monetary Economics', www.ft.com

R. Caballero and L. Hammour (1991) 'The Cleansing Effect of Recessions', www.nber.org

J. Campbell, A. Lo and C. Mackinlay (1997) *The Econometrics of Financial Markets* (Princeton University Press).

F. Canova and L Gambetti (2008) 'Structural Changes in the US Economy: Is There a Role for Monetary Policy?', http://www.econ.upf.edu/

R. Cantillon (1755) An *Essay on the Nature of Trade in General* (http://www.economics.mcmaster.ca/)

Central Bank of Iceland, Monetary Bulletin (2005) 'Economic and Monetary Developments and Prospects', Appendix 2, www.cb.is

L. Christiano, M. Eichenbaum and C. Evans (2003) 'Nominal Rigidities and the Dynamic Effects of a Shock to Monetary Policy', www.nber.org

R. Clarida, J. Gali and M. Gertler (1998) 'Monetary Policy Rules in Practice: Some International Evidence', www.nber.org

J. Cochrane (2001) *Asset Pricing* (Princeton University Press).

W. Coleman (2007) 'Inflation without a Quantity of Money: A Simple Wicksellian Model Outline', http://rse.anu.edu.au/cepr.php

M. Colonna and H. Hagemann (1994) *Money and Business Cycles the Economics of FA Hayek Volume I* (Edward Elgar).

A. Cottrell (1994) 'Hayek's Early Cycle Theory Re-examined', *Cambridge Journal of Economics*, Vol. 18, No. 2, pp. 197–212.

T. Cowen (1997) *Risk and Business Cycles* (Routledge).

T. Cowen (2011) *The Great Stagnation* (Dutton).

A. Damodaran (2011) 'Equity Risk Premiums (ERP): Determinants, Estimation and Implications', www.stern.ny.edu

J. De Gregorio (2010) 'Recent Challenges of Inflation Targeting', www.bis.org

G. Debelle (1999) 'Inflation Targeting and Output Stabilisation', www.rba.gov.au

M. Del Negro and F. Schorfheide (2008) 'Inflation Dynamics in a Small Open-Economy Model under Inflation Targeting: Some Evidence from Chile', www.bcentral.cl

M. Desai (1981) *Testing Monetarism* (Frances Pinter).

M. Desai (1995) *Macroeconomics and Monetary Theory: The Selected Essays of Meghnad Desai* (Edward Elgar).

M. Desai (2002) *Marx's Revenge* (Verso).

T. Di Matteo (2007) 'Multi-Scaling in Finance', *Quantitative Finance*, Vol. 7, No. 1, pp. 21–36.

E. Dimson, P. Marsh and M. Staunton (2002) *Triumph of the Optimists: 101 Years of Global Investment Returns* (Princeton University Press).

R. Djoudad, B. Fung, J.-P Lam and D. Poon (2004) 'How Useful Is the Neutral Interest Rate for Monetary Policy in Canada?', www.bankofcanada.ca

P. Drucker (1993) *Post Capitalist Society* (Harper Business).

P. Drucker (1994) *The Practice of Management* (Butterworth Heinemann).

R. Edge and R. Gurkaynak (2011) 'How Useful Are Estimated DSGE Model Forecasts', www.federalreserve.org

R. Edge, M. Kiley and J.P. Laforte (2009) 'A Comparison of Forecast Performance Between Federal Reserve Staff Forecasts, Simple Reduced-Form Models and a DSGE Model', www.federalreserve.org

A. Einstein (April 1934) 'On the Method of Theoretical Physics', *Philosophy of Science*, Vol. 1, No. 2 (University of Chicago Press), pp. 163–169.

A. Eramo and G. Salleo (2011) 'Securitization Is Not That Evil After All', www.bis.org

J. Estrada, M. Kritzman, S. Myrgen and S. Page (2005) 'Countries versus Industries in Europe: A Normative Portfolio Approach', *Journal of Asset Management*, Vol. 6, pp. 85–103.

Federal Reserve Board (1996) 'A guide to FRB/US', www.federalreserve.org

Federal Reserve Board (2005) 'Federal Reserve System: Purposes and Functions', www.federalreserve.org

Federal Reserve Board 'Minutes of FOMC Meetings', www.federalreserve.org

I. Fisher (1971) *The Purchasing Power of Money* (Augustus M. Kelley).

Fitch Ratings (2010) 'EU Capital Requirements Directive Retention Rule Incentives in Securitisation', www.fitchratings.com

M. Friedman (ed.) (1967) *Studies in the Quantity Theory of Money* (University of Chicago Press).

M. Friedman (1968) 'The Role of Monetary Policy', *The American Economic Review*, Vol. 58, No. 1, pp. 1–17, p. 12.

M. Friedman (1970) *The Optimum Quantity of Money* (Macmillan and Co).

M. Friedman and A. Schwartz (1993) *A Monetary History of the United States* (Princeton University Press).

X. Gabaix (2009) 'Power Laws in Economics and Finance', *Annual Review of Economics*, Vol. 1, pp. 255–293.

J.K. Galbraith (1987) *Economics in Perspective: A Critical History* (Houghton Mifflin).

A. Galesi and M. Lombardi (2009) 'External Shocks and International Inflation Linkages', www.ecb.int

J. Gali (2000) 'New Perspectives on Monetary Policy, Inflation and the Business Cycle', www.nber.org

R. Garrison (2001) *Time and Money* (Routledge).

A. Garratt, J. Mitchell and S. Vahey (2009) 'Measuring Output Gap Uncertainty', www.ecb.int

J. Gleick (1988) *Chaos: Making a New Science* (Viking).

C. Goldin (2006) 'The Quiet Revolution That Transformed Women's Employment, Education, and Family Table', www.nber.org

Goldman Sachs Asset Management (2010) 'Rethinking the Active vs Passive Debate', www.goldmansachs.com

Goldman Sachs Asset Management (2011) 'Linking GDP Growth and Equity Returns', www.goldmansachs.com

C. Goodhart (2010a) 'The Changing Role of Central Banks', www.bis.org

C. Goodhart (2010b) 'Money, Credit and Bank Behaviour: Need for a New Approach', *National institute economic review*, Vol. 214, No. 1, pp. F73–F82.

C. Goodhart (2012) 'Longer-Term Forecasts Are a Step Backwards', www.ft.com

C. Goodhart and B. Hofman (2008) 'House Prices, Money, Credit and the Macroeconomy', www.ecb.int

C. Goodhart, B. Hofman and M. Segoviano (2006) 'Default, Credit Growth and Asset Prices', www.imf.org

J. Gregorio (2010) 'Recent Challenges of Inflation Targeting', www.bis.org

H. Hannoun (2010) 'The Basel III Capital Framework: A Decisive Breakthrough', www. bis.org

J. Hartley, K. Hoover and K. Salyer (1997) 'The Limits of Business Cycle Research: Assessing the Real Business Cycle Model', *Oxford Review of Economic Policy*, Vol. 13, No. 3, pp. 34–54.

R Hawtrey (1932) *The Art of Central Banking* (Longmans).

F. Hayek (1939) *Profits, Interest and Investment* (George Routledge & Sons).

F. Hayek (1941) *Pure Theory of Capital* (University of Chicago Press).

F. Hayek (1946) *Prices and Production* (George Routledge & Sons).

F. Hayek (1966) *Monetary Theory and the Trade Cycle* (Augustus M. Kelley).

A. Herman (2012) *Freedom's Forge: How American Business Produced Victory in World War II* (Random House).

B. Hofman (2001) 'The Determinants of Private Sector Credit in Industrialised Countries: Do Property Prices Matter?', www.bis.org

S. Homer and R. Sylla (2005) *A History of Interest Rates* (John Wiley & Sons).

M. Hume and A. Sentence (2009) 'The Global Credit Boom: Challenges for Macroeconomics and Policy', www.bankofengland.co.uk

IMF (2000a) 'Real Effects of High Inflation', www.imf.org

IMF (2000b) 'World Economic Outlook', www.imf.org
IMF (2006) 'How Has Globalization Affected Inflation', in *World Economic Outlook*, www.imf.org
IMF (2011) 'Global Financial Stability Report', www.imf.org
R. Jarrow and S. Turnbull (1995) 'Pricing Derivatives on Securities Subject to Credit Risk', *Journal of Finance*, Vol. 1, No. 1, pp. 53–85.
O. Jenkinson and M. Pollicott (2002) 'Calculating Hausdorff Dimension of Julia Sets and Kleinian Limit Sets', *American Journal of Mathematics*, Vol. 124, No. 3 (June), pp. 495–545.
L. Jonung (ed.) (1991) *The Stockholm School of Economics Revisited* (Cambridge University Press).
J. Jung and R. Shiller (2006) 'Samuelson's Dictum and the Stock Market', www. econ.yale.edu
G. Kahn (2007) 'Communicating a Policy Path: The Next Frontier in Central Bank Transparency', www.kc.frb.org
S. Kamin, M. Marazzi and J. Schindler (2004) 'Is China "Exporting Deflation"?', www.federalreserve.org
H. Kantz and T. Schreiber (2004) *Nonlinear Time Series Analysis* (Cambridge University Press).
J. Kay (2011) 'Economics: Rituals of Rigour', www.ft.com
J.M. Keynes (1993) *The General Theory of Employment, Interest and Money* (Macmillan Cambridge University Press).
J.M. Keynes (2011) A *Treatise on Money* (Martino Publishing).
C. Kindleberger and R. Aliber (2011) *Manias, Panics and Crashes* (Palgrave Macmillan).
H. Kurz and N. Salvadori (2002) 'One Theory or Two? Walras's Critique of Ricardo', *History of Political Economy*, Vol. 34, No. 2 (Summer), pp. 365–398.
F. Kydland and E. Prescott (1982) 'Time to Build and Aggregate Fluctuations', *Econometrica*, Vol. 50, No.6 (November), pp. 1345–1370.
C. Kyrtsou and C. Vorlow (2009) 'Modelling Non-Linear Co-Movements between Time Series', *Journal of Macroeconomics*, Vol. 31, No. 1, pp. 200–211.
D. Laidler (2003) 'The Price Level, Relative Prices and Economic Stability: Aspects of the Interwar Debate', www.bis.org
T. Laubach and J. Williams (2001) 'Measuring the Natural Rate of Interest', www. federalreserve.gov
J. Law (1705) 'Money and Trade Considered with a Proposal for Supplying the Nation with Money', Chapter 2, http://www.economics.mcmaster.ca/
A. Leijonhufvud (1979) 'The Wicksell Connection', www.econ.ucla.edu
M. Lewis (2010) *The Big Short* (Penguin Books).
E. Lindahl (1970) *Studies in the Theory of Money and Capital* (Augustus M. Kelley).
A. Lo and C. Mackinlay (2007) *A Non-Random Walk Down Wall Street* (Princeton University Press).
J. Locke (1691) 'Some Considerations of the Consequences of the Lowering of Interest and the Raising the Value of Money', http://www.economics.mcmaster.ca/
London School of Economics (2010) 'The Future of Finance', www.lse.ac.uk
R. Lucas (1972) 'Expectations and the Neutrality of Money', *Journal of Economic Theory*, Vol. 4, No. 2, pp. 103–124.

R. Lucas (1976) 'Econometric Policy Evaluation; A Critique', *Carnegie-Rochester Conference Series on Public Policy*, Vol. 1, No. 1.

R. Lucas and L. Rapping (1969) 'Real Wages, Employment and Inflation', *Journal of Political Economy*, Vol. 77, No. 5, pp. 721–754.

R. Lucas and T. Sargent (1978) 'After Keynesian Macroeconomics', www.minneapolisfed.org

C. Mackay (1852) 'Memoirs of Extraordinary Popular Delusions and the Madness of Crowds', www.econlib.org

B. Mandelbrot (1997) *Fractals and Scaling in Finance* (Springer).

B. Mandelbrot and R. Hudson (2004) *The (Mis)behaviour of Markets* (Basic Books).

G. Mankiw (2006) 'The Macroeconomist as Scientist and Engineer', www.nber.org

G. Mankiw, P. Romer and D. Weil (1992) 'A Contribution to the Empirics of Economic Growth', *The Quarterly Journal of Economics*, Vol. 107, No. 2, pp. 407–437.

A. Marshall (1923) *Money, Credit and Commerce* (Macmillan and Co).

A. Marshall (1994) *Principles of Economics* (Macmillan Press).

K. Marx (1990) *Capital Volumes I, III* (Penguin Books).

J. Meaning and F. Zhu (2011) 'The Impact of Recent Central Bank Asset Purchase Programmes', www.bis.org

E. Mendoza and M Terrones (2008) 'An Anatomy of Credit Booms', www.federalreserve.org

McKinsey & Company (2010) 'Basel III and European Banking', www.mckinsey.com

C. Menger (2011) *Principles of Economics* (Terra Libertas).

R. Merton (1974) 'On the Pricing of Corporate Debt: The Risk Structure of Interest Rates', *Journal of Finance*, Vol. 29, pp. 449–470.

D. Miles, J. Yang and G. Marcheggiano (2011) 'Optimal Bank Capital', www.bankofengland.co.uk

H. Minsky (2008) *Stabilising An Unstable Economy* (McGraw Hill).

F. Modigliani and M. Miller (1958) 'The Cost of Capital, Corporation Finance and the Theory of Investment', *The American Economic Review*, Vol. 48, No. 3, pp. 261–297.

R. Morales, T. Di Matteo, R. Gramatica and T. Aste (2012) 'Dynamic Generalised Hurst Exponent As a Tool to Monitor Unstable Periods in Financial Time Series', *Physica A*, Vol. 391, pp. 3180–3189.

MSCI (2010) 'Is There a Link between GDP Growth and Equity Returns?', www.ssrn.com

R. Mundell (1961) 'A Theory of Optimum Currency Areas', *The American Economic Review*, Vol. 51, No. 4, pp. 657–665.

A. Musson (1959) 'The Great Depression in Britain 1873–1896: A Reappraisal', *The Journal of Economic History*, Vol. 19, No. 2 (June), pp. 199–228.

G. Myrdal (1965) *Monetary Equilibrium* (Augustus M. Kelley).

K. Neiss and E. Nelson (2000) 'The Real Interest Rate Gap as an Inflation Indicator', www.bankofengland.co.uk

E. Nelson (2007) 'Milton Friedman and U.S. Monetary History: 1961–2006', www.stlouisfed.org

E. Nelson (2008) 'Friedman and Taylor on Monetary Policy Rules: A Comparison', www.stlouisfed.org

S. Nickell (2005) 'Why Has Inflation Been So Low Since 1999?', www.ssrn.com

R. Novy-Marx and J. Rauh (2010) 'Public Pension Promises: How Big Are They And What Are They Worth', www.ssrn.com
OECD (2011a) 'Macroeconomic Impact of Basel III', www.oecd.org
OECD (2011b) 'Education at a Glance: OECD Indicators', www.oecd.org
OECD (2012) 'OECD Pensions Outlook', www.oecd.org
B. Ohlin (1937a) 'Some Notes on the Stockholm Theory of Savings and Investments I', *The Economic Journal*, Vol. 47, No. 185, pp. 53–69.
B. Ohlin (1937b) 'Some Notes on the Stockholm Theory of Savings and Investments II', *The Economic Journal*, Vol. 47, No. 186, pp. 221–240.
A. Orhpanides (2003) 'Historical Monetary Policy Analysis and the Taylor Rule', www.federalreserve.org
A. Orphanides and S. Norden (1999) 'The Reliability of Output Gap Estimates in Real Time', www.federalreserve.gov
E. Peters (1991) *Chaos and Order in the Capital Markets* (John Wiley & Sons).
E. Peters (1994) *Fractal Market Analysis* (John Wiley & Sons).
A.W. Phillips (1958) 'The Relationship between Unemployment and the Rate of the Change of Money, Wage Rates in the United Kingdom 1861–1957', *Economica*, Vol. 25, No. 100, pp. 283–299.
C. Phillips, T. MacManus and R. Nelson (1937) *Banking and the Business Cycle: A Study of the Great Depression in the United States* (Macmillan).
K. Popper (1974) *Objective Knowledge: An Evolutionary Approach* (Oxford University Press).
C. Reinhart and K. Rogoff (2009) *This Time Is Different* (Princeton University Press).
D. Ricardo (1951) *The Works and Correspondence of David Ricardo*, Ed. P. Sraffa, Vol. 10, 'As Loan Contractor', http://oll.libertyfund.org/
D. Ricardo (1995) *On the Principles of Political Economy and Taxation* (Cambridge University Press).
J. Ritter (2004) 'Economic Growth and Equity Returns', www.ssrn.com
P. Romer (1989) 'Human Capital and Growth: Theory and Evidence', www.nber.org
M. Rothbard (2001) *Man, Economy and State* (Ludwig Von Mises Institute).
M. Rothbard (2006) *Economic Thought Before Adam Smith: An Austrian Perspective on the History of Economic Thought*, Vol. 1 (Edward Elgar).
P. Samuelson (1998) 'Summing Up on Business Cycles: Opening Address', www.bostonfed.org
K. Sawamoto, Z. Nakajima and H. Taguchi (eds) (1995) *Financial Stability in a Changing Environment* (St Martin's Press).
K. Schmidt-Hebbel and A. Werner (2002) 'Inflation Targeting in Brazil, Chile and Mexico: Performance, Credibility and the Exchange Rate', www.bcentral.cl
J. Schumpeter (1961) *The Theory of Economic Development* (Oxford University Press).
J. Schumpeter (1994) *Capitalism, Socialism and Democracy* (George Allen & Unwin).
F. Schwed (2006) *Where Are the Customers' Yachts?* (John Wiley & Sons).
G. Selgin (1995) 'The "Productivity Norm" versus Zero Inflation in the History of Economic Thought', *History of Political Economy*, Vol. 27, No. 4, pp. 705–735.
G. Selgin (1997) *Less Than Zero* (Institute of Economic Affairs).
R. Shiller (2000) *Irrational Exuberance* (Princeton University Press).
C.-H. Siven (2006) 'Monetary Equilibrium', *History of Political Economy*, Vol. 38, No. 4, pp. 665–709.

F. Smets and R. Wouters (2002) 'An Estimated Stochastic Dynamic General Equilibrium Model of the Euro Area', www.ecb.int

A. Smith (1986) *The Wealth of Nations* (Penguin Books).

R. Solow (2010) 'Building a Science of Economics for the Real World', Prepared statement to House Committee on Science and Technology, www.science.house.gov

R. Solow and J. Taylor (1999) *Inflation, Unemployment and Monetary Policy* (MIT Press).

G. Soros (1998) *The Crisis of Global Capitalism* (Little Brown & Company).

S. Snyder (2007) 'The Role of Inflation Targeting in Macroeconomic Effects of Oil Shocks: Evidence from Canada and Australia', www.carleton.edu

M. Spiegel (2006) 'Did Quantitative Easing by the Bank of Japan "Work"?', www.frbsf.org

P. St-Amant and S. Van Norden (1997) 'Measurement of the Output Gap: A Discussion of Recent Research at the Bank of Canada', www.bankofcanada.ca

J. Stiglitz (2008) 'The Failure of Inflation Targeting', www.projectsyndicate.com

J. Stiglitz and B. Greenwald (2003) *Towards a New Paradigm in Monetary Economics* (Cambridge University Press).

L. Svensson (1996) 'Inflation Forecast Targeting: Implementing and Monitoring Inflation Targets', www.nber.org

N. Taleb (2007) *The Black Swan: The Impact of the Highly Improbable* (Allen Lane).

J. Taylor (1993) 'The Use of the New Macroeconometrics for Policy Formulation', *American Economic Review*, Vol. 83, No. 2, pp. 300–305.

J. Taylor (1996) 'The Inflation/Output Variability Trade-off Revisited', www.bostonfed.org

J. Taylor (1998) 'Monetary Policy and the Long Boom', www.stlouisfed.org

J. Taylor (2007) 'Housing and Monetary Policy', www.kcfrb.org

J. Taylor (2010) 'Commentary: Monetary Policy after the Fall', www.kcfrb.org

A. Tebble (2010) *Major Conservative and Libertarian Thinkers – Friedrich Hayek* (Continuum International Publishing).

R. Thaler (1998) 'Giving Markets a Human Dimension', in *Mastering Finance* (Prentice Hall Financial Times), pp.192–198.

H-M. Trautwein (1996) 'Money, Equilibrium, and the Business Cycle: Hayek's Wicksellian Dichotomy', *History of Political Economy*, Vol. 28, No. 1, pp. 27–55.

J.-C. Trichet (2011) 'Remarks at the Farewell Event' (19 October 2011), www.ecb.int

J. Twaddle (2005) 'Evaluating Starting Point Output Gap Estimate Errors', www.rbnz.govt.nz

US International Trade Commission (2010) 'Small and Medium Sized Enterprises: Overview of Participation in US exports', www.usitc.gov

E. Van Der Merwe (2004) 'Inflation Targeting in South Africa', www.resbank.co.za

F. Vibert and T. Aubrey (2007) *Predictive Markets: The End of the Regulatory State?* (European Policy Forum).

L. Von Mises (1981) *Theory of Money and Credit* (Liberty Fund).

L. Walras (2010) *Elements of Pure Economics* (Routledge).

W. White (2006) 'Is Price Stability Enough?', www.bis.org

K. Wicksell (1936) *Interest and Prices* (Macmillan & Co).

M. Woodford (2003) *Interest and Prices: Foundations of a Theory of Monetary Policy* (Princeton University Press).

M. Woodford and J. Rotenberg (1997) 'An Optimization-Based Econometric Framework for the Evaluation of Monetary Policy', www.nber.org

Websites

www.bankofengland.co.uk
www.bloomberg.com
www.bna.com
www.buzzflash.com
www.cnn.com
www.ec.europa.eu
www.ecb.int
www.economist.com
www.fdic.gov
www.federalreserve.gov/
www.ft.com
www.johnbtaylorsblog.blogspot.com
www.r3.org.uk
www.reuters.com
www.texashistory.unt.edu
www.towerswatson.com
www.usgovernmentspending.com
www.wsj.com

Index